MESSAGE OF THE SACRAMENTS

Monika K. Hellwig, Editor

Volume 7

Prophetic Anointing

God's Call to the Sick, the Elderly, and the Dying

by

James L. Empereur, S.J.

Michael Glazier, Inc.
Wilmington, Delaware

First published in 1982 by Michael Glazier, Inc., 1723 Delaware Avenue, Wilmington, Delaware 19806 and distributed outside the USA and Canada by Gill and Macmillan, Ltd., Goldenbridge, Inchicore, Dublin 8

Library of Congress Catalog Card Number: 82-081748
International Standard Book Number
  Message of the Sacraments series: 8-89453-280-4
  PROPHETIC ANOINTING:
    0-89453-233-2 (Michael Glazier, Inc.)
    7171-1139-3 (Gill and Macmillan, Ltd.)

Cover design by Lillian Brulc

Typography by Susan Pickett

Printed in the United States of America

To My Parents
Who Know
How To Close Life Well

Table of Contents

EDITOR'S PREFACE

This volume is one of the series of eight on *The Message of the Sacraments*. These volumes discuss the ritual practices and understanding and the individual sacraments of the Roman Catholic community. Each of the eight authors has set out to cover five aspects of the sacrament (or, in the first and last volumes, of the theme or issue under discussion). These are: first of all, the existential or experiential meaning of the sacrament in the context of secular human experience; what is known of the historical development of the sacrament; a theological exposition of the meaning, function and effect of the sacrament in the context of present official Catholic doctrinal positions; some pastoral reflections; and a projection of possible future developments in the practice and catechesis of the sacrament.

There is evident need of such a series of volumes to combine the established teaching and firm foundation in sacramental theology with the new situation of the post-Vatican II Church. Because the need is universal, this series is the joint effort of an international team of English-speaking authors. We have not invited any participants whose writing would need to be translated. While we hope that our series will be useful particularly to priests, permanent deacons, seminarians, and those professionally involved in sacramental and catechetical ministries, we also address ourselves confidently to the educated Catholic laity and to those outside the Roman Catholic communion who are interested in learning more about its life and thought. We have all tried to write so as to be easily understood by readers with little or no specialized preparation. We have all tried to deal with the tradition imaginatively but within the acceptable bounds of Catholic orthodoxy, in the firm conviction that that is the way in which we can be most helpful to our readers.

The Church seems to be poised today at a critical juncture in its history. Vatican II reopened long-standing questions about collegiality and participation in the life of the Church, including its sacramental actions, its doctrinal formulations and its government. The Council fostered a new critical awareness and raised hopes which the Church as a vast and complicated institution cannot satisfy without much confusion, conflict and delay. This makes ours a particularly trying and often frustrating time for those most seriously interested in the life of the Church and most deeply committed to it. It seems vitally important for constructive and authentically creative community participation in the shaping of the Church's future life, that a fuller understanding of the sacraments be widely disseminated in the Catholic community. We hope that many readers will begin with the volumes in this series and let themselves be guided into further reading with the bibliographies we offer at the ends of the chapters. We hope to communicate to our readers the sober optimism with which we have undertaken the study and thereby to contribute both to renewal and to reconciliation.

Monika K. Hellwig

FOREWORD

Susan Sontag opens her book, *Illness as Metaphor*, with these words:

> Illness is the night-side of life, a more onerous citizenship. Everyone who is born holds dual citizenship, in the kingdom of the well and in the kingdom of the sick. Although we all prefer to use only the good passport, sooner or later each of us is obliged, at least for a spell, to identify ourselves as citizens of that other place.[1]

Her point is that illness is not a metaphor and that it needs to be liberated from the stereotypes that modern culture has assigned to it. As she puts it, "It is hardly possible to take up one's residence in the kingdom of the ill unprejudiced by the lurid metaphors with which it has been landscaped."[2] She wants to purify illness of this kind of metaphoric thinking since that is the "healthiest way of being ill."

It is this author's claim that the ritual of anointing is the liturgical way in which Christians can be freed from their stereotypical and restrictive views of illness. Christians need to have their thinking revitalized regarding sickness. Disease, especially the serious kind, can be seen as the mysterious enemy, the insidious thief of one's life. For this reason sick people are avoided, although the disease may not be

---

[1]Susan Sontag, *Illness as Metaphor* (New York: Farrar, Straus and Giroux, 1978), p. 3.

[2] Ibid.

contagious. For instance, friends and relatives shun those who have cancer. Often they lie to these people about their condition. Their evasive language betrays their bias that cancer contaminates and there is a not very subtle denial of death in this whole affair. But this is a stereotype as much as is the belief that having a heart attack is more respectable. A cardiac patient is merely suffering from a mechanical failure and so is less repugnant. Heart disease becomes a metaphor for weakness as cancer is a metaphor for disgrace and taboo.

It is the hope of this writer that this volume will open up for the reader the more truly traditional understanding of this sacrament as well as offer some suggestions on how anointing can function in the contemporary Church. It is based upon a more holistic approach to sickness, a perspective that is both old and new, drawing upon the meaning of sickness in the New Testament and pristine Church as well as contemporary theology. It is the author's contention that the Christian community can be liberated from much of its dehumanizing metaphoric thinking about illness if the liturgy of anointing is experienced as a celebration of this more fully incarnational approach to being ill in the Church. This more comprehensive view of being sick makes it possible to claim for this way of being a Christian, whether permanent or temporary, a vocational character. For it is not only a view of sickness purged of a dualistic anthropology, but also a recognition of the ministry of the sick person in the Church that makes it possible for Christians to be citizens not only of the kingdom of the well but to identify themselves "as citizens of that other place."

"I have come that they may have life, and have it more abundantly" (Jn 10:10). What is this abundant life about which Jesus is speaking? It depends upon a person's understanding of the meaning of life. In *Age and Grace* the authors pose the problem succinctly:

> If fullness of life means that point at which we are physically most healthy, sexually most gratified, economically most established or socially most accepted, then the years

of our lives, once this point is passed, hold little promise except the inevitability of despair.[3]

The anointing of the elderly provides a sacramental challenge to such an attitude. In anointing an elderly person the Christian community affirms that the abundance of life is what humans are moving toward. The Church as a pilgrim people emerges strongly in the anointing of old people. The liturgy of anointing is a ritualized way of saying that humans never stop, that growth for oneself and others is also characteristic of old age. To give up on life prematurely is to deny oneself the possibility of the fullness of life.

The sacrament of anointing when administered to the elderly brings to expression significant elements in the Christian perspective on human life: 1) that old age has its own merits, beauty, and worth and it must not be marginalized by contemporary society; 2) that reconciliation in the Church includes the acceptance of one's total humanity. This demands reconciliation not only with those who are actually in old age, but reconciliation with one's aging self; 3) that the world's criterion for evaluating the worth of the person needs to be revised. It is not what you do but who you are that counts. The anointing of the elderly should be the liturgical climax of the community's care and love of these people. The celebration must be based upon attempts to integrate them fully as members of the Christian Church. But anointing the elderly says more. It proclaims to all in the Church that life is a continual progress of growth, that each stage of life must be accepted if life is to be lived abundantly.

What this book intends to say about the rites of the sick, elderly, and dying is highlighted in these remarks of Brian Newns:

> We live in an age of doubt and unbelief, where people think in terms of power and strength. The weak, the sick

[3]William Fournier, O.M.I. and Sarah O'Malley, O.S.B., *Age and Grace* (Collegeville: The Liturgical Press, 1980), p. 2.

and the aged are despised and forgotten. . . . Against this modern view the Church sets her face, teaching us that the sick and the aged do matter. They matter in themselves, because they are at a crucial point in their development as followers of Christ and need support, but also because in their sickness and old age, they have much to give the Church and the world.

When death comes modern man tries to banish it to the hospital ward and the undertaker's parlour. But the Church celebrates death; what looks like man's ultimate defeat. . . . is seen by the Church as the ultimate and complete sharing in Christ's death. . . . As Christians we face death in the confidence our faith brings, assured by Christ that if we share in his death we shall share in his resurrection.[4]

[4]Brian Newns, "The Anointing and Pastoral Care of the Sick," in *Pastoral Liturgy*, ed. Harold Winstone (London: Collins Liturgical Publications, 1975), p. 230.

CHAPTER ONE: THE HISTORY OF THE SACRAMENT OF ANOINTING

The Use of Oil in Civil and Religious Anointings[1]

The practice of anointing with oil, especially olive oil, is an ancient one. There is evidence of such a practice among the peoples of the Near East. Sometimes the use of oil was purely utilitarian and on other occasions it involved the symbolism of liturgy. Such liturgical anointing with oil is often found in connection with a specific culture's attempt to give meaning to suffering, sickness, and death. In more primitive and ancient societies, religious rituals, including anointing, were ways in which the mystery of sickness and other forms of human fragmentation could be dealt with. Sickness and death appeared unnatural and contrary to the good order of the universe. Thus, people constructed myths to explain the presence of the limits of sickness and death and made use of rituals to express their belief in an order and life which transcends those limitations.

Because these early people did not make clear distinctions

---

[1]For much of the material in this section I have depended upon the article: "Anointing" by G.T. Kennedy in *The New Catholic Encyclopedia*, 1967 vol. 1. There are further biblical references in this article.

between the physical and the spiritual but took a more holistic approach to the human person, the religious rituals became both a way of providing meaning in these situations of brokenness and a form of medicine to restore a person to health. In this context these rituals took on a strong sacramental character because, while they did not always act as effective medicine, they inevitably offered the sick and dying a meaning of what was going on in their lives.[2] This more holistic perspective while characteristic of ancient Israel and its pagan contemporaries and forebears is not to be considered a naïve worldview. Today, there is an attempt to recapture the same basic insight of human existence by means of a more highly sophisticated psychological understanding.

There is abundant evidence for oil anointing in the bible whether for secular or religious purposes.[3] Its most obvious secular use springs from the dry summer climate of Palestine which required oil for sanitary and therapeutic purposes. Because of exposure to the elements oil was used as the completion of the bathing process (e.g. Ez 16:9). From this most utilitarian need arose the idea of anointing as a symbol of joy (Is 61:3). And conversely, the use of ointment was absent from any person in mourning (2 Sam 14:2). Anointing also was seen as a sign of respect as when the heads of guests (Mt 26:7) or their feet were anointed (Lk 7:46). Those freed from captivity were anointed (2 Chron 28:15) as were the wounded (Is 1:6) and the dead in preparation for burial (Mk 16:1). The practice of anointing in a religious context included both persons and objects. To anoint either was to bless them and set them apart for religious use. The sacred furniture and utensils of Old Testament times were anointed with a specially prepared ointment (Ex 30:22-23).

The ceremony of anointing persons was restricted for the

---

[2] Joseph Martos, *Doors to the Sacred* (Garden City, Doubleday, 1981), p. 371.

[3] For a brief summary see "Anoint" in *Dictionary of the Bible* by John L. McKenzie (Milwaukee: Bruce Publishing Co., 1965).

most part to priests and kings. Such a consecration of priests is described in Exod 28:40-42. In this case, however, the anointing may have been reserved for the high priests. There seems to have been no anointing of the regular members of the tribe of Levi. Prophets would have been anointed (1 Kgs 19:16) based upon the practice of anointing kings. Prophets and priests anointed the heads of kings when they ascended the throne and so they were considered anointed of the Lord (1 Sam 10:1, 16:13). While Israelite kingly anointing resembled that of Israel's neighbors, its significance was seen in terms of the fact that the kings were the "anointed of Yahweh" (1 Sam 24:6). But although such kingly anointing was a civil event, it highlights the religious meaning of anointing in Old Testament times. That is, such anointing meant consecration to God's service. It removed the anointed ones from the arena of ordinary life and they were seen as being directly responsible to God. Such a view of anointing is presumed by the bible. In fact it would be difficult to separate the religious and the non-religious dimensions of Israelite kingly anointing. Its religious character is its true secular meaning in that the king was seen as God's chosen, being given a special commission and strength to carry out Yahweh's wishes.

The biblical practice of anointing, which may have sprung from Egyptian and Canaanite customs, lived on into the middle ages in the enthronement ceremonies of kings, popes, and emperors. The common understanding was the removal of the person or thing from profane reality. This was true both for the anointing in the confirming of the catechumens and the ordination of priests and bishops as well as the crowning of medieval kings. There is ample evidence for this latter anointing throughout the middle ages. Pepin III was anointed by St. Boniface. Leo III anointed Charlemagne and as late as 1825 Charles X of France was anointed. To anoint a king meant exalting him above the laity and giving him a position analogous to priests. Such anointings were a powerful influence in bolstering the prestige of many dynasties. Thus, while the anointing had a strong religious character, it also had great political significance. At times in history there was conflict between the anointing of the bishop and the anointing of the king. The specifically regal anointing spread from France to England and the Holy Roman Empire. In the twelfth century such anointing was understood to have a sacramental character. The anointing of the emperor brought him into the clerical state although the way the anointing was performed (between the shoulders and not on the head) and without the use of chrism, indicated the inferiority of this anointing to that of episcopal anointing. Gradually, theological reflection removed the sacramental character from kingly anointing. At the same time civil authority took care to distinguish the foundation of imperial power from the anointing itself so that the former did not depend upon and flow from the latter.

In the middle ages anointing was closely connected with the consecration of popes. But it was not intrinsic to the elevation to the papacy and was used only to confer episcopal status on the one chosen. Originally, the pope would not have been chosen from among the bishops and so anointing was part of his enthronement. Papal anointing was seen in conjunction with imperial anointing and both symbolized the equality of power of both offices. But in the eleventh century, when papal candidates were chosen from among the bishops, the rite of anointing disappeared from the ceremony of papal enthronement.

New Testament Roots of the Sacrament of Anointing[4]

When looking for New Testament roots to what would eventually become the ministry of healing in the Church,

---

[4]For the material in this section I have made extensive use of the personal notes of professor Joseph Powers, S.J., especially in regard to his use of *Het Heilig Oliesel* by Al Janssens (Nijmegen: N.V. Dekker En Van De Vegt, 1939). The translation used for the biblical references throughout this book is the Revised Standard Version of the Oxford Annotated Bible.

one must look at Christ's own ministry toward the sick. In Acts the first preaching of the kerygma is accompanied by two manifestations of Christ's ministerial powers through others: the preaching in tongues and the cure of the cripple at the Beautiful Gate. In the latter example Peter commands the cripple at the gate of the temple to walk in the name of Jesus Christ. A similar healing by Paul in Acts 14: 9-10 presupposes the faith of the crippled person. In both instances it is the healing of sickness which is a manifestation of care for those burdened with sinfulness. This is a post-resurrectional revelation of Christ's own ministry to the sick whereby he shows his authority over sin, sickness, and death.

The difference between Christ's personal ministry and those who cure in his name is precisely found in the fact that Christ cures in his own name. The cures are achieved through the power given him by God. Thus there is no special symbol or sacramental sign connected with his work. He heals by simple command because he is the sacrament. He is the visibility of grace in the world. He is the epiphany of a power which is properly his. His actions of healing are fully human but they are also acts of the person of the Son of God who has this power in his own right.

The apostolic ministry of healing is clearly found in the New Testament in connection with the preaching of the kingdom. It is a power exercised by Christ and granted to the apostles and disciples. Matthew 10:1 ff., which comes after the demonstration of Christ's own power over sickness and death, speaks of the granting of this power to heal disease and infirmity to the apostles. Luke 10:17 tells of the return of the seventy from their ministry of preaching and healing and that they had power even over demons in the name of Christ. The apostles and disciples, then, exercised a ministry of healing in Jesus' name. And even the exorcisms of Mt 7:22 and Mk 9:30-41 are in the context of a ministry of healing. This ministry and power of healing in the name of Jesus as described in the New Testament finds it clearest example in Peter's miracle at the Beautiful Gate: "In the name of Jesus Christ of Nazareth, walk" (Acts 3:2). It is a power exercised by Christ through the ministry of those who have been sent. Part of this mission is the healing and curing of those in need. It is a ministry exercised in terms of the redemptive mission of Christ.

This New Testament anointing was very much in the Jewish tradition. The uses of anointing which are found in rabbinic literature have their parallels in the Christian Scriptures. Mt 26:7 which tells of Jesus being anointed in Bethany shortly before his death shows that anointing was a sign of honor as well as a means of healing. More often it was used for skin diseases, diseases of the head, and wounds. It was also employed in conjunction with exorcisms. But since illness was often seen as the result of demonic influence, there is no clear distinction between the healing and exorcistic anointings. It is not that the Jewish and New Testament viewpoint was a simplistic connecting of sin and illness. Rather, there was a somewhat unarticulated understanding that physical illness is part of the mystery of evil in the world. Thus, anointing here is more than healing of the body; it is directed to the interior illness of the human person. Biblical anthropology does not make the sharp distinction between body and soul so characteristic of medieval/classical thought. Semitic understanding was more attuned to the psychosomatic, although in an undifferentiated way.

There is no external sign used in conjunction with this ministry of the apostles and disciples. There is a description in Mk 6:7-13 and it is in this text that Trent saw the "insinuation" of the institution of the sacrament of anointing (DS 1695, 1716). Mk 6:13 says: "And they cast out many demons and anointed with oil many that were sick and healed them." In what way is it possible to see here the beginnings of the sacrament of anointing?[5] One can perhaps

---

[5]In dealing with Mark 6:13 it is good to keep in mind the observation made by Joseph Martos: "Scripture scholars point out, however, that this may reflect the practice of the community in which the gospel was written forty years later than the practice of the disciples during Jesus' own life time." *Doors to the Sacred*, p. 371.

defend Trent's implication by using the criterion of E. Schillebeeckx that the apostles appropriated prevalent Jewish religious symbols and employed them in a specifically Christian context.[6] This is what is meant by their doing something in the "power of Jesus." The principle of Schillebeeckx is that an already existing religious symbol is assumed into the history of redemption and thus becomes a sacrament by its reference to the power of the mystery of Christ.

Another biblical reference which is often understood as being a place where the sacramentality of anointing is implicitly emerging is Mt 9:35: "And Jesus went about all the cities and villages, teaching in their synagogues and preaching the gospel of the kingdom, and healing every disease and every infirmity." This text has not been employed for supporting the foundation of the sacrament of anointing but the reference has been seen as an anticipation of what the Church would later articulate as a sacrament. This is based on the idea, already noted, that Jesus' ministry of healing was passed on to his apostles (Mt 10:1, Mk 6:7, Lk 9:1). Reference to Mk 6:13 has already been made as supporting this claim.

Traditionally, the primary scriptural evidence for this sacrament has been chapter 5:13-16 of the epistle of James. Set in the context of the norms for Christian living, James recommends an approach to the time of illness:

> Is anyone among you suffering? Let him pray. Is any cheerful? Let him sing praise. Is any among you sick? Let him call for the elders of the church, and let them pray over him, anointing him with oil in the name of the Lord; and the prayer of faith will save the sick man, and the Lord will raise him up; and if he has committed sins, he will be forgiven. Therefore confess your sins to one another, and pray for one another, that you may be

---

[6]E. Schillebeeckx, O.P., *Christ the Sacrament* (London: Sheed and Ward, 1963), paperback, p. 147.

healed. The prayer of a righteous man has great power in its effects.

This text has been understood as referring to someone who is seriously ill but not dying. (Cf. similar references: Jn 4:46, "the curing of the official's son"; Jn 11:1-6, "the raising of Lazarus.") The presbyters here are not charismatic healers but leaders in the local Church. They are members of an incipient hierarchy. The fact that the plural is used is not an indication of some kind of early concelebration of this sacrament. The ritual is simple; it is a prayer made in the name of the Lord accompanied by anointing with oil. It is a Christian rite in that the Christian is anointed in terms of his/her baptism through the invocation of the name of Jesus. Charismatic and miraculous healing is not implied in this text.[7]

What is the meaning of the "prayer of faith" referred to in verse fifteen? Does it mean simple prayer done in a faith context? Probably so, since this prayer takes place in a community setting. And this prayer "will save" the sick person. The meaning of "will save" and "will raise" would appear to refer to physical health according to some exegetes. They would not exclude spiritual healing but would see that as secondary in emphasis.[8]

If the first two effects of the sacrament according to James are physical and spiritual healing, the third effect of anointing is clearly spiritual: the forgiveness of sins. The rite is concerned primarily with the physical restoration of health which may have a spiritual dimension. But the secondary effect is the removal of grave sin. There have been varying interpretations of the relationship among these various effects. These interpretations tend to discount any necessary connection between sin and sickness, either the text meaning that it is not necessary to be in sin to engage in

---

[7]Raymond Brown, Joseph Fitzmyer, Roland Murphy, eds. *Jerome Biblical Commentary* (Englewood Cliffs, N.J.: Prentice Hall, Inc., 1968), 59:36.

[8]Ibid., 59:39.

this rite, or that the forgiveness of sin is the eschatological effect of this rite.

Some have seen in this last part of the text a reference to sacramental confession.[9] The Council of Trent (DS 1679) does refer to this verse when speaking of that sacrament but makes no further specification regarding the precise meaning of the text. It would be going beyond the meaning of this passage to conclude that the confession of sins must be made to presbyters. Rather, this is an exhortation that Christians should confess to each other. Perhaps it is a call to those present to acknowledge their sinfulness before they pray for the sick person. The text ends with "that you may be healed." This can refer to both bodily and spiritual healing. The forgiveness of sins also qualifies as the healing that is taking place. One author suggests that the connection between the anointing of lepers with oil and the forgiveness of sin as found in Lev 14:10-31 may have influenced this passage in James.[10]

The major biblical problem regarding this sacrament is the question of its institution, especially whether or not it was instituted by Christ. Following the teaching of the Council of Trent one would have to say that the origin of the sacrament of anointing can be discerned in the passage of James. The Council states: "This holy anointing of the sick was instituted by Christ our Lord as a true and proper sacrament of the New Testament. It is implied in Mark's Gospel (6:13), and it is commended to the faithful and promulgated by the Apostle James, the brother of the Lord" (DS 1695). But even at the time of Trent, there was a recognition of the exegetical problems regarding this text. It adds: "In these words (Jas 5:14-15), as the Church has learned from apostolic tradition transmitted to her, he teaches the matter, the form, the proper minister, and the effect of this salutary sacrament" (ibid).

---

[9]Much in this section is dependent upon "Theology of Anointing of the Sick" by J.P. McClain in *The New Catholic Encyclopedia*, 1967.

[10]Ibid., p. 569.

The theological tradition differs on how to establish the authenticity of the institution of this sacrament. This point will be discussed more fully in Chapter Two which analyzes the teaching of the Council of Trent. Suffice it to say that some theologians put forward a hypothesis that Christ instituted the anointing of the sick in the Easter period when he spoke of the kingdom of God with his apostles. In effect, this would mean an indirect institution by Christ. This means that while he did not denominate a specific sign, e.g. anointing with oil, he did indicate what it was that he wished to be accomplished on the level of grace and that this be achieved through some symbolic process. The point being that what the apostles received from Christ was the command of dealing with those who were sick in terms of symbolic encounter so that they might be healed. The apostles as Jews had the experience of using oil therapeutically and so chose this as the way of placing sick people in a grace-filled situation. This is but one example, a fairly conservative one, of the attempt on the part of theologians to articulate an answer to the question of the institution of this sacrament. Such an indirect institution at least avoids the problems of ascribing this specific rite to the historical Jesus, but even how one would understand what actually developed in a post-resurrectional situation will depend upon one's hermeneutical approach to the post-resurrection narratives.

Summary

In sum, what can be said regarding the New Testament roots for this sacrament is that in these biblical times the early Christian community showed a concern for its sick members. This was a concern which was consonant with the healing ministry of Jesus. Later centuries would see a liturgical organization of this ministry of the primitive Church. But the New Testament does not provide the answers to questions it did not ask, such questions as what is the matter and form of the sacrament, who is the proper minister and the like. The New Testament simply wishes to affirm that the sick Christian is in need of assistance from the community and in providing this help, the community is continuing the work of Jesus Christ.

Anointing of the Sick in The First Five Centuries[11]

There are very few clear indications of a special sacrament of anointing in the early centuries of Christianity. Some of the reasons would be: 1) the relatively late idea of what a sacrament is in terms of theological definition; 2) the considerable variation in the prayers used in conjunction with anointing; 3) the ritual which tended to be private and as a result, the lack of much in the way of public commentary; and 4) anointing's relatively subordinate importance in comparison with baptism and eucharist. In the writings of the Fathers of the Church some references to the ministry of the sick are too vague to be useful. And when there is any reference it is more in terms of penance and reconciliation even in regard to the text of James. There are, however, uses of the James text which are situated in the context of the anointing of the sick. But Paul Palmer points out that the Epistle of James did not have much influence on the Western theological tradition until relatively late and so there are few commentaries on it.[12] Rather, the documentation from the early centuries is in the way of liturgical texts, formulae for the blessing of the oil.

The Didache
The *Didache* probably presents the earliest blessing over oil. Based on a Coptic fragment from the beginning of the fifth century, this document indicates that the following

[11]Also in this section I have relied heavily on the notes of Joseph Powers whose expert knowledge of the Dutch language has made Janssens' excellent book a valuable resource for me. The sections quoted from this volume have been translated by Professor Powers.

[12]Paul Palmer, "The Purpose of Anointing the Sick: A Reappraisal," *Theological Studies.* 19 (1958): 309-44.

prayer is to be added to the end of the anaphora:

> . . . . but allow the prophets that they should give thanks
> according to their will. But concerning the words with the
> ointment give thanks thus as we say: "We give thanks to
> you, O Father, concerning the ointment which Thou hast
> made known to us through Jesus, Thy Child: glory to
> Thee unto the Ages. Amen."[13]

Although it is not clear whether this is part of the original
text of the *Didache*, it is of ancient origin. It is found in the
Apostolic Constitutions (c. 400).

The question here is the nature of the oil used. That is, is
the text dealing with sacramental oil? Its location after the
anaphora places it in the same location as the consecration
of oil used for the sick which can be found in other Church
Orders such as the *Apostolic Tradition* of Hippolytus, the
Euchologion of Serapion, and *The Testament of Our Lord
Jesus Christ*. The words used are of the thanksgiving type,
and they correspond to those used for the blessing over the
chalice and bread as found in the *Didache*: "We thank you,
our Father, for the holy vine of David your servant which
you have revealed to us through Jesus your Child."[14] Similar phrasing of the prayer to that which is used in the
eucharist would indicate that the blessing of the oil occurred
in a sacramental context.

Apostolic Tradition (c. 215 A.D.)

The importance of this third century liturgical order is
found not so much in its antiquity as in the influence it had
on the Church Orders of the third and fourth centuries in
Africa and the Near East. Here is the text dealing with the
offering of oil:

---

[13]This text can be found in "A New Papyrus Fragment of the Didache in
Coptic," *Journal of Theological Studies* 25 (1924-25): 230. See also: Paul Palmer
Sacraments and Forgiveness (Westminster: The Newman Press, 1959), p. 277.

[14]Lucien Deiss, *Springtime of the Liturgy* (Collegeville: The Liturgical Press,
1979), p. 74.

> If anyone offers oil, (the bishop) shall render thanks in the same way as for the offering of bread and wine, not saying it word for word, but to similar effect saying: "O God, sanctifier of this oil, as you give health to those who are anointed and receive that with which you anointed kings, priests, and prophets, so may it give strength to all those who taste it, and health to all that are anointed with it."[15]

It seems clear that this is a formula for the blessing of the oil of the sick.

The text mentions "if anyone *offers* oil." This raises questions about the use of the oil. Who administered the anointing of the sick? A later document, *Canons of Hippolytus*, a fifth century codification of Ethiopian and Arabic practices, distinguishes two uses of the oil that is blessed in the eucharist. Canon 219 says: "The sick receive cure if they visit the church and receive from the *water of prayer* and the *oil of prayer*, except for the case of the one who is dangerously sick; he should be visited daily by a cleric who knows him."[16] The term, oil of prayer, is the Greek name for this sacrament. What one can gather from this canon is that private families brought oil to be blessed for the use of the sick and that they used this oil themselves. However, in the case of more serious illness, a visitation of the sick took place. This is described in Canon 199-200:

> Let one deacon accompany the bishop, and let him inform him about each one, especially about the sick man—that he knows him. For it is a great thing for the sick to be visited by the "principes sacerdotum" for it is from them that he received respite from his illness, if the bishop comes to him, and especially if he prays over him (for the shadow of Peter cures a sick man) unless the end is come.[17]

---

[15]Geoffrey J. Cuming, *Hippolytus: A Text for Students* (Bramcote Notts: Grove Books, 1976), p. 11.

[16]Janssens, *Het Heilig Oliesel*, p. 35.

[17]Ibid., p. 36.

This canon reflects the text of James in terms of the leadership of priests and the praying over the sick person.

In the visitation of the sick mentioned here there is no reference to any kind of anointing. It would be cavalier to conclude that no anointing was involved. The evidence of the Church Orders of the third to fifth centuries show that oil was blessed specifically for the anointing of the sick. The absence of any reference to anointing here need not indicate the lack of any anointing; it could also indicate that it was presumed because the practice was so general. However, one must be careful not to overprove the case for anointing in the ministrations to the sick since there does not seem to have been a uniform practice. There was a tradition which saw the prayer over the sick in terms of the laying on of hands which probably springs from Mk 16:18: "...they will lay their hands on the sick and they will recover." Whether an anointing was also involved cannot be verified.

There is considerable patristic evidence regarding this laying on of hands. St. Ephrem advises the sick to go to "visitors" who are to pray over them. One visitor lays hands on the sick person and the other makes the sign of the cross (with oil?). Praying with imposition of hands is clearly indicated. Gregory of Nazianzen writes in one of his poems: "I am your servant, I who lay hands on your gifts (in the eucharist) and on the heads of those who kneel before me and call me 'healer of the sick.' "[18] Augustine is spoken of as one who never hesitated to lay hands on the sick. The saint's biographer, Possidius, said that Augustine "was accustomed to visit the sick who desired it in order to lay his hands on them and pray at their bedside."[19] It is, of course, speculation that on such occasions Augustine personally made use of oil. Ambrose in his *De Poenitentia* refers to this practice. He is concerned with the refutation of the Novatians and so makes the point that this practice is an exercise of divine power entrusted to the Church:

[18]Ibid., p. 39.
[19]Ibid., p. 40.

He has given everything to His disciples to whom he says: "in my name they will cast out demons — they will place their hands on the sick and they will be well." Thus, He has given them everything, but there is nothing of man's power in these matters, in which the grace of a divine office is at work. Why, then, do you impose hands and put your trust in the work of a blessing, if (so that) the sick might perhaps recover?[20]

Because Ambrose goes on to apply this same principle to baptism and penance, he places this imposition and prayer in a clearer sacramental context.

The Apostolic Constitutions

The *Apostolic Constitutions* (fourth and fifth centuries from Palestine and Egypt) has the following prayer for the blessing of oil and water (to be performed by the bishop or by the priest in the absence of the bishop):

God of Hosts, God of power, Creator of water and giver of oil, merciful and kind toward men; you who have given water for drink and for cleansing, and oil that our face may rejoice in gladness and joy, sanctify this oil and this water through Christ, in the name of him or her who offered it, and grant to these things the power to bring forth health, to chase away sickness to make devils flee, and to foil every snare through Christ, our hope, with whom you have glory, honor and praise and your Holy Spirit forever. Amen.[21]

The *Apostolic Constitutions* is derived from the *Traditio Apostolica* of Hippolytus. This and other Church Orders which spring from Hippolytus have this ritual for the blessing of oil and water which is offered by the faithful to be used in time of illness.

[20]Ibid. See also: Palmer, *Sacraments and Forgiveness*, p. 282.

[21]Ibid., p. 36. *Apostolic Constitutions* VIII, 29. See also: F.E. Brightman, *Liturgies: Eastern and Western* (Clarendon Press, 1896), pp. 3-30.

The Testament of Our Lord Jesus Christ

There are similar references to blessing water and oil in this document which may go back to Monophysite circles of Syria in the second half of the fifth century. Apparently the water and oil are blessed separately:

> As the priest consecrates the oil for the healing of pain, let him take it before the place of the altar and say in a low voice: "Lord God who has given us the Spirit, the Advocate, Christ, who has sanctified us.... you who cure every sickness and pain; you who have given the charism of healing to those found worthy through you for this gift; send over this oil, the representation of your abundance, the help of your bountiful mercy, so that it may heal the sick, and sanctify those who repent, after they have drawn to a closer faith. For you are powerful and filled with glory forever. Amen."[22]

The water is blessed with the same prayer.

The Euchologion of Serapion

The *Euchologion of Serapion* (bishop of Thmuis in Egypt, who died after 362 A.D.) contains prayers for the blessing of oil. The following prayer, which is taken from a collection of blessings, is for both oil and water:

> We bless these creatures in the name of your only Son, Jesus Christ. Let the name of Him who suffered, was crucified and rose and sits at the right hand of the Unborn God, come over this oil and water. Give to these creatures the power to heal, so that every fever, every devil and every sickness may disappear by this drink and this anointing; so that the use of these creatures may be the means of healing and complete health, in the name of your only Son, Jesus Christ, through whom to you belong glory and power in the Holy Spirit forever.[23]

The *Euchologion* contains another blessing entitled:

[22]Ibid., p. 38.
[23]Ibid., p. 37.

"Prayer for the oil of the sick or for bread or for water." The point of the prayer is seen in the words: "so that it may become a means of removing every disease and sickness...unto health and soundness of soul and body and spirit, unto perfect well-being...."[24] The Gelasian Sacramentary also contains such a blessing.

The Church Orders of the first five centuries contain two kinds of prayers in conjunction with oil: (1) they are prayers of thanksgiving and (2) they are prayers of blessing. Both apparently are said over oil which has been offered by the faithful for the use in the healing of the sick. This healing is seen as part of the life of the Church. Such prayers do not contain a developed notion of sacrament, certainly not a medieval scholastic one. Nor is there a uniformity of ritual involved. They are epicletic in nature, that is, they are a calling upon the healing power of God to enter into the oil. The oil so blessed is used by the faithful both in the privacy of their homes as well as in the ritual visitation of the sick by the presbyters.

What is clear from these prayers is the presence of a ministry of healing in the Church. The power of this ministry is found in the blessed oil and in the use of the name of the Lord. This ministry was practiced in many ways either by the faithful themselves or by the visiting priests. There are no liturgical formulae for the rite of anointing itself. This should not be surprising since, during the early centuries of the Christian Church, the eucharistic anaphora itself was improvised. Presumably, in the case of anointing also, the form of the prayer was left to the inspiration of the individual ministers.

The usual rule regarding the oil was that it had to be consecrated by a bishop. Apparently, the oil was considered a kind of permanent sacrament in similar fashion as the eucharist. There was "reserved" oil. This, of course, raises the question of who was the minister of this sacrament. Was

---

[24] *The New Catholic Encyclopedia* v. 1, p. 570. Bernard Poschmann sees this prayer as influenced by the Epistle of James. *Penance and the Anointing of the Sick* (New York: Herder and Herder, 1964), p. 238.

there such a thing as lay anointing? That there were lay people who anointed with oil can be verified.[25] Whether this was considered strictly sacramental is another question. One theory is that there were two parallel practices of anointing. One was done by a priest or bishop and it involved both forgiveness of sins and restoration of physical health. This was considered sacramental. The second practice which was non-sacramental strictly speaking was administered by lay people and would be primarily concerned with the recipient's health. The custom of lay anointing fades away from history about the beginning of the eighth century. Church councils of the Carolingian period refer to this and so according to some scholars these references tend to emphasize the sacramentality of anointing by the clergy.

Despite the lack of any consistent formula or ritual for anointing, there are present the elements of sacramental ministry to the sick. Blessed oil in conjunction with the prayer of the Church is seen as the instrument of the healing power of God. What spontaneity took place was practiced by the community under the permissive direction of competent authority. This ministry continued in the history of the Church along the lines laid down in the New Testament, although characterized by freedom and spontaneity present in early liturgical practice.

Early Use of the Text of James

This text is used in both a spiritual sense of healing the sinful soul as well as the more corporal sense of the healing and sanctification of the sick person. Origen in his *Homilies of Leviticus* (c. 244 A.D.) cites the James text with an emendation. He substitutes "let them *impose hands on him*" in place of "let them *pray over him*." The context here seems to be the visiting of a sick person in the ministry of forgiveness of sins rather than healing. Most probably Origen

---

[25] *The New Catholic Encyclopedia* v. 1, p. 570. For a more extended discussion see "Who Can Anoint the Sick?" by Paul Palmer in *Worship* 48:2 (February 1974): 81-92.

simply adapted the text to fit the penitential practice.[26] Chrysostom uses the text in the same sense in his *De Sacerdotio* (c. 385 A.D.). He is comparing the power of the priestly ministry to forgive sins with that of parents to protect their children. Thus, the sickness and disease referred to here would be sin.[27] Hesychius, a presbyter of Jerusalem, also uses the text in identical fashion in his commentary on Leviticus. The prayer is efficacious for the forgiveness of sin and healing of spiritual illness. In *De Adoratione in Spiritu et Veritate* (c. 428 A.D.), Cyril of Alexandria cites James in the context of physical illness.[28] The same is found in Victor of Antioch in his commentary on Mark. In speaking of Mark and James with regard to the use of oil in healing, he says that prayer is the agent of healing and oil is the symbol of God's mercy. Anointing is both a healing of sickness and an illumination of the heart (sanctification). There are some references to James in the Western Fathers of the first five centuries. However, as already noted, it seems that this text came into Western theology slowly. One finds citations in Hilary, Ambrosiaster, Pope Damasus, Jerome, Rufinus, the Council of Carthage and Innocent I. Pope Innocent deserves a special treatment on his own.

Pope Innocent I

Innocent gives the most explicit testimony to the practice of the Roman Church in this early period.[29] In a letter to Decentius, bishop of Gubbo (March 19, 416), he answers a number of questions proposed to him such as: when is the kiss of peace to be given in the eucharist, when are the diptychs to be read, who anoints the baptized with the oil of chrism, should Saturday be a fast day, must a deacon or priest have the bishop's permission to exorcise the pos-

---

[26]Palmer, *Sacraments and Forgiveness,* p. 278.

[27]Ibid., p. 281.

[28]Ibid.

[29]*Epist.* 25:8, PL 20: 559-60.

sessed, what is the required length of time of public penance. Innocent complains that too many bishops are doing as they please in these matters. He says that the Roman practice should be the norm since it stems from Peter. He is defending the rights of bishops against a form of presbyterianism.

On the matter of anointing Innocent seems to be answering three questions put forth by Decentius: 1) what is the meaning of the James text: physical or spiritual illness, 2) who performs the anointing: priests or bishops, and 3) can "penitents" be anointed? The pope's answers to the first two questions can be stated in this way: 1) the James text shows that only those faithful who are sick can be anointed and 2) the oil must be blessed by the bishop but can be used by the priest as well as by the faithful for their own needs of their families. He also asserts that both bishops and presbyters may anoint when they visit. Innocent interprets the presbyters of the James text as those who are standing in for the bishop when he is impeded by his other duties. The pope describes the visitation as including a blessing and an anointing with chrism. The bishop's visitation is a *liturgical* one which includes the imposition of hands with a prayer and anointing with blessed oil. There is no distinction (as is the case today) in the oil used here and that used in baptism. Both are referred to as chrism. The prayers indicate the effects of the sacrament as 1) healing and enabling those who are sick and 2) remitting their sins.

Innocent addressed the third question by stating that public penitents are excluded from anointing. Since penitents are barred from the eucharist, so much the more is it the case in anointing. While there is evidence from a letter of Innocent to Exuperius, bishop of Toulouse (February 20, 406) indicating that reconciliation and communion were granted to those in danger of death, there is no mention of anointing. As a matter of fact, the older practice was to grant reconciliation alone. Viaticum was granted when the discipline was rendered more mild.

Innocent refers to two anointings: one by the sick person or some relative and another one by the bishop or priest. But this should cause no difficulty since the sacramental nature of the anointing by priests and bishops is clear from the letter. Nor was there any restriction on the laity to refrain from touching blessed objects such as the blessed oil. Presumably, whatever sacramentality there was in lay anointing came from the fact that they used oil blessed by the bishop.

It is appropriate to note at this point that Venerable Bede cites Innocent as an authority in his commentary on James.[30] Bede affirms that anointing of the sick has been carried out since the time of the apostles. In his commentary he states:

> In the Gospel we read that the Apostles also did this, and even now the custom of the Church holds that the sick are to be anointed by presbyters with consecrated oil, and to be healed by the accompanying prayer. Not only presbyters, but, as Pope Innocent writes, all Christians as well may use this same oil for anointing, when their own needs or those of their family demand. However, this oil may be prepared only by bishops. For the saying, "with oil in the name of the Lord," means oil consecrated in the name of the Lord. At least it means that when they anoint the sick man, they ought to invoke over him the name of the Lord.[31]

Summary

Interpretations of these various early Church documents vary. Most authors are very cautious about asserting that the anointing that was practiced in the Pre-Nicene Church could be a sacrament strictly speaking. It is a matter of how one confronts the evidence. Clearly there was no anointing of the dying. James does not propose anointing as a sacrament of the dying. But on that fact one cannot conclude that there was no sacrament of anointing for the sick. Also, the

---

[30] *Super Divi Jacobi Epistolam* 5 (PL 93:39-40).
[31] Palmer, *Sacraments and Forgiveness*, pp. 286-7.

fact that anointing was employed in non-sacramental situations does not allow one to conclude that there was no sacramental ritual. Nothing can be proven from the fact that the faithful used blessed oil as a means of healing in their sicknesses. The question is whether in this early period there is an anointing of the sick by priests and bishops which involved not only physical healing but also was considered to be a means of grace because it corresponded to the healing ministry of Christ.

The evidence does substantiate that while there is mention of penance and viaticum in the case of death, there is no reference to anointing. There is some evidence that the minister of anointing is the bishop or priest. In such cases as the healing practiced by monks, there are two possibilities: either they were acting as presbyters exercising this ministry in the name of the Church or they were engaging in charismatic healing. In one case it would be a grace-conferring sacrament and in the other it would be a personal charismatic gift. In reality, it would probably have been difficult to distinguish the two functions completely. Thus, it is not possible to link the question of sacramentality to *priestly* performance in any exclusive way at this time. The documents of the fifth century such as the Letter of Innocent look back to the text of James as a justification of the contemporary practice. Innocent traces the Roman practices to the earliest period of the Church in Rome. The prayers of consecration dealing with oil do so in a manner similar to those dealing with bread and wine. The healing power of the oil is seen in terms of a victory over Satan and evil.

The honest judgment is that the evidence for the existence of this sacrament in these early centuries is quite scarce. One reason that has already been mentioned is that the James text was slow in entering the West. There was doubt about its canonicity at the time of Origen and Clement of Alexandria. Charismatic anointings were more widespread during this time than at any other time in the history of the Church and such more flamboyant cures would be the ones that were recorded. Because of Origen's influence in the history of theology, his spiritual interpretation of sickness in the James text as sinfulness prevented people from seeing a distinct sacramentality of anointing of the *sick* in this epistle. Finally, in the fourth and fifth centuries there was the practice of postponing baptism until immediately prior to death. People remained catechumens most of their Christian lives. Thus, a large part of the Christian community could not receive anointing. In addition, this sacrament was not given to penitents. And so the number of possible candidates for anointing lessened. Only when the Roman See began to promote anointing did such practices change.

One might sum up this period of the first five centuries of development of anointing in the words of Joseph Martos, keeping in mind that his is an optimistic assessment:

> During the patristic period, therefore, oil was indeed a sacrament of physical and spiritual health, at least in some parts of the Roman Empire and perhaps in others. It was a sacrament in the broad sense, for it symbolized the healing power of the Holy Spirit, whose activity was often described as a spiritual anointing.[32]

Anointing From the Sixth to the Tenth Century

The teaching of Innocent I became normative. His letter is listed in papal collections from the fifth to the eleventh centuries. It is found in the *Collectio Decretorum Pontificum Romanorum* of Dionysius Exiguus (448-514). But in this case a normative practice does not mean a uniform ritual. An examination of the several sources of evidence proves the case. There are three major kinds of sources: 1) formulae for the consecration of the oil, 2) liturgies of the anointing of the sick, and 3) literary sources.

---

[32]Martos, *Doors to the Sacred*, p. 374.

The Consecration of the Oil

The Gregorian and Gelasian sacramentaries both contain such consecrations. The older sacramentary, the Gelasian, contains material assembled in the latter half of the sixth century. The source seems to be Gallican and the materials are probably pre-sixth century. There are several versions of the Gregorian sacramentary. The two that are relevant here are the *Gregorianum Cameracense* which dates from the eighth century and the Gregorian Sacramentary of Hadrian which was introduced into the empire in the time of the Carolingian reform.

The formulae found in these sacramentaries are similar to those in the *Apostolic Tradition* of Hippolytus. There is an amazing unity in the text of Hippolytus, the two sacramentaries and the pre-Vatican II *Pontificale Romanum*. According to the *Apostolic Tradition* the purposes of the consecrations are comfort and health. Some commentators interpret the use of these two words as referring to the total person, including both a spiritual and a physical effect of the anointing. The Gelasian and the Roman rites stress protection of body, mind, and spirit to avoid all sickness of mind and body. The Gregorian Sacramentary seems to emphasize more the bodily effects although the spiritual dimensions mentioned in the other texts are also present. All the sacramentaries speak of a spiritual power having both a spiritual and corporal effect.

The *Gelasianum, Gregorianum* and the pre-Vatican II *Pontificale* present the Roman practice of blessing the oil at the Chrism Mass on Holy Thursday. However, other practices are referred to such as that by Bonitho of Piacenza (1095) in Italy. He states that the oil can be blessed on any day. The *Apostolic Tradition* allowed for the blessing of oil at any mass. According to the Ambrosian ritual the oil is blessed by the priest at the time of the visitation. Such is still the practice among the Greeks. Both the Gelasian and Gregorian sacramentaries presume the use of oil by the faithful as well as by priests and bishops. Some manuscripts clearly indicate that this oil is for the general use of the people as well as for the sick.

Liturgical Sources

The first ordinals for the adminstration of this sacrament date from the ninth century. Between the ninth and mid-tenth centuries there are many such books. The best historical evidence is that the ritual of anointing as found in the Roman Rite evolved in the Frankish kingdom in the ninth century. As already noted, before the ninth century there existed two parallel practices: 1) anointing by a priest and 2) the private anointing of the sick by the faithful with oil blessed by the bishop. The rites accompanying this second practice were unspecified. Some historians speculate that it was similar to the form used in the anointing of catechumens of the newly baptized.

While all the rituals indicate considerable variety, they bear witness to two facts: 1) the supernatural effect of the rite and 2) that the rite is carried out in accordance with the command found in the James text. The predominant idea of the rite is well expressed in the prayers of the *Sacramentarium Gregorianum* of Menard (end of tenth century).[33] This is a combination of the Sacramentary of St. Eloi (late tenth century) and the Sacramentary of Rodred (c. 853 A.D.). It contains the following prayer:

> Lord God, who has spoken by your Apostle James, saying: Is there anyone sick among you? Let him call in the presbyters of the Church, and let them pray over him, anointing him with oil in the name of the Lord...cure, we beseech thee, our Redeemer, the weakness of this sick man, heal his wounds and forgive his sins.[34]

There is a growing consensus in what the Church is aware of in anointing the sick, namely, that it is fulfilling a divine imperative and that the effect is forgiveness of sins and healing of weakness. But there is no uniformity regarding the rites that are recorded in the liturgical books. There is still present in some rites the inclusion of anointing as part

---

[33]Edited by Menard in 1642. PL 75: 25-240.
[34]Palmer, *Sacraments and Forgiveness*, p. 294.

of reconciliation. In some cases the anointing is seen as satisfaction for sin and reconciliation follows. In other cases, the anointing follows reconciliation and communion since, according to Innocent I, it cannot be given to penitents.

It is safe to say that this period demonstrates a clear historical relationship between the sacrament of anointing (if one may refer to anointing as a sacrament at this time) and the sacrament of penance. This is seen in the movement from public to private penance in the middle ages. Public penances in the early part of this period were extremely severe. As a result the reception of penance was frequently delayed until the nearing of death. Public penance was accomplished in two steps. First there was the admission into the order of penitents. Then after a more or less lengthy period of time there was the rite of reconciliation. Each stage was properly ritualized. The rite of anointing was often associated with the second stage of reconciliation. Eventually public penance ceased to exist in the Church. Private penance became the norm. Some of the rites that were formerly associated with the penitential anointing were now assigned to what would be later called the sacrament of anointing. This helped the solidifying of the anointing ritual. Private penance, introduced into the Frankish kingdom from Ireland, became common by the early ninth century. Whether or not the priest was the sole minister of penance at this early stage is a disputed point. Evidence pointing to the existence of women confessors is vague.

The prayers that accompany the anointing vary in form, some being a simple invocation of the Trinity. The anointings range in number from five to fifteen and more. The prayer formulae tend to resemble the anointing prayers connected with baptism and confirmation, as found in Hippolytus' *Apostolic Tradition*: "I anoint you with holy oil in our Lord God, almighty Father and in Christ Jesus and in the Holy Spirit." This is the most ancient of the anointing formulae. As with the other prayers in the sacramentaries, such formulae are older than the time of the compilation of these liturgical books. These formulae may well go back to the sixth century. The sacramentaries came into existence between the seventh and ninth centuries. Prior to the sixth century, there was considerable spontaneity in the composition of liturgical prayers.

An example of consensus on the purpose of anointing while admitting variety in the ritual practice would be the Gregorian Sacramentary of St. Eloi whose origins are traced back to the late 900's. For instance, although the priest who does the anointings does not say the accompanying prayer and is to visit the sick person for seven days with communion and the repetition of the anointings, the effect is clearly stated in the opening prayer: "cure the weakness of the sick person, heal his wounds, forgive his sins." The prayers which accompany the anointing states: "that the unclean spirit may not remain hidden in you. . . . cured and warmed by the Holy Spirit, may you merit to receive your former and even better health."[35] The practice on the part of the ministering priest may be somewhat unique, but the prayers speak of a common understanding of the desired effects of the anointing.

A closer look at two of the rites of anointing will give some idea of the morphology of this sacramental ritual in this period. Probably the earliest liturgy of anointing is of Roman origin, the Carolingian Unction Order. It developed in the Frankish kingdom between 815 and 845 A.D. In this rite Roman, Frankish and Mozarabic components can be seen in combination. H. Boone Porter has demonstrated the strong Spanish influence on this rite.[36] He discusses in detail the version given in Menard's edition of the Gregorian Sacramentary.[37]

Not only is this rite a combination of elements from different parts of Europe, it is also a compilation of compo-

[35]Ibid., pp. 294-5.

[36]H. Boone Porter, "The Origin of the Medieval Rite for Anointing the Sick or Dying," *Journal of Theological Studies* 7 (1956): 211-225.

[37]PL 78: 231-66.

nents from different existing liturgies. In this case, it would have been the rites of the visitation of the sick into which the rite of anointing had been inserted. The liturgy itself began with the blessing of the water. The sick person and the home were sprinkled with it. Then followed five prayers for the healing of the sick. These prayers were taken from Alcuin's Ordinal for visiting the sick. One prayer, *Domine Deus, qui per apostolum tuum Jacobum*, was of Carolingian origin and is still preserved in the pre- and post-Vatican II rituals. Its importance lies in giving the apostolic authority for this rite as well as declaring the effects of the sacrament. This prayer was followed by three antiphons with their psalms and these were concluded with a prayer. This led into the anointing itself. The formula was in part derived from the ceremony of exorcism for catechumens. Various parts of the body were anointed: back of the neck, throat, between the shoulders, the chest, and the particular area where pain was felt. The Menard text, however, directs anointing for back and front of neck and back and front of chest only. Other anointings were added later. Two Mozarabic prayers concluded the anointing. The eucharist was then to be administered. There is a directive that the rite could be repeated in seven days if necessary. In a possible later addition there is an alternate rite in which only the five senses are anointed.

Because this Carolingian liturgy is so elaborately developed, it most probably was first used in a monastic setting. It was a rite that had great influence in western Europe in the ninth, tenth, and eleventh centuries. From it spring the late medieval and modern rites. However, it was not the only existing rite of anointing at its time. The city of Milan had its own Ambrosian order. Britain also had its own unction of the sick. The ninth century Stowe Missal contains Celtic texts of this rite. The Celtic practice emphasized the mass of the sick with an anointing inserted before the *pater noster*. This Celtic rite is of particular interest because it had some influence on some of the sacramentaries in use on the continent. The texts indicate that anointing was administered to hopeless cases in which there was no possibility of a cure.

Porter points out that the Carolingian rite was not seen as a rite for the dying up to the tenth century and even then the prayers used still spoke of recovery.[38] The Celtic influence was also felt in particular forms of anointing in special cases such as the curing of someone who is the victim of demonic possession.

A second example of an anointing rite during this period would be that as described by Theodulf in the *Capitulary of Theodulph of Orleans*.[39] Theodulf died in 821. What should be especially noted is that while the rubrics refer to the performance of the rite in the church, there are also rubrics which are suitable for the administration of the rite in the home of the sick based on the older tradition of the visitation of the sick. The order of the rite is as follows:

1. Penance is to take place first. This would not be public penance since this is already the period of the Carolingian reform with its Celtic penitential discipline.

2. The sick person is washed and clothed in white in remembrance of the anointing in baptism. He/she is brought to the church and laid on an ash covered sack-cloth.

3. Three priests say the prayer: "Peace to this house and to all who live in it." One of them puts some holy oil in water and sprinkles the sick person. In effect this is a concelebration of the rite. Suitable music is sung during this sprinkling.

4. The sick person is signed in the form of a cross on the head and chest with blessed ashes with the formula of Ash Wednesday. There are chants which accompany the imposition of ashes.

5. Then follows the seven penitential psalms and a litany.

6. One priest anoints the sick person fifteen times: a great cross on the back, between the shoulders from shoulder to neck and across the shoulders; on the neck from the

[38]Porter, "The Origin of the Medieval Rite....," p. 225.

[39]PL 105: 220-222. According to J.P. McClain in *The New Catholic Encyclopedia* v. 1, the Ritual of Theodulf of Orleans probably represents a later period in liturgical history than the ninth century. For a complete analysis of the matter see H. Boone Porter, "The Rites of the Dying in the Early Middle Ages, I: St. Theodulf of Orleans," *Journal of Theological Studies* 10 (1959): 43-62.

shoulders to the skull; across the top of the head to the forehead and across to the ears; on the eyelids; on the nostrils; on the lips; on the ears; on the throat; on the chest; on the outside of the hands; on the feet. Theodulf says this was done with prayer, but gives no text. There were accompanying chants.

7. The priest and sick person jointly pray the Lord's Prayer, the Creed, the Commendation of the Soul to God, various blessings and a farewell blessing. The dying person takes leave of the living.

8. Absolution of the sick person: "May he be granted peace." There may have been a kiss of peace in conjunction with this absolution.

9. Communion.

10. A closing prayer: "Let us bless the Lord."

The priest is instructed to visit the sick person for seven days with communion and to pray over him/her in the rite just described.

This rite has been the object of considerable scrutiny by H. Boone Porter. Several of his conclusions seem to be beyond challenge and they must be taken into account when referring to this order as descriptive of anointing practices during this period. Some of his conclusions are:[40]

> a) Theodulf is not the author of this ritual.
>
> b) This ritual does not represent Carolingian practice but most probably is descriptive of late tenth or early eleventh century procedures.
>
> c) This ritual which is addressed to the dying person cannot be used as evidence that Theodulf is the "father of extreme unction."
>
> d) Prior to the time of Theodulf the practice of anointing refers to unction for the obtaining of a physical cure or as some form of exorcism.
>
> e) In these pre-Theodulf anointings there was no uniform method of anointing with the oil. Lay people or the sick

[40]Ibid.

person could apply it. And preparation for death was a secondary consideration.

f) Extreme unction, on the other hand, was sacerdotal in character with no provision for lay anointing. There was an elaborate anointing of the senses and the service had a strong penitential character.

While it is not possible in the opinion of this writer to contradict Porter's findings, there is still value in including this rite attributed to Theodulf in this section of the chapter. It does represent a practice which was most probably characteristic of the anointing ritual at the end of this historical section and at the beginning of the next period of the eleventh century on. This liturgy also illustrates the movement from anointing being directed toward the sick to it becoming a service exclusively performed for those who are dying. That extreme unction as a specific rite developed later than had previously been believed is significant, but ultimately not that important for the contemporary understanding of the sacrament. What is of both historical importance and of contemporary significance is the change itself in the meaning of anointing: from a form of ministry to the sick to a universally accepted ministry to the dying. Whether the bishop of Orleans is the originator of extreme unction or not, does not change this regrettable theological and pastoral development.

Porter also points out that not only was this rite not fathered by Theodulf, but that it is "little more than blundering, disjointed pedantry."[41] He asserts that the author, whoever that may be, was not attempting to introduce a new rite but to simplify one which had already become too complicated for use on the pastoral level. The Carolingian experience of anointing as healing unction is now a matter of history. The author is trying to give some helpful rubrical advice to the clergy about the incumbent sacrament of extreme unction. The importance of this document has been aptly expressed by Porter:

[41]Ibid., p. 57.

This order for the dying thus has not the slightest value as a witness to the liturgical and pastoral practices of the time of Charlemagne. On the other hand, this document still is of great interest. For the first thousand years of Christian history, the rites of the dying in Western Christendom had become increasingly elaborate; then a change slowly set in. In the order of Pseudo-Theodulf, we have the unique record of one of those who inaugurated that new trend towards simplicity which has continued from his day right down to our own.[42]

There are some common characteristics of anointing practices during this time especially as reflected in the rituals of Menard and the Pseudo-Theodulf. There is one central idea: anointing and prayer for the purpose of care for the sick and the forgiveness of sins. In Menard there is a clear connection with the James text. It is less so in the Pseudo-Theodulf. The rite was usually administered at home. It was also administered in church, probably because of the eucharist. Anointings by a single priest took place although the more usual practice was by several. One did the anointings while others read the prayers. Another practice would be that each priest performed one of the anointings with the accompanying prayer. There seems to have been little uniformity in the number of parts of the body that were anointed. There was no universally established order.

For a time there was concern not to re-anoint those parts of the body which had already been anointed. Thus parts adjacent would be anointed instead. But eventually all anointings were dropped in favor of the five senses and the feet. The formulae that accompanied the anointings varied considerably. But as the experience and theology of the sacrament became more for the dying than the sick, references to physical healing were dropped and the emphasis was placed on the forgiveness of sins. This change took place around the same time that the ordinals reflected a change in the order of the administration of these last rites

---

[42]Ibid., p. 60.

from penance, anointing, viaticum to penance, viaticum, anointing. That is the order of the last rites in the Frankish Church by the tenth century.

The ninth century was a time of great liturgical activity in the Frankish kingdom. A number of the rites were receiving a more definite form and were becoming fixed formulae. This is certainly true for the sacrament of the sick. At this time the canonical evidence is that private anointings are proscribed and sacramental anointing is reserved to the priest.[43] This priestly anointing develops in terms of the contemporary priestly functions of the visitation of the sick and the administration of penance and viaticum. Thus, the end of lay anointing, the restriction of this sacrament to the priest, and the clerical ministrations to the dying led to the combination of anointing and penance on the deathbed. Apparently reform efforts to restore the visitation of the sick which had fallen into desuetude in the dark ages had a massive influence on moving anointing from the sacrament of the sick to the sacrament of the dying. Celtic practices may have been the initiators in this case. In the Celtic practice both penance and viaticum as sacraments of the dying joined anointing to become a unified rite for the care of the sick who were proximate to death. This prepares for the practice beginning around the eleventh century of calling anointing "extreme unction."

Literary Sources

There are two principal sources for the literary information of this period. They are: 1) the commentary of Venerable Bede on James and Mark and 2) the hagiographers. Two of the literary bits of evidence before Bede might be noted.[44] Caesarius of Arles (d. 543) in his sermons exhorts women in the time of their children's sickness to come to church to receive the eucharist and anointing. In one place

---

[43]Martos gives some examples which indicate that private lay anointing continued till the beginning of the ninth century.

[44]Palmer, *Sacraments and Forgiveness,* pp. 284-5.

he writes: "As often as sickness occurs, let the sick one receive the Body and Blood of the Lord and afterwards anoint his body so that what is written might be fulfilled in him.....See to it, brothers, that the one who goes to the church in time of sickness receives the healing of the body and the forgiveness of sins."[45] Along the same lines St. Eloi (Eligius) of Noyons exhorts the sick to put their trust in God, receive the eucharist, and let themselves be anointed.[46] In this way the promise of the gospel and of James will be fulfilled.

Venerable Bede in his commentary on James speaks of the faith of the Church in his time, namely in the eighth century.[47] In this context he gives the basis for the anointing of the sick. Sickness is described as something both corporal and spiritual and in this sense there is a continuation of the tradition of Origen. And while there is still the custom that it is "priests" who pray over the sick, there is still the recognition that the faithful may use the oil for themselves. Confession of sins to the priests is recommended, although the forgiveness of sins through the daily prayers of the community is recognized in the exhortation: "Wherefore confess your sins to one another." The basis of anointing is the interpretation of the James text that here we have a grace-giving ministry done by the Church in the name of Christ. Bede's commentary was very influential in the middle ages.

The hagiography of the period gives evidence of a shift in popular understanding. As might be expected it is a movement from a sacrament of the sick to a sacrament of the dying. The lives of the saints after 700 A.D. present the final hours of the saints in terms of the sacramental ministrations of penance, eucharist and *anointing*. For instance, Paschasius Radbertus (d. 865) in his life of Adelard indicates a practice which lasts into the later middle ages and would be characteristic of the latter part of this period between the

[45]*Sermo* 225, PL 39:2238.

[46]Palmer, *Sacraments and Forgiveness*, p. 285.

[47]Ibid., p. 286-7.

sixth and tenth centuries. At the time of Adelard's final hours, the bishop of Beauvais comes to Corbie to visit him and asks if it is necessary to anoint him. The bystanders ask Adelard if he wishes anointing, although they know he is without sin. He requests anointing.[48] Again, in the *Acta Sanctorum* (February 1, 866) Rimbertus (bishop of Hamburg 865-888) asks for anointing on the seventh day before his death and receives it, with the eucharist on each of these seven days.

The eighth and ninth centuries present further evidence that anointing has become a sacrament of the dying. The *Statutes of Bonifacius* instructs priests not to go on a journey without the oils and the eucharist.[49] The *Capitulary of Charlemagne* says: "that the dying might not pass away without an anointing" (*General Capitulary*, 769-771) and "before the close of life" (*Capitulary of Aachen*, 801), they should receive both viaticum and anointing. Martos points out that Alcuin of York added to the Gregorian Sacramentary imposed by Charlemagne a supplement of prayers which contained a newly composed rite for priestly anointing of the sick. It was placed in the section which contained the prayers for the dying and the rite of final reconciliation. Ironically, when the Gregorian Sacramentary returned to Rome and replaced the original Roman one, Rome adopted the French Church's order of the last rites which concludes with anointing rather than the eucharist.[50]

From the eighth century on, the private use of oil for anointing decreases. Capitularies, synods, and bishops are stressing the importance of people confessing, communicating and receiving anointing when their lives are in danger. Priestly anointing is emphasized as the bishops desire to adopt what they think is the Roman practice. Priests are ordered to be ready at any time to provide eucharist and anointing to the sick and dying. The leaders of the Church

[48]PL 120: 1547.

[49]Palmer, *Sacraments and Forgiveness*, p. 292.

[50]Martos, *Doors to the Sacred*, p. 377.

complain of a general negligence in this matter. The liturgical reforms of the Carolingian period are directed toward this restoration of anointing. The Council of Aachen insists that bishops are to consecrate the oil for the sick at the Mass of Chrism.[51] The councils of this period also stress the biblical foundation for this practice in the James text. The Councils of Chalon, Aachen, and Pavia make it clear that anointing is of more than ecclesiastical origin. The interpretation of Bede on the text of James is more universally accepted as time goes on.

The effects of this sacrament as they are presented in the writings of this period are both corporal and spiritual. However, the shift to the spiritual dimension is more evident. To take but a few examples is all that is necessary. Amalarius in his *De Ecclesiasticis Officiis* says that the oil energizes the weary and gives the light of grace. Thus God makes visible what happens invisibly in this anointing. The sick are assisted by the grace of God in the anointing by the priest. Anointing is the source of the curing of physical illnesses. In this sacrament Christ overcomes the devil. The Council of Chalon II (813) identifies the remedy as that which "heals the weakness of body and soul."[52] The Council of Pavia (850) sees the corporal effects working through the spiritual: "It is a great mystery and greatly to be desired; through it, if one asks with confidence, sins are remitted and as a result, bodily health is restored."[53]

It was during this period that the number of anointings increased.[54] Different traditions were molded together and so there does not seem to be any logical development. Rather it was merely a matter of accumulation. The most simple and perhaps the most original form was to anoint the head as a symbol of the whole person. Anointing the

---

[51]Palmer, *Sacraments and Forgiveness*, p. 291.

[52]Ibid., p. 290-1.

[53]Ibid., p. 292.

[54]For more information on this matter, cf. Porter, "The Origin of the Medieval Rite for Anointing the Sick or Dying," p. 221.

extremities would have been an alternate practice with the same intent: unction addresses the whole person. Anointing the place of ailment would be the result of seeing anointing with a strong therapeutic purpose. The ninth century witnessed the practice of the anointing of the hands of the sick person. This most probably came from the parallel practice of anointing hands in ordination ceremonies. The anointing of the senses is the practice that ultimately triumphed in medieval Europe. Anointing the senses was already a custom in baptism and this practice easily moved into the liturgy for the sick. The emphasis on anointing as the sacrament of forgiveness of sins committed by means of the senses reinforced this practice of multiple anointings.

Summary

This period is one of both enriching growth and confusing complications. However, some summary statements are possible.

1. Before the time of Charlemagne, the Roman liturgy had no special rite for administering oil to the sick. There is no eighth century evidence for a priestly or clerical anointing of the sick in Rome. The same is true for those Roman books in use in Northern Europe. The only liturgy of anointing would have been the formulae for blessing the oil.

2. Merovingian times (sixth to eighth centuries) provide evidence for a blessing of oil on Maundy Thursday. This oil was provided by the laity who took it home with them and either drank it or anointed themselves with it as they pleased. The oil would have been blessed by an epicletic prayer offered by the bishop.

3. By the middle of the ninth century an elaborate and unified rite had developed. It was a composite of rites and prayers from several sources: the visitation of the sick, special rites for the sick, and prayers referring to anointing itself.

4. Before the ninth century the rite of anointing is directed to the sick and is not for the dying, although one cannot exclude the latter possibility on the level of pastoral practice.

5. Before the ninth century there is evidence for lay anointing, self anointing and presbyteral anointing in various parts of Christian Europe.

6. Before the ninth century anointing is directed to the healing of the whole person, the health of body and spirit. It is not anointing for life after death, nor is it associated with the forgiveness of sins.

7. The Carolingian practice of anointing is part of a larger Church renewal and liturgical reform. Clergy are urged to care for the sick. Lay anointing is probably suppressed to overcome abuses and in deference to the emphasis on the priestly ministry. From the late ninth century on the priest is the proper and probably the only minister of the sacrament. Early Carolingian anointing involved a number of priests.

8. During the ninth and tenth centuries the anointing is directed primarily to those who are close to death. One of the main reasons for this change of direction is the mentality regarding the sacrament of penance. Because of the harsh penances connected with public reconciliation, many put off the sacrament of penance until the very end of their lives. But since one could not receive anointing until after penance, anointing itself was associated with the death-bed penitence.

9. As a result of the pastoral practice of postponing anointing until the final hours of one's life, there was a theological change. Since in such cases there was little hope of a physical cure or the restoration of health, in the ninth, tenth, and following centuries anointing was redirected from the healing of the body and spirit to human death. The effect of the sacrament was seen as a spiritual one: the forgiveness of sins. This practice and this theology will eventuate in the naming of this anointing as "extreme unction" since it is given *in extremis*. This change also meant a renewed emphasis on the James text where it says: "and if he has committed sins, he will be forgiven."

10. A greater stress was placed on the relationship between sin and sickness. Bede had made a passing reference to this relationship. More was made of it in these

centuries. This partly sprung from a decreasing sense of the importance of the human body. Physical healing was relegated to a position subordinate to spiritual grace.

Anointing of the Sick
From the Eleventh Century
To the Council of Trent

During this period the sacrament takes on the shape it will have until the Second Vatican Council's reform of the rite. The thirteenth century concludes with the practice of anointing becoming general in the Western Church. A fully developed theology of the sacraments in general is characteristic of the high middle ages or that period between the eleventh and thirteenth centuries. As was to be expected with the development of scholastic theology in the twelfth century, greater precision was given to defining the sacramentality of anointing of the sick. And as was the case in other theological areas there were differing views. In fact, however, since Peter Lombard listed anointing as a sacrament in his book of *Sentences* and because his list of sacraments became normative, "extreme unction" was accepted as one of the seven sacraments.

The medieval theologians, because they did their reflections in terms of the concrete practices they experienced, described anointing as the sacrament of the dying. Because anointing was now restricted to the final hours of one's life, certain somewhat bizarre attitudes surrounded its administration. For instance, according to some theologians, once anointed a person was pledged to a life of penance, was forbidden the use of matrimony, and could not eat meat. For these reasons as well as the fact that the ordinary person dreaded the sacrament because of its connection with death, anointing of the sick fell into disuse. The twelfth century *De Sacramentis infantium morientium* says that this sacrament has been virtually abolished. It seems that the leaders of the Church and the theologians did not agree with the strongly penitential character that surrounded anointing. However, the practice of connecting anointing and final reconciliation only reinforced such an attitude. The use of sack cloth and ashes, the extraction of a promise to "keep this Holy Anointing" should the person recover, could only point to a life of penance. A more pedestrian, non-theological reason for the rarity of anointing at this time was the expense. Ordinary simple people could not afford the honoraria for several priests gathered for an anointing.

In the systematic theologies of the eleventh to the thirteenth centuries anointing is universally accepted as a sacrament in terms of the rather univocal definition of a sacrament prevalent at that time. But there was both a variety of opinions as well as a variety of practices regarding the nature of this sacrament, the manner of its institution, whether it could be repeated, and the requirement of a minister. First, the theologians called the early scholastics will be considered.

The Early Scholastics[55]

It is only in the eleventh and twelfth centuries that sacramental theology takes on its own form which clarifies the nature of anointing. There are several representative theological figures who have contributed to the development in this area. Bonitho of Piacenza is one of the earliest scholastic authors who deals with the sacraments. In his *Libellus de Sacramentis ad Gualterum*, he divides the sacraments into three classes. He accepts the Augustinian definition of a sacrament as a visible form of invisible grace. In the first class are those sacraments instituted by Christ: baptism and eucharist. The second class includes those sacraments instituted by the apostles: salt for the catechumens and the three oils of chrism, catechumens, and the sick. The third class consists of those sacraments which the Church uses based on the example of Christ: the breathing on the person in the exorcisms, the ephpheta or prayer over ears and mouth in

[55]For further referencing of this material the reader should consult Janssens, *Het Heilig Oliesel*, p. 91ff.

baptism, the imposition of hands in the anointing of catechumens as well as in absolution and ordination. For Bonitho, anointing of the sick is a sacrament instituted by the
apostles.

Nicholas, secretary to Bernard of Clairvaux, lists twelve
sacraments: baptism, confirmation, *anointing of the sick*,
consecration of a bishop, consecration of a king, consecration of a church, confession, canonicate, the state of monks,
the state of hermits, consecrated virgins, and marriage. Here
anointing is described as the help of the Spirit in time of
death to release dying people from their sins. The oil heals
and forgives sins and the priest raises up the body and stills
the bodily desires.

Geoffrey, bishop of Vendome (d. 1132), treats the eucharist and anointing together. As a unit they heal the soul from
the wounds of sin and effect eternal salvation and union
with Christ. For Geoffrey anointing is not only of apostolic
origin but is so great a sacrament that it cannot be repeated.
This was an opinion held by many in the eleventh and
twelfth centuries. Some even ascribe a character or indelible
mark to anointing.

The anonymous *Summa Sententiarum* reiterates the
common position that this sacrament was instituted by the
apostles. In classical distinctions, the *sacramentum* or out-
ward sign is the anointing. It speaks of the sign and the effect
of the sacrament. The *res sacramenti* or interior grace is the
forgiveness of sins. Although the *Summa* admits that this
sacrament is repeated, this is viewed as contrary to Augustine. However, in fact, according to the *Summa* there is no
recognition of the sacrament because the oil is not
reconsecrated.

Hugh of St. Victor's position is more in accord with that
of the original meaning. That is, he does not view anointing
as a sacrament of the departing. He says that "this sacrament was instituted for a twofold reason, namely, both for
the remission of sins and for the alleviation of bodily sickness."[56] He also sees the sacrament as instituted by the

[56]Palmer, *Sacraments and Forgiveness*, p. 297.

apostles. And he allows for its repetition upon request. The sacrament always heals. It cures physical illness when this is appropriate. But the rite always heals in that it forgives sins. Physical illness comes to some so that they will turn back to God and thus forgiveness means a kind of healing of the body. The point is that the soul is always healed. And if someone becomes sick because of their sins why should they not be repeatedly anointed. Hugh's position is important because it was embraced by later theologians and his theology was influential for centuries.

Twelfth and Thirteenth Century Theologians

The work of the early scholastics was the basis for the theologizing on anointing in the twelfth and thirteenth centuries. This is a very rich time both in the number and quality of theologians. Rather than treat individual theological positions, it will be more helpful to summarize positions under the principal questions that were treated by these theologians.

Anointings

Lombard lists three anointings: the principal anointing called Chrism, the anointing of the catechumens on the back and chest, and the anointing of the sick. Peter Cantor (d. 1197) adds to this list the ordinary anointing of the sick by the faithful. He notes that the last anointing is no longer in use. A change of practice occurs in the twelfth century which would have provided theologians with a different understanding of the meaning of the anointing. Justification for this latter anointing is found in Mk 6:13. Robert of Courcon has four anointings: baptism, confirmation, for the sick, and the anointing of the sick with consecrated oil of any sick person by the faithful. He notes that the last anointing is no longer in use. A change of practice occurs in the twelfth century which would have provided theologians with a different understanding of the meaning of the anointings. As the sacrament took on more the purpose of the forgiveness of sins, the oil that once was applied to the places of the body that were in need of healing, now is applied to the five senses through which the sins are committed.[57]

Institution of the Sacrament
The majority of the twelfth century *Summae* attribute the institution of the sacrament to the apostles. This is based on the text of James. This is simply taken as a fact. There is no real theological reflection on this point. There is no attempt to explain how the apostles instituted it or what the sacrament's relationship to Christ is. This may be a case of *lex orandi, lex credendi* because the prayers of the sacramentaries refer to the James text for the basis of the sacramentality of anointing. There was a school of thought at this time, to which Geoffrey of Vendome belonged, which attributed the institution of all the sacraments to the apostles. The other school would have followed Bonitho's division of the sacraments in which they are divided into three classes. Robert of Courcon is unique in his position in that he says that Christ instituted the sacrament of anointing in his mission to the apostles in Mk 6:13.

Ministers
The opinions reflect the diversity of practice. For instance, Peter Cantor says that there must be several priests. Anointing by a single priest is contrary to James and must be discontinued. Robert of Courcon, however, allows for administration by a single priest but only in the case of necessity.

Effects of the Sacrament
The high scholastics had only limited documentation upon which to do their theological analysis. It is universally the text of James which was used, although the letter of Innocent I is quoted with some regularity. These theologians list three effects of anointing: (1) the forgiveness of sins, (2) physical healing, and (3) protection of the sick

[57]Martos, *Doors to the Sacred*, p. 379.

person from the powers of evil at the time of death. But the theologians are not agreed on what the sacrament primarily causes.

One view was that anointing is clearly a sacrament primarily for those who are seriously ill. Using the cause/effect model these theologians assigned the cure of the body as the proper effect of this rite. A more noble effect of anointing would be the forgiveness of sins. Some of the proponents of this view were Hugh of Saint-Victor (d. 1141) and William of Auxerre (d. 1231). But others also promoted this view of the sacrament: Roland Bandinelli (d. 1181), Omnebenne (d. 1185) and Alanus of Rijssel.

The second theological position understood anointing more to be the sacrament of the dying and so the primary effect of it would deal with spiritual healing or the forgiveness of sins. This view was represented by the well-known medieval theologian, Peter Lombard (d. 1160). Apparently, he was one of the first to use the name, "extreme unction." The *Summa Sententiarum* as well as Lombard speaks of anointing in terms of the soul which implies an increase of virtues. The *Epitome* of the school of Abelard and Rolandus held that *some* sins are forgiven. Peter Comestor and John Belethus held that only venial sins are forgiven. The *Epitome* says that since this sacrament is like penance, a person's senses are anointed since a person sins through his/her senses. Master Simon (possibly a contemporary of Hugh of St. Victor) and William of Auvergne (c. 1249) furthered the stress on the spiritual effect of anointing by seeing it as preparation for the beatific vision. The second position was the one adopted by the stars of medieval theology: Albert the Great (d. 1280), Thomas Aquinas (d. 1274), Bonaventure (d. 1274), and Duns Scotus (d. 1308).

How this sacrament actually effected its results was the source of theological differences between the Franciscans and Dominicans. While both school espoused the idea that extreme unction prepares one for the after life, the Franciscans saw this preparation taking place through the removal of venial sins. The Dominicans saw it in terms of the removal of the remnants of sin. Such remnants were not sins themselves but the aftereffects of sin which impeded one from a deeper union with God. Aquinas, who followed the Dominican position, argued that the sacrament should not be given to children and those who could not understand what the anointing and the words meant. Bonaventure, in the Franciscan tradition, added that it should not be given to people who might recover from their illness; otherwise the purpose of the sacrament would be defeated. John Duns Scotus in stressing the automatic efficacy of the sacrament maintained that the best recipient for this sacrament is someone who can no longer sin. This position prepared the way for administering anointing to the unconscious.

The Repeatability of the Sacrament

There was no unanimous position in the medieval theological community on this point. Those who do not permit the repetition of anointing base it on Augustine's teaching regarding baptism, confirmation, and orders which are three sacraments which involve an anointing and cannot be repeated. Anointing of the sick is assimilated to these anointings and thus this sacrament takes on the same character as the others. Ugguccio in claiming to follow St. Augustine's principles asserts that this sacrament has a *character* and so cannot be repeated. Praepositinus also maintains that this sacrament has a character but asserts that it lasts for only a year. Yves of Chartres sees anointing of the sick to be parallel with public penance and both are unrepeatable.

Since theology tends to follow practice, such pluralism in opinions merely reflects the pluralism on the practical level. Lombard and the *Epitome* state that the custom of each place should be followed. There are those who admit that the sacrament can be repeated but even they are divided on how often this repetition may take place. Cluny was most influential here in permitting the sacrament to be received only once a year. In the synods of the late twelfth century more frequent administration is permitted. The summists of this period are agreed that the oil used must be blessed by the bishop on Holy Thursday and that even in the case of necessity, the sacrament may not be administered by a deacon.

The Meaning of "to be infirm"

The almost universal opinion at this time is that the sickness must be mortal. Thus the sacrament is called the sacrament of the dying or extreme unction. There were those such as Peter Cantor and Robert of Courcon who advised that the sacrament be administered while the person could consciously receive it, thus permitting the possibility of some corporal effect. Others disagreed, maintaining that this is the sacrament that brings the Christian life to a close. These would also maintain that sexual intercourse is not permitted after anointing. Peter Cantor and Robert of Courcon both agreed that an explicit and active intention for the reception of the sacrament is required, that it was to be given only to those who asked for it, and that administration to the unconscious, the insane, and possessed is invalid. While some theologians advocated giving the sacrament to infants, the synods and capitularies of this time insist that it be restricted to those who have reached the age of reason.

Anointing displaces Viaticum

The logical and inevitable result of this historical development through the eleventh and twelfth centuries was that anointing replaces viaticum as the final sacrament. The older order of the sacraments: penance, anointing, viaticum was firmly transposed to penance, viaticum, anointing. There are without question non-theological reasons for this displacement. The fact that anointing became too costly to be received more than once in one's life, or the common belief that once anointed certain human experiences such as marital relations were no longer permitted, helped to push anointing to the last moment of a person's life. Theological reasons such as anointing for heavenly glory are also important in understanding this displacement. It is not obvious whether the non-theological reasons brought on a theological articulation or whether the reflections of theologians changed popular practice. Probably it was a matter of mutual interaction and influence.

It appears, however, that the major reason for this shift in understanding of the sacrament was the inability to see its relationship to physical healing. Because the theological question was posed in terms of the cause/effect model, the dominating question was: what does this sacrament do?[58] Formerly, the answer was seen in terms of the restoration of physical health. But since this effect was so infrequently realized, it seemed that the very sacramental efficacy of anointing was being called into question. A solution was found in terms of the larger theological framework of grace. Sacraments produce grace and grace is a supernatural reality. From such a perspective it was easy to conclude that the remission of sin is the primary effect of this sacrament. And since other sacraments were seen as having the same purpose, e.g. baptism and penance, it became incumbent on medieval theology to specify the kind of remission from sin, namely, those sins committed prior to death but not removed by the sacrament of penance. And even more specifically, anointing's task was to purify the person of the final remnants due to sin. Inevitably, this theological articulation had the effect in practice of pushing the sacrament to the last moments of life. As the historical survey of this period reveals, many forces conspired to turn the sacrament of the sick into extreme unction. Needless to say, this was reflected in ritual changes. Martos puts it this way:

> Since the anointing was rarely given to people who were expected to recover from their illness, the prayers for physical healing were gradually dropped from the rite and were replaced with ones which spoke only of the remission of sins and the hope of salvation. Sometimes

[58]See Thomas Talley, "Healing: Sacrament or Charism," *Worship* 46:9 (November 1972): 518ff. for a good discussion in contemporary terms of how this sacrament *causes* an effect.

these prayers were borrowed from exorcism formulas in old liturgical books; sometimes they were composed by those who inserted them into the rites themselves. But they were always attempts to make the words of the ritual correspond more closely to what it appeared to be: an anointing in preparation for death.[59]

By the thirteenth century the sacramentality of anointing is firmly established and the Council of Lyons (1274) speaks of it as a sacrament of the Roman Church. The Council of Florence in the *Decree for the Armenians* and the Council of Trent state clearly that the sacramentality of the anointing of the sick has always been the faith of the Church based on the authority of scripture, especially the text of James.

From the High Middle Ages to Trent

In its historical development the rite of anointing became extremely lengthy. This elaboration of the ritual contributed to its falling into desuetude since its length meant that it was used less often. A reform of simplification was inevitable. The Benedictines of Cluny engaged in a reform of this rite that made it less complicated. This Benedictine reform in turn influenced that of the rite found in the Pontifical of the Roman Curia of the thirteenth century. This ritual is the confluence of many other ritual developments of the previous centuries. The Romano-Germanic pontifical of the tenth century which contained five rites dealing with Christian death and burial fed into this pontifical. Two of these five rites: visitation of the sick and a rite for anointing also appeared in the Breviary of the Franciscans. And since the Franciscans traversed Europe and had considerable influence on the dissemination of liturgy as mendicants, these two rites received considerable exposure. In this same Breviary there is a threefold ritual for anointing, viaticum, and commendation of the dying. All these modifications influenced the structure of the thirteenth century Roman Pontifical. This Ordo became part of the *Liber Sacerdotalis* of Alberto

[59]Martos, *Doors to the Sacred*, p. 379.

Castellani (d.c. 1522) and the Ritual of Cardinal Santorio (d. 1602). From this latter ritual, it passed into the Ritual of Paul V (1614) to become the Roman Ritual of Anointing. This was a simplified rite to be used by one priest and with more emphasis on the forgiveness of sins than physical healing. With this ritual local variations ceased.

Summary

The major changes that occurred in this period can be summed up as follows:

1. Anointing moves from being a sacrament of physical healing to being a means of the forgiveness of sins. This is due to the desire both on the part of the theological community as well as popular understanding to stress the spiritual effects of the sacrament so that anointing always achieves what is claimed for it. Physical-psychological well-being becomes secondary.

2. There is considerable variety of ritual practice until the sixteenth century, although by the thirteenth the order of the last rites had been changed so that anointing displaced viaticum.

3. Theological pluralism was still characteristic of this period. However, the various theories of the purpose of this sacrament had the same pastoral result in that anointing was usually administered in the last hours of one's life.

4. Non-theological reasons such as penitential practices associated with the sacrament of penance as well as anointing were operative, as were the more theological influences listed in the previous three points, to make anointing into a sacrament directed primarily to the dying, a last sacrament, an extreme unction. Once this was achieved, the best of the medieval theologians attempted to view the sacrament in a more positive way as an anointing for final glory. This in turn gave support to one of the necessary conditions for the reception of this sacrament: the danger of death.

5. The sacraments of penance and anointing are brought into closer existential association in the life of the Christian and the relationship of sin and sickness and healing and

forgiveness is highlighted. Anointing receives its meaning from a context of a theology of sin.

From the Council of Trent To Modern Times

The sixteenth century saw the great upheavals of the Protestant Reformation. The reformers made radical changes in the medieval sacramental system. The sacramentality of anointing was rejected because there was no biblical warrant for it and it was playing only an insignificant place in the life of the late medieval Christian since so few people received it. In reaction, the Council of Trent felt compelled to stress certain points about this sacrament. Reactions of some of the major figures of the Reformation are summarized here.

Martin Luther

Luther denied that the James text could be used to support anointing's sacramentality. James was talking about healing and the scholastics were talking about preparation for death. However, Luther did think anointing might be practiced as a way of experiencing confidence in God and forgiveness of sins. While Luther permitted anointing, he considered it a human invention.[60]

Melancthon

Melancthon took up Luther's position adding that the sacrament originated in Patristic times. Since it is analogous to the healing charisms of the primitive Church, it ceased when those charisms did.

Calvin

Calvin distinguished what he said was actually described by James and what the Roman priests were actually doing.

[60]*Luther's Works* 36 (Philadelphia: Fortress Press, 1959), pp. 117-123.

James did not indicate that the oil forgave sins but the priests attributed the remission of sins to the anointing itself. Calvin maintained that the elders of the James text refer not to priests but to the older members of the community. He attributes the origin of anointing to Innocent I. His fundamental judgment about the sacrament of anointing is that it is a kind of playacting.[61] The apostles's gift of healing was only temporary.

Other Protestant judgment regarding anointing would be in the direction of either Luther or Calvin. Bucer, for example, rejected anointing but not communion to the sick. Chemnitz claimed that Felix IV (526-530) was the originator. Liberal Protestant historians of theology have tended to place the beginnings of this sacrament in the ninth century. Earlier rituals were directed solely to physical care. Later, the forgiveness of sins was added and so the twelfth century theologians could include it in the list of sacraments. Protestant theologians would view anointing in the history of the Church as a devotion rather than a sacrament in the strict sense.

What continued on in Protestantism in place of the sacrament of anointing was the visitation of the sick. Some Churches had more formal forms of visitation with special prayers and even confession. The early Methodists celebrated communion in the sickroom. In the eighteenth century the Church of the Brethren made use of anointing. It probably involved an anointing on the head.

Anglican

The Church of England's position on anointing is characterized by some variety and change. The 1549 Prayer Book continued the rite of anointing. The twenty-fifth of the thirty-nine articles lists it among the five sacraments which are not of divine institution.[62] But the 1552 Prayer Book no

---

[61]*Institutes of the Christian Religion* IV. xix, 18 (Philadelphia: The Library of Christian Classics 21, 1960), p. 1466.

[62]*The Book of Common Prayer* (The Church Hymnal Corporation, 1977), p. 872.

longer contains a rite for anointing. In the later nineteenth century some Anglicans attempted to restore this rite to their communion. And in 1928 attempts were made to reintroduce an anointing rite.

The 1549 rite was modelled after the Sarum usage for visiting the sick. Procession to the house of the sick person, penitential psalms, auricular confession, and imposition of penance would be some of the elements omitted from the Sarum rite. The theological emphasis moves in the direction of viewing sickness as a visitation from God to try or punish the person. Repentance and patient submission is the response that is expected by one who shares in the sufferings of Christ through baptism. The person renews his/her baptismal promises by reciting the Apostles' Creed. Then follow the articles of faith. The anointing itself is quite simplified. Only one anointing is made on forehead or breast with a sign of the cross but without an accompanying psalmody. The prayer which is said at this time emphasizes the restoration of health and the triumph over suffering. Although it refers to the forgiveness of sins and spiritual strengthening, it is in marked contrast to medieval extreme unction with the emphasis on preparation for death. This would be in accord with earlier official Anglican statements regarding unction. However, early in the rite there is a homily dealing with the fear of death. The communion of the sick which follows presupposes the reservation of the eucharist. The reception was to be under both forms and on the same day as the celebration in the church.

Sixteenth century Anglicans accepted the views of Martin Bucer, the Calvinist reformer, regarding anointing as something which was meant only for apostolic times and so the possibility of anointing was removed from the 1552 Prayer Book. Any further references to healing were deleted in the 1662 revisions. There was still the visitation of the sick with prayers and a benediction but reservation of the eucharist was in effect ruled out. The non-jurors of the eighteenth century and the Tractarians of the nineteenth promoted the use of anointing. They laid the groundwork for the modern revisions of the Anglican Church.[63]

The Council of Trent

Since even contemporary Roman Catholic theology must reflect upon the major doctrinal statements of the Roman Catholic Church, the pronouncements of this Council regarding the sacrament of anointing will be analyzed and explored in Chapter Two which deals with the theology of anointing. But some preliminary observations need to be made here. The Council of Trent's statements about this sacrament do not reflect any change in direction of theology. The bishops of the Council were convinced that the problems with anointing were more pastoral than theological and so were concerned with clarification and improvement of the way the sacrament was administered. In fact, Trent's statements on anointing are a concluding summation of the line of thinking that preceded the Council. Fortunately, the final decree of the Council was revised from the first draft which took the extreme view of reserving the administration of the sacrament for those about to die. It is to be given "only to those who are in their final struggle and have come to grips with death and are about to go forth to the Lord."[64] The approved decree was more balanced. "It is also prescribed that this anointing is to be used on the sick, especially on those who are so dangerously ill that they are thought to be departing this life."[65] While this is in some discontinuity with the view of the early Church, it does not canonize the extreme medieval position on the sacrament. Danger of death was not considered by the Council of Trent to be a necessary condition for this anointing. Martos well summarizes Trent's rather negative explanation of the sacrament:

> The bishops unequivocally condemned all those who

[63]Charles Gusmer, "Anointing of the Sick in the Church of England," *Worship* 45:5 (May 1971): 262-268.

[64]*Acta Genuina SS Oecumenici Concilii Tridentini*, ed. Theiner, 1:590.

[65]DS 1698.

contradicted the true Catholic doctrine by teaching any of the following: that extreme unction was not a sacrament instituted by Christ; that it did not confer grace, forgive sins, or comfort the sick; that in times past it had only been for physical healing; that the present practice of the Roman Church was not what the apostle James had in mind; that the "presbyters" mentioned in his epistle were not ordained priests but lay elders of the Church; that anyone besides priests could be proper ministers of the sacrament.[66]

While the Council Fathers probably considered anointing as the sacrament of the dying, in fact, the council documentation preserves some of the emphasis of the Council of Florence (1439) which was sensitive to the practice and understanding of the Eastern Churches which considered anointing more directed to physical healing rather than death and preparation for final glory in heaven. At least on the level of official teaching Trent can be seen as a partial recovery of the idea of anointing as a sacrament of the sick. The catechism of the Council of Trent moves in this direction when it regards it as a "very serious sin to defer holy unction until, all hope of recovery being lost, life begins to ebb and the sick person is fast verging into a state of insensibility."[67]

Pre-Vatican II Roman Rite of Anointing

This is the rite as found in the *Rituale Romanum* of Paul V (1614). It has been referred to as the modern ritual until the recent revision inspired by Vatican II.[68] This ritual is an historical reconstruction. It makes use of an independent rite for the visitation of the sick in adopting the "Pax huic domui" and three prayers which do not refer to anointing.

[66]Martos, *Doors to the Sacred*, pp. 386-87.

[67]Palmer, *Sacraments and Forgiveness*, p. 315.

[68]This rite can be found in any of the standard rituals available before the Vatican Council II. A helpful reference book for this section which contains both an English and Latin text is Walter J. Schmitz, S.S., *Collectio Rituum* (Milwaukee: Bruce Publishing Co., 1964).

These three prayers are all of ancient origin. The first, *Introeat*, is from a ninth century ordinal. The second, *Oremus et deprecemus*, is from the Roman Ordinal of the tenth century. And the third, *Exaudi nos*, is from the prayer for the blessing of water in the Gelasian sacramentary.

The rite of penance has left its mark on this ritual in the confession and *confiteor*, the penitential petitions, and the litany. The prayer, *In nomine patris*, was originally associated with the anointing. But the anointing was replaced by the imposition of hands in 1925. This ritual allows two types of anointing: the five senses with a formula for each sense and another one for the case of necessity which is an anointing on the forehead with a formula which does not refer to any particular sense. The three concluding prayers are taken from the ancient sacramentaries: Gregorian, Hadrianum, and Gelasian.

This ritual also provides prayers to be said at the bedside of the dying person without in any way derogating from the fact that viaticum is the chief preparation for death. The prayers for the dying included: the apostolic blessing, the *commendatio animae* (the commendation of the departing soul), and prayers at the hour of death. The term, *commendatio animae*, originally referred to the prayers for the dead. Beginning with the Carolingian period it was the name given to the prayers for the dying. The practice of reciting prayers at the bedside of the dying Christian probably existed from the beginning. There is evidence for this kind of prayer in the Gelasian sacramentary. In this modern ritual there are fourteen prayers for the recommendation of the departing soul and for at the hour of death. Later additions would be prayers to St. Joseph (1913) and to the Blessed Virgin (1922). A number of the prayers in the rite made their first appearance in the ritual prescribed by Paul V. But other prayers can be traced back to the twelfth century Roman Pontifical. There one finds two different series of prayers. The first group followed viaticum. These consisted of the reading of the passion, the psalms, and a litany. The second series of prayers were for recitation when death was imminent. Many of these prayers are quite ancient coming from the sixth, eighth, ninth, and tenth centuries. The practice of granting a plenary indulgence at the time of death had been in existence for centuries. The privilege of the Apostolic Blessing for those dying was decreed in the papal bull of Benedict XIV, *Pia Mater* (April 4, 1747).

Theology and Practice after Trent

The theological picture between the time of Trent and the second Vatican Council is primarily characterized by a gradual restoration of the idea that this is the sacrament of the sick rather than of the dying. In effect, what happened was a broadening in the interpretation of the kind of danger of death required for the administration of this sacrament. Such a growing benign interpretation ultimately undermined the thinking that supported this sacrament as extreme unction. For those theologians who would still require danger of death, this danger is now remote rather than proximate and probability is sufficient so that even in the case where no real danger is actually present, the sacrament can still be given. Such an approach received official Vatican approval in the Apostolic Letter, *Explorata Res*, of February 2, 1923: "It is not necessary either for the validity or lawfulness of the sacrament that death should be feared as something proximate, it is enough that there should be a prudent or probable judgment of danger."[69] Such a movement culminated in the Second Vatican Council which changed the name from extreme unction to the anointing of the sick. Pastoral preaching today is restoring the notion that this anointing is for the sick more than for the dying.

The more balanced articulation on the part of Trent and the gradual change on the part of theologians proved insufficient to reverse the pastoral practice of treating anointing as the sacrament of the dying. It was too firmly entrenched in popular understanding so that the visitation of the priest

[69]Pius XI, AAS 15, 105. See also, McClain, *The New Catholic Encyclopedia*, p. 571.

was tantamount to the announcement of imminent demise. And the ritual of the last rites had remained unchanged with anointing still displacing viaticum as the last of the sacraments. There were some changes in pastoral practice. But these tended to reinforce the notion of an *extreme* unction. In the seventeenth century the custom of giving the sacrament only to those who had attained the use of reason became firm but in trying to decide the question of how long the seemingly dead person may still be alive and so a proper subject of this sacrament, canonists chose the safer way and priests were advised to anoint conditionally those who were not certainly dead. In 1747 Pope Benedict XIV resolved the Dominican/Franciscan debate regarding the effect of the sacrament by making a plenary indulgence available to all those who had been anointed. That meant that those who died were forgiven their sins and the remnants of their sin were also removed. It also removed the controversy but only temporarily, since there are elements of it in the modern theological position of Kerns, which is treated later in this chapter.

Some attention was given to anointing in the latter part of the nineteenth century by the modernists who claimed that unction was not sacramental for James. It was more in the way of a devotion. What sacramentality anointing has comes from Christian tradition. There is some foundation in the gospel for it, but as a specific dimension of the power to forgive sins. The medieval theologians claimed too much for it. Overtones of the Protestant reformers are heard here. But the Modernists made some suggestions which anticipate contemporary Roman Catholic theology of the sacrament.

The twentieth century has seen a new emphasis on the ministry to the sick. There are many reasons for this such as the liturgical movement which began in France in the nineteenth century, a better understanding of the sacramental life of the patristic Church, the advances in the human sciences of psychology and sociology, and more attention to a holistic approach to health and healing. The charismatic revival is one of the more recent influences which places this sacrament in a different perspective. The early part of the twentieth century witnessed a new consciousness about the ministry of healing in many of the Churches not in communion with Rome. This is especially true of the Anglican Church. Percy Dearmer (1867-1936) in his *Parson's Handbook* (1899) advocated the restoration of anointing in the Church of England. His studies were oriented toward healing and he wrote about the importance of the ancient practices of laying on of hands and anointing. The rites which were inspired by him were simpler than the liturgies of the Prayer Book. They included periods of silence and the participation of the sick person's family and friends. Lengthy exhortations and numerous psalms are absent from these rites.

The 1928 proposed Prayer Book took up some of Dearmer's suggestions. But it did not restore anointing. 1928 is an improvement over 1662 in that due to its brevity some of the sickness as punishment theology has been omitted. The emphasis is more on the sick person's connection with the suffering Christ. Auricular confession with absolution has been restored. The psalms are more hopeful than penitential. There is a laying on of hands during the final prayers and blessing. There is a litany for the sick, additional prayers, and biblical texts, all of which may be used by or with the sick person. An attempt was made to allow for reservation of the eucharist for the communion of the sick. In general the changes were positive and more in accord with the contemporary needs of the pastoral care of the sick. However, the book was not approved. Ten years later the Convocations of York and Canterbury authorized services of anointing and laying on of hands. Individual groups within the Anglican Church have composed their own services of healing. These guilds of healing display their own theological emphases, as for instance, a High Church tendency or one of a more psychological bent. The important thing here is that all of these "grassroots" movements eventually fed into the reformed rites of the Anglican Church.

However, despite this gradual change in theology and

practice in the larger Christian Church, in the Roman Catholic Church in the last two hundred years of this pre-Vatican II period, the theology of the sacrament has been under the domination of the medieval understanding. Often this was in opposition to pastoral practice which was becoming more liberal and oriented toward the sick, that is, those *only probably* gravely ill. But for many theologians anointing was little more than an appendage to the sacrament of penance. And what appeared to be an attempt at creatively theologizing about this sacrament actually contributed to an obscuring of its meaning both theoretically and pastorally. This is especially true of the position that this sacrament is "an anointing unto glory." Adolf Knauber puts it this way:

> Down to Vatican II, with but few exceptions, the high Scholastic thesis about "preparation for glory" is constantly trotted out and refurbished, more recently in existential-eschatological clothing. This conception, though untenable in the light of biblical and liturgical theology, has, especially in the modern period, been widely circulated in the Church through popular literature, very much to the detriment of an authentic understanding of the sacrament in pastoral practice.[70]

Knauber refers to the work of Eugene Walter, Michael Schmaus, and especially Joseph Kerns, who describes anointing as a "sacrament of consecration for death." Kerns wrote a celebrated book, *De Sacramento Extremae Unctionis*, in which he saw the sacrament primarily as a means of avoiding purgatory. The main effect of the sacrament according to him is removing the temporal punishment due to sins which have been forgiven. In the early 1940's H.A. Reinhold popularized Kern's position in an address that he gave at a National Liturgical Week.[71] One contemporary

---

[70]Adolf Knauber, *Pastoral Theology of the Anointing of the Sick*, trans. Matthew J. O'Connell (Collegeville: The Liturgical Press, 1975), p. 25A.

[71]"The Sacrament of Extreme Unction in Parish Life," *National Liturgical Week* 1941 (Newark, 1942), pp. 135-141.

theologian, Aloys Grillmeier, has spoken of anointing as "the sacrament of resurrection," and as "the Christian fulfillment of the whole man." To compare anointing to baptism, as Grillmeier does, makes it a sacrament of initiation into the heavenly Church. These strongly eschatological positions enforced the indefensible viewpoint that anointing is a sacrament primarily for the dying.[72]

The beneficial aspect of this approach to anointing has been the reaction to it by theologians who have stressed that this is a sacrament of the sick and not of the dying. Their argumentation flows from the rite itself which does not indicate imminent death, from the history of the sacrament which for ten centuries does not find the sacrament being administered to those about to die, and from present pastoral needs.

Ironically, one of the things which may have been most influential in turning anointing away from being the sacrament of the dying to that of the living, sick, or elderly, was a more Christian understanding of death. Catholics dreaded asking the priest to come and anoint because it meant hope of recovery was gone. The Requiem Mass of old with its black color and with its "dreadful" prayers seemed at times to contradict the very texts of the liturgy which spoke of resurrection. But biblical scholars have been speaking of death in terms of life and the kingdom of God. Liturgists have pointed out the discrepancy between the centrality of the resurrection in theology and the off balance of the same doctrine in liturgical celebrations. A resurrection-centered view of death inevitably understands the act of dying of a Christian in a community context. Christian death is a eucharistic action. The community celebrates the passing over of one of its members by giving thanks for the life of that person. The Christian consciousness intuitively has come to the conclusion that eucharist-viaticum is more appropriately the sacrament of the dying than is anointing.

---

[72]For a helpful critique of Kern's position see Charles Davis, *The Study of Theology* (London: Sheed and Ward, 1962), chapter XIX.

Summary

What can be said in summary of this section from the Council of Trent to modern times can also conclude this chapter on the history of anointing. The first moment of the history of this sacrament, the first five centuries, culminated in the letter of Innocent. The theological and liturgical developments of the following age found expression in the medieval theologians. Medieval theology and practice has dominated the Roman Church until the second half of the twentieth century, despite Christianity's traumatic experience in the sixteenth century which triggered the Council of Trent and the Counter-Reformation. Some observations can be made regarding this post-Reformation period:

1. Post-Tridentine theology was primarily concerned with the principal effect of the sacrament whether it be the removal of venial sin or the removal of the consequences of sin. Official teaching avoided the extreme medieval position of limiting the sacrament to the final hours of human life, although many theologians embraced a strongly eschatological view of the sacrament.

2. Although often in practice anointing remained the final sacrament of the Christian life, there were benign interpretations which made it more available to the Catholic who was not at the door of death. A parallel insight in the other Christian Churches promoted the healing ministry on the pastoral level and Christian theologians and liturgists called for a restoration of such practices as anointing and laying on of hands.

3. The Baltimore Catechism, published in 1885, represented the mainline Roman Catholic position until only recently. It was a bare minimum approach to anointing. The catechism omits references to scripture or the Fathers. There is no discussion of the institution of the sacrament. There is no mention of grace as an effect. The concern is for the matter, form, method of administration, and the minister. Fortunately, most of these omissions are corrected in the revision of 1941. In substance it repeats Trent: the sacrament is to comfort the sick person and strengthen

him/her against temptations; it remits venial sin and the remains of sin; and if God wills, the person is restored to health.

4. The liturgical practices in the Orthodox Churches, which kept the Patristic stress on physical healing as well as the ecclesial nature of the sacrament in that it was performed in church rather than on the deathbed, have raised questions about how *traditional* Western practices really were.

5. Despite theological differences and canonical restrictions, which often distorted the true nature of the sacrament, a positive assessment of this period between Trent and Vatican II is also possible. It would be difficult to deny that anointing functioned during this period in the lives of Roman Catholics as a source of consolation in a sorrowing time, as a symbol of the Christian victory over death and suffering, as an affirmation of their belief in a gracious God, as a concrete way of placing their trust in this God, and as an experienced creed in the meaning of life in a Christian perspective.

BIBLIOGRAPHY: HISTORY OF THE SACRAMENT OF ANOINTING

Books

Janssens, Al. *Het Heilig Oliesel*, Nijmegen: N.V. Dekker En
Van De Vegt, 1939. (Although this book appeared some-
time ago and has not been translated into English, it is
included here because it contains the most comprehensive treatment of the history of this sacrament known to
this writer. For those who can read Dutch, it will be
invaluable.)

Knauber, Dr. Adolf. *Pastoral Theology of the Anointing of
the Sick*, trans. Matthew J. O'Connell, Collegeville: The
Liturgical Press, 1975.

Martos, Joseph. *Doors to the Sacred*, Garden City: Doubleday and Co., Inc., 1981.

Palmer, Paul, S.J., ed. *Sacraments and Forgiveness: History
and Doctrinal Development of Penance, Extreme
Unction and Indulgences*, Westminster: The Newman
Press, 1959.

Poschmann, Bernard. *Penance and the Anointing of the
Sick*, trans. Francis Courtney, S.J., New York: Herder
and Herder, 1964.

Schmitz, Walter, S.S., ed. *Collectio Rituum*, Milwaukee:
The Bruce Publishing Co., 1964.

Articles

The New Catholic Encyclopedia, 1967. S.v. "Anointing" by
G.T. Kennedy and J. Gaudemet; "Anointing of the Sick I
(Theology of)" by J. P. McClain; "Anointing of the Sick,
II, (Liturgy of)" by J. P. McClain; also: Supplement
for 1967-1974. S.v. "Anointing of the Sick, Liturgy
of" by C. Gusmer.

Palmer, Paul. "The Purpose of Anointing the Sick: A Reappraisal" *Theological Studies* 19 (1958): 309-44.

Palmer, Paul. "Who Can Anoint the Sick? *Worship* 48:2 (February 1974): 81-92.

Porter, H. Boone. "The Origin of the Medieval Rite for Anointing the Sick or Dying." *Journal of Theological Studies* 7 (1956): 221-225.

Porter, H. Boone. "The Rites of the Dying in the Early Middle Ages, I: St. Theodulf of Orleans." *Journal of Theological Studies* 10 (1959): 43-62.

CHAPTER TWO: THE THEOLOGY OF THE SACRAMENT OF ANOINTING

In this chapter the theology of anointing is seen from the perspective of Church doctrine and official teaching. The theological understanding as articulated in the Councils of Trent and Vatican II as well as the theology found in the revised rite itself are the subject matter of this second chapter. Chapter Three will deal with the primary biblical text that has been associated with this sacrament: James 5:13-16. Since most preaching and catechesis about the sacrament of anointing will refer to this primary text, it seems important to have a commentary on this section from the Epistle of James which both the preacher and catechist can depend upon for bringing the Church's theology of anointing to bear on the pastoral situation.

The Council of Trent

Traditional Roman Catholic theology of the sacrament of anointing has been articulated by the Council of Trent in its statement that the effect of the sacrament:

> is the grace of the Holy Spirit, whose anointing takes away sins, if there are any still to be expiated, and removes the traces of sin; and it comforts and strengthens

> the soul of the sick person. It gives him great confidence
> in the divine mercy. Encouraged by this, the sick man
> more easily bears the inconvenience and trials of his
> illness and more easily resists the temptations of the devil
> who lies in wait for his heel (Gn. 3:15). This anointing
> occasionally restores health to the body if health would
> be of advantage to the salvation of the soul.[1]

This is the clearest statement from a Church council on the
sacramentality of anointing. Its context is Trent's reaction
to the denials of the Reformation theologians. However,
this was not the first time that the Church had reacted to
those who questioned the sacramentality of anointing. The
Council of Verona in 1148 had made an allusion to anointing because of the denial of the sacraments   by the
Albigensians.

Martin Luther had rejected the Epistle of James because
of its stress on good works along with justification by faith.
He did not think that James wrote it or that it was part of the
canon of inspired scriptures. Trent presumes the canonicity
of James. Luther rejected the sacrament of anointing as he
experienced it: given only to the dying and only once. In
reaction Trent adopted a more benign attitude toward
anointing in the pastoral situation, but continued to see it as
a sacrament of the dying. This was done with careful qualifi-
cation as Chapter One has pointed out. Luther could find no
scriptural foundation for a sacrament for the dying. And
this is true, since the James text refers to the sick and not to
the dying. In this sense there is no biblical foundation for the
medieval position and for Trent's position in so far as it
subscribes to the medieval understanding of anointing as
primarily directed to the dying Christian.

Trent treated anointing in conjunction with the sacrament of penance. The Fathers of the Council no doubt saw
the two sacraments as closely related in that anointing was
the culmination not only of the sacrament of penance but of
the Christian penitential life. This is reflected in the intro-

[1]DS 1696.

ductory paragraph. Here the sacrament is presented as "a culmination not only of penance but of the whole Christian life which itself ought to be a continual penance."[2]

On November 25, 1551, the fourteenth session of the Council treated both anointing and penance together. Since it regards anointing as a sacrament of the dying, it sees Christ providing this sacrament to Christians who are departing this life. In the words of Trent: "He prepared great helps in the other sacraments to enable Christians to keep themselves throughout their lives untouched by any serious spiritual harm, and likewise he protected them at the end of life with the invincible strength of the sacrament of extreme unction."[3] This clearly reflects the thought and theology of the period.

Chapter One (DS 1695) deals with the institution and structure of the sacrament. Christ instituted this sacrament as implied in Mk 6:13 and promulgated by the Apostle James. The text of James gives the matter, form, minister, and effects of this sacrament. The matter is the oil blessed by the bishop and the form is "By this holy anointing and his most loving mercy may the Lord forgive you whatever sins you have committed by the use of your sense of _____."

Chapter Two (DS 1696) explicitly deals with the effects of anointing. The primary effect is the grace of the Holy Spirit. Whatever sins need to be remitted are forgiven and the remains of sin are removed. This is an official acceptance of the view of the high Scholastics on this point. Anointing brings about the trust in God's mercy and so the sick person can bear his/her illness more easily and can resist the temptations which accompany this weakened state. Healing of the body may take place if it "would be of advantage to the salvation of the soul." A very important point to note is that

---

[2]DS 1694. The explicit statements of Trent regarding anointing are catalogued in the *Enchiridion Symbolorum* by H. Denzinger and A. Schoenmetzer, S.J., edition XXXVI. This is distributed in the United States by *Christian Classics* (205 Willis St., Westminster, Md. 21157). English translations of the texts quoted are from *The Church Teaches* (London, St. Louis: B. Herder Book Co., 1955).

[3]DS 1694.

there is no mention of death among the effects of the sacrament, although the introduction refers to it as the sacrament to consecrate the end of the Christian life of penance.

Chapter Three (DS 1697-1700) is concerned with the minister and conditions of administration. The minister is the presbyter, not the older people in the community. Presbyter means the bishop or the priest ordained by the bishop. The sick person anointed in this sacrament is one who is so gravely ill as to seem to be in the danger of death. The sacrament can be received again in the event that the sick person recovers.

The canons which follow the chapters anathematize the teachings of certain of the reformers. Canon one (DS 1716): The sacrament is instituted by Christ (against Luther and Calvin). It is promulgated by James (against Luther). It was not the creation of the Patristic period (against Melancthon). It is not of human invention (against Calvin). Canon two (DS 1717): It confers grace, remits sin, and relieves the sick (against Melancthon). It is not simply charismatic curing no longer present in the Church (against Calvin, Melancthon). Canon three (DS 1718): It is not repugnant to the text of James (against Luther, Melancthon, Calvin). It cannot be changed (against Luther, Melancthon, Calvin). It cannot be disregarded by Christians (against Luther, Melancthon, Calvin). Canon four (DS 1719): The presbyters mentioned by James are priests and not simply the older members of the community (against Calvin). The priest is the proper minister of the sacrament.

The Roman Catechism or the Catechism of the Council of Trent which was published in 1566 reflects faithfully the doctrine of the Council. It carries on Trent's ambiguity: it is definitely presented for the dying, but with the realization that it should not be delayed until the moment of unconsciousness. The institution by Christ and the priest as minister are two points emphasized by the Catechism. This is in tune with the general theological perspective of Roman theologians of the time. Despite the slowly changing theological climate between Trent and Vatican II, the teaching of Trent remained the official position of the Roman

Catholic Church until Vatican II. Contemporary theology must continue to review the meaning of the definitions of Trent. More references to this Council will be made under individual topics later in this chapter.

The Second Vatican Council

An important change of theology regarding anointing emerged with the Second Vatican Council in which the ecclesial dimension of all the sacraments is stressed. Anointing is no exception to this emphasis on the normativity of the communal celebration of the sacraments. Once again the visible rite, the symbol itself, is highlighted in sacramental theology. The direction for the reformed rite was set by the Vatican Council's *Constitution on the Sacred Liturgy*.[4]

> Extreme unction, "which may also and more fittingly be called "Anointing of the Sick," is not a sacrament for those only who are at the point of death. Hence, as soon as anyone of the faithful begins to be in danger of death from sickness or old age, the fitting time for him to receive this sacrament has certainly already arrived. (73)
>
> In addition to the separate rites for Anointing of the Sick and for Viaticum, a continuous rite shall be prepared in which a sick man is anointed after he has made his confession and before he receives viaticum. (74)
>
> The number of anointings is to be adapted to the occasion and the prayers which belong to the rite of Anointing are to be revised so as to correspond to the varying conditions of the sick who receive this sacrament. (75)

It is clear that the Council wanted this rite placed in the larger context of the pastoral ministry to the sick and elderly. The title and text of the new rite make it certain that anointing is the sacrament of the sick. The misleading phrases of "extreme unction" and "last rites" have been

[4]The translation given here is found in Austin Flannery, O.P. *Vatican Council II* (Collegeville: The Liturgical Press, 1975), p. 22.

replaced. Even the ordering of the chapters in the ritual of anointing shows that the emphasis is on the larger ministry to the sick. The Study Group XXIII of the liturgy Concilium, the group set up by the Council to implement its liturgical reforms, presented a schema for the new rite of anointing. This was done in October, 1969. It was revised during the following year. On December 7, 1972, the official text for the *Rite of Anointing and Pastoral Care of the Sick* was published by the Congregation for Divine Worship. The implementation date was January 1, 1974. Between those dates the Latin text was translated into the vernacular languages of the local Churches and appropriate adaptations were made by the national hierarchies.

The rite contains seven chapters:

1. Visitation and Communion of the Sick
2. Rite of Anointing a Sick Person: Ordinary Rite Viaticum
4. Rite of the Sacraments for Those near Death: Continuous Rite of Penance, Anointing, and Viaticum
5. Confirmation of a Person in Danger of Death
6. Rite for the Commendation of the Dying
7. Texts for Use in Rites for the Sick

The most important change in the reformed Roman Catholic rite has to do with the matter and the form. In the Apostolic Constitution, *Sacram Unctionem,* of Paul VI which accompanies the rite, it is stated:

> The sacrament of anointing is administered to those who are dangerously ill by anointing them on the foreheads and hands with blessed olive oil or, according to the circumstances, with another plant oil and saying once only these words: "Per istam Sanctam Unctionem et suam piissimam misericordiam adiuvet te Dominus gratia Spiritus Sancti, ut a peccatis liberatum te salvet atque propitius allevet." (Through this holy anointing may the Lord in his love and mercy help you with the grace of the Holy Spirit. May the Lord who frees you from sin save you and raise you up.)[5]

[5] *The Rites* (New York: Pueblo Publishing Co., 1976), pp. 580-81.

The anointing no longer takes place on the five senses and the new formula expresses a fuller theology. The old formula mentioned only the forgiveness of sins.

Another very significant point is that the danger of death has been omitted as a condition for reception of the sacrament. Rather, those seriously infirm from illness and old age are proper recipients of this sacrament. Repetitions of anointing are permitted if the sickness becomes progressively worse. The priest may administer the sacrament conditionally in the case of real doubt. If the person is dead, the priest is to pray for the dead person but should not anoint.

One of the far-reaching effects of the new rite is that it is placed in the context of the pastoral ministry of the sick. The opening paragraphs of the Introduction to the rite (1-4) touch on the meaning of sickness in the mystery of salvation. Human struggle and victory in regard to sickness and evil must be seen as part of the participation in the paschal mystery of Christ's death and resurrection.

In sections 32-37 the offices and ministries for the sick are described in a most comprehensive way. All people who minister to the sick, all those who belong to the Christian community, the family and friends of the sick or elderly person, participate in administering this sacrament. It is not only the priest who does so, although it is clear that he is the proper minister. In 42-45 the entire community is asked to participate in the visitation of the sick and they are encouraged to do so with the reading of scripture and common prayer.

The ecclesial nature of this sacrament is emphasized in the recommendation of the communal anointing service. Rather than private anointing being the normative practice, the liturgical setting which involves the sick person's family and friends is seen as paradigmatic. The possibility for communal anointings involving several sick and elderly persons is now a reality. These communal celebrations may take place at the appropriate time in a eucharist, namely, after the homily or they may be held in conjunction with a communion service. There is a rather limited provision for a concelebration of anointing by several priests.

This sacrament presupposes faith. Thus it prohibits the delaying until the moment of death or until the person is so weak as to make involvement in the ritual difficult. The beginning of a serious illness, benignly interpreted, is the fit occasion to administer this sacrament. The present Roman Catholic practice requires that priests urge the worshippers to request the sacrament on their own initiative rather than delaying until they are too enfeebled to do so. More is being asked of the clergy in the matter of catechizing regarding this sacrament. Far from the emergency setting of the hospital, this rite, like all good liturgy, requires planning in the selection of readings, prayers, and music. Massive reeducation must take place if anointing is to cease to be the harbinger of death and become a time of strength and comfort.

Thus far this chapter has dealt with the two major Church councils which have spoken on the topic of the sacrament of anointing. Some general observations have been made regarding the theology of the new revised rite of anointing which is the product of the second of these Church councils. In order to enter more specifically into the theology of this sacrament the remainder of this chapter will take up two of the major questions surrounding anointing, the institution of the sacrament and the effects of the sacrament, and then enter into detail regarding the administration of the sacrament of the sick in so far as the actual performance of the rite brings to the fore certain theological presuppositions. In other words, first follows two major questions regarding anointing that are found in the tradition but are still the preoccupation of sacramental theologians today and then the theology of anointing as it is found in the rite will be articulated.

While this book was in its final stages of completion, the author received word that the International Commission on English in the Liturgy (ICEL) had proposed a revision of the 1974 *Rite of Anointing and Pastoral Care of the Sick*. It is expected that this revised ritual will appear shortly. Most of the revisions are of a pastoral nature dealing with the structure of the rites, new prayer texts, and pastoral notes. The title has been changed to *Pastoral Care of the Sick — Rites of Anointing and Viaticum.* Since the revision does not involve any significant theological change, the comments in the chapter on the rite itself will follow the division of material as found in the 1974 rite. But since the final two chapters deal with the pastoral application of the rite, they will follow the chapter outline of the revised ritual. This present chapter is primarily concerned to indicate a movement in the theological understanding of anointing.

Institution of the Sacrament

This has been the major theological question in the history of anointing. It is still a question although there has been a movement away from this point in the writings of liturgical and sacramental theologians. There are two dimensions to this question: 1) the apologetic and 2) the theological. First, the apologetic needs to be considered.

The Reformers of the sixteenth century, the Modernists, and the liberal Protestants all asserted that anointing was of human origin. Some of the doctrinal divergences here can be explained in terms of historical misunderstanding. For instance, Modernist and liberal Protestants tended to equate Trent with one or other scholastic theological position. But all that Trent asserts is that the anointing of the sick is a sacred sign which is grace-giving. Anointing and prayer are seen as gifts which forgive sin. In response to the Reformation Protestant theology which continues to present this sacrament as of human origin, it can only be pointed out how close and unbroken is the line between this ritual of anointing and the text of James. The liturgies are based on the command of James. The theologizing is done in terms of this text. Synodal and pontifical documents use James as the basis for their statements. As a matter of historical fact, the anointing of the sick was present in the Church before Innocent I or the Carolingian reform. To assert that early anointings were purely charismatic in character is to ignore the James text where the anointing is carried out by elders.

It was something done in the name of the leaders of the community. Further, the forgiveness of sins which has been tied to this anointing is never attributed to charismatic ministry. The Council of Trent, as the solemn teaching authority of the Church regarding this sacrament, based its teaching on the text of James. In this sense the Council defined the text. Its articulation of the faith of the Church is developed in terms of the various elements of the text of the epistle.

However, the Council of Trent did not resolve all matters regarding the institution of this sacrament. While it states that anointing was instituted by Christ, it does not say what that means. It does not even define what it means by a sacrament. The theological question of the institution of anointing remained open. Questions that have remained unanswered by Trent are: 1) what is meant by this sacrament being instituted by Christ; 2) what part did the apostles play in the emergence of this sacrament; and 3) what is the role of the Church in the origin of this sacrament?

In order to understand the reason for these remaining open questions at the time of Trent, it is important to recall some of the historical background already discussed. Prior to the twelfth century a presentation of the belief of the Church regarding anointing can be found in the liturgy. The prayers of the sacramentaries indicate that this sacrament is a command of the Lord through the apostle James. This same note is found in the synodal decrees. The early Scholastics attributed the institution to the apostles. Such was the general teaching in the twelfth century. Later, the Franciscans, Alexander of Hales and Bonaventure, follow this tradition. It was Thomas Aquinas who asserted that this sacrament must have been instituted by Christ since it is efficacious of grace. On the one hand, the Franciscans maintained that the apostles under the guidance of the Holy Spirit instituted this sacrament; on the other hand, Aquinas maintained that these apostles merely promulgated a sacrament which had its origins in Christ. He would allow that the actual form of the sacrament could have been done by the apostles. With such diversity of theological opinion, it is understandable why the Fathers of the Council would refrain from becoming any more specific on this point.

The apologetic question is at a dead end today. It is necessary to address the question of the institution of the sacrament from a purely theological stance. Since Trent, the Roman Catholic position has been that all the seven sacraments have been instituted by Christ. But theologians have distinguished the meaning of institution: 1) immediate specific, 2) immediate generic, and 3) mediate. The institution question relates to the question of what is the substance of a sacrament, that is, what comes from Christ. It cannot be equated with the matter and the form because there are instances in the history of the sacraments where these have been changed. For instance, Pius XII determined that the matter and form of ordination are the imposition of hands and the prayer of consecration. Thus, it is impossible to maintain that Christ immediately and specifically instituted the matter and form of every sacrament.

The question of the institution of the sacrament has been dealt with by some theologians in terms of the sacramental sign. The presumption is that Christ gave a command that a specific sanctification is to take place by means of some visible sign. The theologians maintaining this position say that Christ did this in the period immediately following the resurrection. There is no scriptural support for this position. The presupposition here is that the institution of a sacrament is concerned with the sacramental sign itself. And for a sign to be connected with the grace of salvation, divine power must be at work in connecting this sign to salvation. However, it can be argued, and is in fact so argued, that this does not prohibit this bond being established historically at some later time whether in the apostolic age or even later.

There seems to be little if any evidence that Christ instituted the sacrament of anointing directly. However, he did give to the Church through the apostles the mission to heal the sick in the context of the proclamation of the Good News. This is one of the signs of the Church as seen in Mk

6:13 and 16:17-18. Ministry to the sick is closely tied to the more general ministry of the apostles to the world. It is a ministry which involves a visible sign and a calling upon the name of Jesus. The anointing with oil which was used in Jewish healing ministry now signifies the outpouring of the Holy Spirit. The imposition of hands in this situation retains its basic sacramental meaning of the exercise of power. What can be stated with certainty is that this sacrament of anointing was instituted by Christ in so far as it is part of a larger ministry in the context of the name and power of Christ and a sign which expresses that power. Healings not performed in the context of this sign such as that of Peter at the Beautiful Gate and Paul at the gate of Lystra cannot be definitely established as sacramental.

There is no evidence that Christ enjoined the use of oil in healing, although such was an ancient practice. From the time of the primitive Church there is great diversity in the way anointings are performed. From the earliest times it was done with oil which had been blessed by an invocation that the Holy Spirit empower this oil. The letter of James at least indicates the antiquity of the practice of anointing. It is clear from the chapter on the history of anointing that there is no way to prove conclusively that the commission of ministry to the sick in the Church implied the use of anointing with oil. One could maintain the probability of anointing with oil in primitive Christian times based on an analogy with baptism. In any event, it would be more prudent to claim the probability of such a practice than attempt to establish a specific institution of this ritual on the part of Christ. No one would claim that the prayer that accompanies the anointing was instituted by Christ. The traditional Roman formula is traced back to the monastic practice of Cluny or to the successors of Cluny in the middle ages.

The specific institution of this sacrament is little discussed today by theologians. It is dealt with in terms of the institution o such it is in terms of the James text and the healing ministry of Christ. The power of the Risen Christ is seen to be working among the early Christian community and this same power is having an impact on the sick people. This is seen to be in continuity with the healings recorded in the gospels but now done in the light of the paschal mystery. The redemption of the cross is seen more comprehensively in that it also strengthens and renews those who are weakened or devastated by illness.

One example from contemporary theology should suffice. Karl Rahner in his *The Church and the Sacraments* is concerned not to approach history with an *a priori* position that Christ must have instituted this sacrament directly. He deals with the historical institution of anointing in terms of his general ecclesiological framework of the Church as the primordial sacrament, the eschatological presence of grace in the world. Any action of the Church which touches one of its members in a fundamentally salvational way is a sacrament. That is, the action flows from the basic nature of the Church and since the Church is a sacrament, so is that specific action. Such an institution of a sacrament requires no specific injunction on the part of Christ which can be explicitly found in the scriptures. This is becoming a commonly accepted theological position for dealing with the question of the historical origin of the sacrament.[6]

In summary, as regards the theological problem of the institution of the sacrament of anointing, it is resolved in terms of the facts that a ministry to the sick was entrusted to the Church, power was given to perform this ministry in the name of Christ, and this power implies the grace of redemption. Grace comes to the Christians, in this case, those in need of healing. Through this ritual the victorious power of Christ's redemption confronts the power of evil apparent in the sick person, whether such sickness be classified as spiritual or physical. The purpose of this sacrament is to allow the sick person to share in this victory of Christ. Because the power of God is present in this person in terms of a sign (anointing) of the sending of the Spirit, the Christian is no

---

[6]Karl Rahner, *The Church and the Sacraments* (Montreal: Palm Publishers, 1963), pp. 41ff and 112ff.

longer under the power of sickness whether this be manifested physically or whether this take place on the spiritual
dimension primarily. The one saving action of God in Christ
is particularized in the case of a human being in terms of
his/her special need: sickness and its accompanying
problems.

The problem of the institution of this sacrament is not
only a question of historical fact but of the grace signified in
this sacrament: what power of God is made manifest here in
a context of anointing and prayer? There is still lack of
complete agreement in these areas of the institution and the
conferral of grace and so there is need for continual theologizing, especially in terms of the greater question of how
grace is realized in the world. This leads to the next major
theological question in the history of this sacrament: its
effects on the person anointed.

The Effects of the Sacrament

Charles Gusmer has pointed out that article 73 of the
Constitution on the Sacred Liturgy which speaks of the
purpose of anointing is a compromise.[7] It is the result of two
conflicting theologies: a sacrament of the dying and a sacrament of the sick. The article refers to extreme unction while
giving a preference to the title: Anointing of the Sick. It
requires the danger of death but this is more broadly stated.
As noted in chapter one the immediate historical background for this ambiguity is that the approach that the
sacrament prepares one for death was given impetus
through the thesis of Joseph Kerns while at the same time
there has been a growing consensus that anointing is primarily directed to the sick and the elderly. There is still some
of the ambiguity of Trent found in the Second Vatican
Council. Martos sums up the ambiguous situation, at least
as far as the public teaching of the Church is concerned:

It is as though there were now two sacraments of anoint-

[7]Charles Gusmer, "Liturgical Traditions of Christian Illness: Rites of the Sick,"
Worship 46:9 (November 1972): 528.

ing in Catholicism, one which corresponds in form and meaning to the patristic and early medieval anointing of the sick, and one which corresponds in form and meaning to the late medieval and modern anointing of dying.[8]

Despite the ambiguity, the new Roman Catholic Rite for the Sick speaks of the effects of the sacrament in a different way from Trent while remaining in continuity with the latter council.

> The sacrament provides the sick person with the grace of the Holy Spirit by which the whole man is brought to health, trust in God is encouraged, and strength is given to resist the temptations of the Evil One and anxiety about death. Thus the sick person is able not only to bear his suffering bravely, but also to fight against it. A return to physical health may even follow the reception of this sacrament if it will be beneficial to the sick person's salvation. If necessary, the sacrament also provides the sick person with the forgiveness of sins and the completion of Christian penance.[9]

The theological change from the time of Trent to the 1972 Rite of Anointing is enshrined in the ritual itself. It is possible to see the difference in the prayer for the blessing of the oil (n. 75): "may your blessing come upon all who are anointed with this oil, *that they may be freed from pain and illness and made well again in body, mind, and soul.*" And this emphasis is carried through in the prayers that accompany the anointing on the forehead and hands. "Through this holy anointing may *the Lord in his love and mercy help you* with the grace of the Holy Spirit. May the Lord who frees you from sin *save you and raise you up*" (n. 76). In order to grasp more fully the theological change, despite the ambiguity of the official texts in places, it is helpful to revisit some of the background to the contemporary theological understanding of this sacrament.

[8]Martos, *Doors to the Sacred*, p. 393.
[9]*The Rites*, pp. 583-84.

As indicated in the statement from Trent quoted at the beginning of this chapter, the council affirmed that there are two effects of the sacrament: the forgiveness of sins and some kind of bodily effect. The sacrament forgives sins both mortal and venial. It is, however, considered a sacrament of the living in that it ordinarily presupposes the absence of mortal sin and the presence of sanctifying grace. But this increase is not the primary purpose of the sacrament. In the other sacraments of the living such as marriage and orders, the forgiveness of sins is an indirect and accidental effect. But anointing is different in that, if for some reason the person anointed has no access to the sacrament of penance, all his/her sins will be forgiven through anointing. Such is the view of Trent.

The most balanced of the Catholic tradition has maintained that the proper effect of this sacrament is related to bodily well-being. The distinction between the two effects of the sacrament: a physical and a spiritual one, or physical healing and grace, has created a dichotomy between the two, both on the theoretical as well as the practical level. But such a separation makes no sense theologically since one is dealing with a single reality which is bidimensional. This theological isolationism, however, follows the kind of Christian anthropology which was current during the middle ages. A view that divides the human person into the corporal and spiritual held together somewhat tenuously will be reflected in a sacramental action such as anointing. A recovered sense of the incarnate nature of the human person which keeps unified the physiological, psychological, and transcendent dimensions has brought about a renewed appreciation for the synthetic experience that this sacrament is about. In that sense, there are not two distinct effects: bodily and spiritual, but rather a single effect which is brought about when the physical and spiritual work in and through each other. In other words, there is only one subject of this sacrament: the whole person. There is no question of one effect referring to the body and another bringing about a change in the soul alone. While one of the advantages of scholastic theology is its precision, a handicap of such a method is that the total reality, which is always larger than the distinctions indicate, is inadequately expressed.

The best of the traditional theological approach tried to preserve the unity of the person on the supernatural level of grace. The effect of the one grace was twofold: remission of sins and alleviation of physical infirmity. The former effect has never been a theological problem, but how something such as supernatural grace can lessen one's bodily infirmity has been problematic for the most enlightened of the scholastic and Tridentine theologians. But attempts were made so that the best of theology took a holistic approach to the person. What happens in anointing is that the Church commends the sick person to God and in so doing makes the person's illness a source of grace. This is possible because illness is more than a mere physical phenomenon. It entails a change in the personality. It involves the kind of alteration in a person which makes it difficult for the person to move toward God. In this view illness is considered to be an evil, both on the physical and spiritual levels. It is part of the disorder in the universe which is the result of original sin. Usually, this approach does not attempt to tie sickness and actual sin together, but the very fact of sickness in this world is seen to be the result of the original loss of innocence.

The nature of sickness is such that it consumes a person's vital energy to such a degree that it becomes a powerful obstacle to a person's spiritual growth. And in the case of serious illness there is the added possibility of death with all its concomitant fears of the unknown and the loss of meaning. Confrontation with physical dissolution raises questions about the significance of human life. These questions are surrounded with anxiety. Such anxiousness can impede one's further movement toward God.

The sacrament of anointing is supposed to make it possible for sick persons not only to manage spiritually during the trials of illness but also to intensify their growth process, their orientation toward God. Traditional Roman Catholic theology has sometimes spoken of this as a form of restoration of the original gift of integrity. Effectively what this means is that the supernatural vitality, grace, so permeates the human body, mind, and imagination that the persons can more readily follow the promptings of the Spirit which guide them along the right path. In some sense this is seen as a partial restoration of the original harmony destroyed by the first sin. In a more harmonious working together of the physical and material in the person there emerges the kind of strength and peace which frees the soul to continue on its way to grace with freedom and spontaneity. This main line Catholic thinking presupposes that there are remains of sin in the human person, whether it be from original sin taken away in baptism or from actual sin now forgiven. These remnants are spoken of as the reluctance to lead a good life, the depression and fear that emerge because of one's sinful past, and the inhibitions one finds in oneself because of one's history and tendencies.[10]

Traditional theology connected the spiritual effect of anointing, harmonious spiritual freedom, with the cure of or recovery from physical illness. At times spiritual improvement assisted in a cure or at least accelerated the recovery. But even in the cases where the illness remained, the primary effect of the sacrament obtained. For although the suffering person was called to endure the illness, this infirmity could not impair his/her relationship with Christ. The physical debility could not render his/her spiritual life dysfunctional. If death was the result of the illness, then anointing assisted the person to enter into the paschal mystery more deeply by being conformed to the suffering and death of Christ.

Both in the teaching of Trent and the Second Vatican Council as more fully expressed in the Introduction to the new rite of anointing, physical healing is not primary and there is no certainty about whether it will eventuate. One

---

[10]For much in this section I am dependent upon McClain, "Anointing of the Sick, I," *The New Catholic Encyclopedia*: 572ff.

can only wonder in what sense physical healing is really an *effect* of this sacrament. Thomas Talley has well pointed out the disparity in which this sacrament is being understood at a time when there is a changed comprehension of the other sacraments.[11] Baptism and eucharist are seen in a larger ecclesial context whereas there is still a tendency to emphasize the effect of anointing on the individual recipient. Talley suggests that much of this is due to a confusion between charismatic healing and the kind that is appropriate to a sacrament. In other words, this sacrament should not be surrounded with the kind of implicit hope or expectation that something miraculous might happen, even if it is only a happy side effect. While both charismatic and sacramental healings will take place in the context of a deepened faith and can effect a transformation of the person and while both hopefully will be approached in such a way that the paschal mystery of Christ's death and resurrection is central, usually the sacrament of anointing when done properly will emphasize certain elements more than charismatic healings do such as, the ongoing pastoral care of the sick and cooperation with the medical profession. There will be less concern with the individual therapeutic results and less preoccupation with the "miraculous effects."

This is in no way to deny that healing, even physical healing, is part of the Christian tradition. One need but be acquainted with reliable hagiography for a demonstration of this point. However, what may be the relationship of charismatic healing to liturgy is another question. It appears that the two have not been together from the beginning. In the *Apostolic Tradition of Hippolytus* there is an explicit denial of ordination for those who claim the gift of healing. Their actions speak for themselves.[12] Healing does not belong to status roles in the Church. Baptism, Confirmation, and Orders refer to sacramental structures of the com-

---

[11]Thomas Talley, "Healing: Sacrament or Charism?" *Worship* 46:9 (November 1972): 518-27.

[12]Ibid., p. 522.

munity. Healing is a charism which some of those ordained may have, but need not and often will not have.

More recent contemporary theologies of anointing would be in continuity of what has been just described as main line Roman Catholic theology.

They would, of course, have their own emphases. This author gives his personal perspective on this sacrament in Chapter Four. There are a number of common accents found in these theologies. One theologian who manifests a number of these common points in regard to anointing is Joseph Powers, S.J.[13] For him, as for other theologians today, this sacrament brings the saving reality of Christ's redemption to the human reality of old age and sickness. It is a sacrament of and for the sick. It is not for any sick person, but is the ritual that the Church reserves for its sick members. It is for those who are *sick in the Church.* Just as life in the Church cannot be equated or reduced to the physical reality of human life, so the Church's concern for the sick must transcend their physical condition of sickness. Life in the Church is of a special kind; it is the life of salvation. The person in the Church is in need of redemption, is a sinner, and one whose Christian life is constantly in need of repentance. Sickness is part of this context of human sinfulness. Sickness is part of the incarnate existence that the person in the Church has. Being elderly can also be seen as part of the mystery of evil that is part of human existence, at least of physical if not moral evil. Thus, the Church's concern in this sacrament is directed to the salvific dimension of human experience. In strongly Christological terms, because Jesus has conquered the mystery of evil in his redemptive life, death, and resurrection, this sacrament is the way that the Church brings the power of Christ to bear on this mystery of evil. Thus, the meaning of this sacrament is seen in the focussing of the power of Christ on a limit situation, a need-situation of the particular Christian. Through this sacramental prayer the sick Christian hopes to

[13]For this section I am very much indebted to the personal notes of Joseph Powers.

obtain the victorious power of Christ. In this sense, the sick person is also victorious over his/her own sickness. In the case of recovery, it is a physical victory or authority. And even without such physical healing, it is a spiritual authority or mastery over this sickness.

A concluding comment to this specifically theological section before moving to the detailed matter of the administration of the sacrament seems to be in place. Anointing, like all sacraments, does not live in theological concepts in the minds of theologians. Their meaning is not necessarily best expressed in the traditional symbols connected with them. The most effective understanding of these symbols is found in the actual experience of those participating in them. In this there is a basic similarity between all the forms of anointing whether for one or many, whether for the sick, the elderly, or the dying. In all cases it is the Church saying that there is more than disease and death, that as Christians it is important to live through sickness, old age, and death without fear although they cannot be escaped. It says that Christians are not alone in these times but that the community is with them in a more specific sacramental way. It proclaims that personal self-integration and reconciliation with other and themselves is the meaning of salvation. Such is the theme of Chapter Four of this book.

The Administration of the Sacrament[14]

What follows is not a detailed commentary on the Rite of Anointing and Pastoral Care of the Sick. Rather, it attempts to bring out some of the theology which is found in the various components of the ritual. The procedure is first to comment on the individual chapters and then to refer to some specific ritual questions connected with the administration of this sacrament. This chapter concludes with some

[14]For further details regarding the administration of this sacrament, especially concerning certain canonical conditions regarding validity and liceity, the reader is referred to Nicholas Halligan, O.P. *Sacraments of Reconciliation* (New York: Alba House, 1973), pp. 197ff.

observations regarding anointing in the other Christian Churches.

Chapter One: Visitation and Communion of the Sick

This chapter, as well as nos. 32-37 of the Introduction, gives what is probably the greatest departure in this new rite from the previous Roman Catholic tradition. It is the call to all Catholics to share in the care for the sick by visiting and comforting them. Pastors and those who professionally care for the sick should convey to them the Christian understanding of the role of suffering in human life and how it finds its meaning in terms of the paschal mystery, They are to pray with the sick, read and reflect on the scriptures with them, and encourage them in a lively sacramental life.

Pastors are to encourage the elderly to receive communion frequently especially during Eastertime. They may receive under the form of wine if they cannot receive the bread (95).[15] Those who work with the sick may also receive communion with them. Communion under both kinds is permitted to the person being anointed and to those present (99). The attempt to restore the fullness of the sacramental sign to these marginal people is obvious. Often these sick and elderly persons cannot participate in the most adequate sign of Christ's presence, the eucharistic assembly, and so the rite tries to make up for that deficiency by stressing the importance of the sacramental sign in terms of *bread and wine*. The ritual contains both an ordinary rite for the communion of the sick as well as a shorter form.

Chapter Two: Rite of Anointing a Sick Person

This rite offers a number of alternatives and options since it is directed not only to three classes of Christians, the sick, the elderly, and the dying, but also to many different situations in each of these three categories. What this chapter furnishes is a normative way of administering this sacra-

[15]The numbers in parentheses refer to the sections of the rite.

ment to an individual. But the pluralism found here — the ordinary rite, anointing during mass, anointing in a large congregation with a celebration outside of mass or during mass — attests to the fact that a norm is a norm and not an absolute. In this spirit of adapting to the local scene the priest who is to anoint should try to know the condition of the sick person and provide instruction regarding the sacrament. Sacramental confession should be made available before the anointing. Separating the penitential aspect of the sacramental life of the sick and elderly would help to restore some of the more positive and supportive aspects to the sacrament. It should be more an occasion of appreciative joy rather than of penance.

While anointing may need to be performed on someone confined to a sickbed and in homes for the sick as well as rest homes, it can also be administered in Church or some other suitable place (66). If the condition of the sick person, allows, anointing may be done during mass in which case it is administered after the homily (80-82). The concern here is to stress in as many cases as possible the ecclesial nature of the sacrament. That anointing, like any sacrament, is the word of God made visible is exemplified in the requirement that anointing takes place after the proclamation of this word.

Communal anointings are acceptable (83-85). And in accordance with the more general liturgical principles, such communal anointings should be the norm which gives meaning to individual anointings. There should be pastoral preparation and catechesis for these communal events and the sacrament of reconciliation should be available. Here again, one would hope that the two sacraments would not be so closely related that the ambiguity regarding this sacrament is further promoted. If several priests are involved in the anointing rite, each one imposes hands and anoints with the formula some of those who come forth for this sacrament. Each person is to receive the imposition of hands and anointing singly. It may well be that there are still remnants of legalism behind this prescription. However, it also stresses the importance of personal contact by means of these two gestures. More on this will be said in the following chapters. The communal rite may take place within or outside of the eucharistic liturgy (86-92). The revised formula for the blessing of the oil has an obvious eucharistic character. This stress on the paschal character of the use of oil in the life of the Christian makes this blessing similar to the one used for the baptismal water.

What is more obvious about the revised rite (which will be least adverted to and yet is probably the most important aspect of the revision) is that anointing takes place in the context of a liturgy of the word. It is no longer a bare sacramental act. And not only do the scripture readings, the homily, and the prayers restore the proper liturgical understanding of the relationship between word and sacrament, but they also presuppose that the person to be anointed can participate in the celebration. The person needs to be more than merely conscious.

Chapter Three: Viaticum

This chapter deals with that special sign of sharing in the paschal mystery: the eucharist received when one is in proximate danger of death. It is a wish of the new rite that people receive the sacrament when in full possession of their senses. Viaticum may be administered within or outside of mass. That viaticum may be administered in a eucharistic celebration presupposes that the people are not on the verge of breathing their last breath. Again, there are several regulations which emphasize that viaticum takes place within the larger context of pastoral care: the opportunity for sacramental confession, that all present may receive under both forms of bread and wine, that wine alone may be given to a dying person, that while the minister for viaticum and anointing are the same, viaticum may also be administered by a deacon or properly appointed lay person when there is no priest. Lay persons use the usual rite for distributing communion but pronounce the special formula for viaticum (29). What comes through clearly amidst all these details is concern for the pastoral context and the importance of the sacramental sign.

Chapter Four: Rite of the Sacraments for Those Near Death

In effect this will usually mean the administering of reconciliation, anointing, and viaticum on one occasion and in that order. It may be possible to have the person receive the sacrament of reconciliation at some previous time. Anointing cannot be refused if the person chooses not to go to confession. In general, the person should be given the benefit of the doubt. The plenary indulgence for the dying may be given at the conclusion of confession or the penitential rite (122). In urgent cases, the person is anointed with one anointing and given viaticum. If not all the sacraments can be given the dying person, viaticum is offered (116). One can notice a change of emphasis in these situations of the person being near death. Hopefully, the need for the continuous rite will become less and less as a deeper understanding of anointing permeates the Catholic community. Ordinarily, persons will have received reconciliation and anointing previously so that only viaticum is the sacrament given in these hours close to death. It is helpful to note that when all the sacraments cannot be given, viaticum is to be preferred. The theological change is that the important concern for the dying Christian is not the forgiveness of sins or the removal of the remnants of sin to avoid purgatory, but union with the paschal Christ by means of the eucharistic meal.

Chapter Five: Confirmation of a Person in Danger of Death

Confirmation may be conferred in danger of death but it should usually be given separately from reconciliation, anointing, and viaticum. In the absence of a bishop the faculty to confirm is given to others such as pastors and curates. In case of necessity any priest can confirm (31). There is an anointing in both confirmation and in anointing of the sick. This argues against doing both in a continuous rite. If necessary, however, confirmation is conferred before the blessing of the oil of the sick and the imposition of hands of the anointing rite is omitted (117). Ordinarily, the entire rite is used, but in urgent cases an abbreviated rite can be substituted (136-137).

The inclusion of the provision of confirmation at the time of death is an example of the rite trying to provide for as many situations as possible as well as broadening the ministry to the dying person. One can question the value of introducing confirmation at this time. No doubt the rite wishes to "cover all bases" and make it possible for any Christian to receive as many sacraments as possible. In the case of a lengthy but terminal illness the administering of confirmation could be significant. But to introduce it too close to the time of the reception of anointing would surely be confusing and counterproductive.

Chapter Six: Rite for the Commendation of the Dying

The intention of the Church here is to accompany dying people until their last moments and to create an atmosphere of prayer around them. The living are called upon to assist the dying in dealing with death by recommending the person to God. This chapter is a collection of biblical readings and prayers which may be chosen for the occasion when the community expresses this fellowship with a dying brother or sister. The importance of the commendation is that even after viaticum the Christian community is not without liturgical resources. Those who are present with the dying person have here a collection of litanies, psalms, readings, and prayers which will assist the dying but conscious person to face the anxiety of death. Some form of reminder of baptism, such as the use of the sign of the cross, is recommended. These prayers are to be used in accordance with the situation which may call for a repetition of some of the prayers as well as for periods of silence. The use of the prayers which most Catholics learned in their youth can be most effective at this time. Immediately before death there is a need to return to one's origins, to the early years of one's life. After death, it is recommended that all kneel and recite the prayer to be used immediately after death (151). Both clergy and laity are urged to assist the dying in reciting these recommended prayers. In the case where the dying person is unconscious, these prayers can be of assistance to those present and grieving.

The Subject of Anointing

The person who receives this sacrament must be baptized, must have the use of reason, and must be seriously ill due to sickness or must be in a weakened condition due to old age. All of these conditions are necessary for the valid administration of the sacrament. The reason why this sacrament is limited to those with the use of reason, why, for instance, infants are excluded, is that it is seen as analogous to the sacrament of penance. This is still the predominant canonical viewpoint, although the theological position may be moving away from joining penance and anointing together so readily.

Much of the pastoral concern of the past focussed on what constituted a true danger of death. Because of canon law there was a concern about establishing the reality of this danger. Even the *Constitution on the Sacred Liturgy* retains the clause: "danger of death." On the one hand, prisoners to be executed could not receive the sacrament since the danger of death had to come from either illness or old age, but on the other hand, if the person who is ill, or some other person, reasonably judges that death might result from an illness, the norm of the canon was fulfilled. Contemporary theologians do not make an exclusive connection between anointing and dying that would require that it be delayed until the final moments of life. The new rite clearly moves away from earlier teaching regarding the necessity of some kind of danger of death. Danger of death is no longer necessary. Those who are prudently judged to be seriously ill and those weakened by old age can be anointed. The rite goes out of its way to caution against a scrupulous attitude in discerning who may be the subject of this sacrament. Small children may be anointed if they can be comforted by this sacrament. It is not necessary that they be at the chrono-logical age usually referred to as the "age of reason." Their response to the sacrament is the determining factor. The 1974 rite does not address the matter of anointing the mentally ill, but, the American Bishops' Committee on the Liturgy states: "It is clear that a person who is mentally ill and at the same time judged to be seriously sick (physically) may be anointed."[16]

Halligan gives a helpful and succinct summary of the conditions for anointing that readily apply in pastoral practice.

> The sacrament may be given as long as there is true illness which is presently and actually dangerous, thus, for example, excluding the person simply insensible merely from inebriation. Thus a sick person may be anointed before undergoing a surgical operation, as long as a dangerous ailment is the reason for the surgery. Elderly people whose strength becomes very much weakened, even though no dangerous illness is observed, may be anointed. Since the danger of death must arise from intrinsic causes, no other cause justifies the conferral of the sacrament, e.g. shipwreck, sentence of death, impend-ing air raid or battle, the mere accumulation of years; a pregnancy must present an extraordinary difficulty or danger.[17]

In actuality most of the time the priest will have to make a prudential judgment that the person is seriously ill due to sickness or old age. This will include other situations such as surgery to correct a serious illness. This author would include such situations as a person suffering from alcohol-ism or drug abuse, noticeable depression, and other psycho-logical problems such as discouragement and scrupulosity. Ideally the person should request the sacrament so that he/she can take part in it. It should not be left to the family to make such a request.

[16]*Newsletter* 10:3 (March 1974).
[17]Halligan, *Sacraments of Reconciliation*, p. 202.

Repeated and Conditional Anointings

Number nine of the Introduction states: "The sacrament may be repeated if the sick person recovers after anointing or if, during the same illness, the danger becomes more serious." The sacrament may be repeated in the course of a person's life should there be other situations of serious illness. Anointing may be repeated if the same illness becomes more dangerous. It should not be repeated during the same crisis of serious illness or death. The rubric is trying to achieve a balance between making the sacrament more available to persons who undergo either a protracted illness or one which is characterized by significant changes, and what might be called indiscriminate anointings. The danger of such lack of discretion in anointing people beyond the criteria set forth by the ritual would probably arise most frequently in the case of communal anointings where people from the parish are invited to come forward for anointing without some method of discrimination. In cases of doubt, one may always anoint.

The sacrament is conferred without condition on an unconscious or demented person who at least implicitly would have requested it while conscious or possessing the use of reason. Those who die in the act of sinning as in the case of a quarrel or a shooting can be anointed conditionally. Those who refuse the last sacraments before lapsing into unconsciousness should not be anointed. If the person is dead by the time the priest has arrived, that person should not be anointed, but rather the priest should pray that the person might be joined to God and find new life in God. If the priest is in doubt whether the person is dead, he may anoint conditionally (15). Many canonists are of the opinion that conditional anointing may be given up to one hour after apparent death in the case of a sudden death. Others would extend it to two or three hours. In the event of death after a lingering illness, anointing may be given up to one half hour after apparent death.

The idea of conditional anointing is based upon a medieval anthropology whereby the human person is divided into body and soul. Since even in the scholastic understanding it is not possible to tell when the soul leaves the body, differing opinions arise as to how long anointing may be delayed. The theological presupposition behind conditional anointing is that this may be the only means of salvation left to the apparently unconscious person. There appears to be a movement away from this position on the level of pastoral practice. As anointing clearly becomes the sacrament of the sick rather than the dying on the level of theological understanding, the pastoral change will accelerate. One can raise the question whether for someone who can no longer receive viaticum due to unconsciousness, would it not be better to use the prayers of the dying to show the community's support and concern at this time? But strictly speaking, a priest can anoint conditionally an apparently dead person when he is uncertain about the person's state.

The Minister of the Sacrament

In the Roman Catholic Church the priest is the minister of the sacrament. No one other than someone in presbyteral orders may confer the sacrament (16). The ordinary ministers are the bishop, the pastor of the sick or elderly person as well as associate pastors, priests who minister in hospitals and institutions for the sick and elderly, and clerical religious superiors. The obligation to anoint rests on the sick person's pastor. Ordinarily if another priest anoints, he should have the pastor's permission.

Number 19 provides for a minimal form of concelebration of this sacrament. When several priests are present, one says the prayers including the sacramental form and does the anointing. The others may participate by performing the introductory rites, the readings, the imposition of hands, and whatever explanations might appropriately be given. What the ritual has in mind here is the anointing of a single person. However, it does implicitly acknowledge the value of the presence of more than one priest at an anointing. In a true concelebration all priests would be involved in the imposition of hands, the prayers, and the anointing itself.

But this presupposes a communal celebration. More about communal anointings can be found in Chapter Five.

A welcome stress in the revised rite is the change in catechesis, namely, that Catholics should be encouraged to ask for anointing and that they should not misinterpret this eacrament by delaying it. Number 13 continues: "All who care for the sick should be taught the meaning and purpose of anointing." Furthermore, number 17 reminds the ministers of the sacrament that they have the responsibility to prepare the sick, the elderly, and others who will be present at the anointing so that they may all the more completely enter into the celebration.

Requisite Material

Traditionally, the oil to be used was olive oil. Such oil had to be blessed before it could be validly used. As has been noted in the chapter on the history of the sacrament, the consecrated oil itself was considered to be the sacrament without any reference to actual use. The blessing of this oil takes place on Holy Thursday at the Chrism Mass. For pastoral and liturgical reasons it is becoming more prevalent to have these masses some time before the Sacred Triduum. The new rite has broadened the legislation regarding the oil. Another plant oil may be substituted for olive oil and the oil can be blessed by any priest who has the faculty. In case of need the oil can be blessed by any priest. Again, the ritual tries to be as accommodating as it can so that the sacrament can both be rendered more accessible in varying circumstances and be as intelligible as possible.

As regards the actual anointing itself, number 23 provides that oil be spread on the forehead and hands or another suitable part of the body, if the condition of the person so requires. In case of necessity one anointing suffices. Individual national Churches may provide for additional anointings. While the forehead is being anointed, the minister says the prescribed formula: "through this holy anointing may the Lord in his love and mercy help you with the grace of the Holy Spirit. Amen." And while the hands are being anointed, he says: "May the Lord who frees you from sin save you and raise you up. Amen." In all cases, even in that of a single anointing, the entire formula is pronounced. It has already been noted that the form of the sacrament reflects a change of theological understanding as regards the purpose of the sacrament. This movement away from the stress on the forgiveness of sins is also seen in the dropping of the anointing of the five senses "through which the person sinned."

Reviviscence

Although contemporary sacramental theologians tend to be silent on this topic and although there is no reference to it in the ritual, the traditional Roman Catholic teaching on reviviscence still applies and so a word about it seems to be in place. This doctrine says that if a person validly receives a sacrament but it is not fruitful because of the presence of some obstacle such as sin or lack of sufficient attrition for such sin, that once the situation is rectified, the person receives the grace of the sacrament. The inhibiting obstacle could be posited inculpably or culpably. If the latter case obtains, then the reception of the sacrament is considered sacrilegious. In such a case can the effects revive? The sacrament cannot be repeated. Common theological opinion is that there is a reviving of the graces of this sacrament. If the obstacle is grave sin, it must be remitted by the sacrament of reconciliation or by perfect contrition. Because of the possibility of reviviscence, the minister should confer the sacrament absolutely even though he is in doubt about the proper dispositions of the recipient. To do otherwise would endanger the possibility of reviving the effects. Conditional administration of this sacrament is reserved for those situations where there is doubt whether the sacrament can be received validly. Such cases would include whether the person is dead, baptized, has the use of reason, or is lacking the proper intention.

Needless to say, these questions arise out of a more classical theological understanding. The notion of reviviscence is included here since the theological view supporting it is still present in the Church. More contemporary sacramental theologies would make many of these points theoretically irrelevant and pastorally less pressing. The major reimaging in theology today which affects one's understanding of reviviscence is in the understanding of grace. With the relational character of grace being stressed, it is also necessary to see the "reviving" of a sacrament in terms of a relationship. One can still speak of "obstacles" to the human relationship which serves as the analogy for understanding grace. But reimaging from other areas of theology comes into play here. The meaning and nature of "grave sin" and "perfect contrition" would be but two examples. Also, as the pastoral situation regarding conditional administration changes, the theological question in this regard will become less significant. Reviviscence is an example of a way of speaking which made sense in a certain theological framework. However, this framework is receiving less and less support from the theological community and may be passing into history.

The Obligation to Receive the Sacrament

A traditional theology which would view the sacrament as being instituted by Christ would see that there is some obligation to receive it. Such an obligation is not a grave one. Contempt for the sacrament would involve serious sin. If not receiving the sacrament would cause grave scandal, there would be an equally grave obligation to receive it. Another reason for speaking of the obligation to receive the sacrament is based on the idea that traditional theology sees this sacrament as the only means of salvation for the unconscious person who is in serious sin.

The question of obligation even more than that of reviviscence is of little concern for Catholic theology today. Few theologians would speak of the institution of the sacrament by Christ in such a way that it would imply an obligation to receive it. Concern about the sacrament being received with proper dispositions and with proper respect spring more from a Counter-Reformation mentality than one of the twentieth century. Again, the notion of sin that is usually implied when speaking about sin being forgiven in the unconscious person is one that depends upon an "act morality" rather than one of fundamental option or basic orientation. When there are changes in theological imaging in the other disciplines, it is to be expected that sacramental theology and sacramental practice will feel their influence. However, with all of that said, there is one way in which the point of obligation is the *most contemporary question* concerning anointing. It is the matter of the way in which this sacrament is going to play a significant part in the lives of Catholics. In moving away from the idea of the "last sacrament" to the anointing of the *sick and elderly* will this sacrament be one which will existentially ritualize important aspects of the Christian mystery? Or will it be left in some kind of theological limbo and pastoral ambiguity as is the case with the sacrament of reconciliation in many places in the Christian Church today? There is no point to sacraments unless they are received.

Anointing in the Other Churches

There is considerable diversity among the various Churches and only a few general observations can be made. With the exception of the Nestorians, all Orthodox groups accept anointing as a sacrament. Each has its own ritual and in general they would be more elaborate than that found in the Roman Rite. The Orthodox position can be summed up thus: 1) The principal effect of the sacrament is related to bodily health. 2) In addition to the anointing of the sick, there is a penitential anointing that complements the sacrament of reconciliation. There seems to be a distinction made between the two. A Western theologian would probably apply the sacrament/sacramental distinction. 3) The person who is to receive this sacrament must be seriously ill but danger of death is not required. 4) Concelebration of the sacrament by several ministers is the liturgical ideal. One minister will suffice according to pastoral need. 5) The sacrament has fallen into desuetude among certain groups such as the Ethiopians. It appears that the scarcity of olive oil in some places has been a contributing factor.

Among the Greeks this sacrament is administered to the healthy person as a preventative measure. Related to that is the fact that often anointing is given as a preparation for communion. In such cases it would be administered to the healthy. The Russian Church is more ambivalent in its position. Sometimes illness is required; sometimes it is not. In the Coptic Church the custom is to gather the sick in church on Monday of Holy Week to receive the anointing, although individuals can be anointed at other times. Although the Ethiopian Church has a ritual for anointing, it is rarely used. Syrian Jacobites anoint the dead, especially the clergy but this is a burial rite rather than a sacrament of the sick. The practice among the Nestorians is obscure. The Chaldeans of Mesopotamia were united to Rome in the sixteenth century. At that time they accepted the Roman rite of anointing and translated it into Syriac.

There is remarkable convergence between the Anglican Church's and the Roman Catholic Church's approach to the ministry of healing. In 1962 the Revised Catechism in the Church of England spoke of the sacramental ministry of healing in which God's grace is given "for the healing of spirit, mind, and body, in response to faith and prayer, by the laying on of hands, or by anointing with oil."[18] While the distinction in this ritual, which was in use at this time, between the anointing and the laying on of hands is not completely clear, the majority opinion seems to be that unction is more definitely sacramental. Perhaps, for that reason the minister of anointing is the ordained priest or bishop while a layperson who has the gift of healing may lay on hands. The subject of anointing is any sick person, even a child. The sickness may be either physical or mental. The danger of death is not a requisite and the anointing may be repeated. The anointing is a single one on the forehead in the

[18] *The Revised Catechism* (London: S.P.C.K., 1962): 18.

sign of the cross with the prayer for anointing. The purpose of this anointing has been succinctly summed up by Charles Gusmer: "Unction is the sacrament whereby the Holy Spirit is conferred for the restoration to wholeness of body, mind and spirit."[19] What is significant about the practice of sacramental healing in the Church of England in recent decades is that it is placed in the larger pastoral ministry to the sick. On this point, especially, are the Anglican and Roman traditions together.

The more recent liturgical revisions regarding the ministry to the sick in the Church of England follow these lines. The service of the laying on of hands and the anointing are intended to be public services in conjunction with holy communion and evening prayer. There are provisions for adaptation to individual use, but there is a shift in attitude from earlier rites in that there is a stronger connection between a sick person and the whole body of the faithful. Nor is there any longer a separation of the service of the visitation to the sick from the explicitly sacramental ministrations of the Church. No provision for auricular confession is made but there is a brief general confession. Prayers and readings are added for specific occasions and for additional use. The brevity of the rite manifests a sensitivity to the state of the sick person.

The American Episcopal Church has a new rite for ministration to the sick as found in the new Prayerbook (1979). It is composed of three parts: 1) Ministry of the Word, 2) Laying on of Hands and Anointing, and 3) Holy Communion. The parts can be used individually or together. The Service of the Word is a simplified one containing readings, prayers for specific occasions, places where the celebrant may make comments, and a provision for confession either general or individual. In part two the laying on of hands is seen as an act of blessing whereby there is established contact between the sick person and the healing power of God.

---

[19]Charles Gusmer, "Anointing of the Sick in the Church of England," *Worship* 45:5 (May 1971):271.

It is a symbol of the communication of the Holy Spirit. Anointing is understood to be of similar symbolic content. Part three provides for the eucharist. There is also a selection of prayers that can be used for the sick person or by the sick person.[20] This Prayerbook contains a "Ministration at the time of Death." Theologically, the Episcopal and Anglican Churches have the same emphasis as the Roman Catholic Church. Illness is part of the mystery of the Christian life and these sacramental ministrations speak of the health and wholeness of the unified person. The rites are intended to convey a sense of hope and community solidarity rather than a preparation for death. No longer is it God visiting the sick person with judgment. Now it is the community visiting the sick Christians to celebrate their special manifestation of the paschal mystery.

Protestant Churches do not accept the sacramentality of anointing in the same sense as they do baptism and eucharist. That does not mean that there have been no forms of the visitation of the sick in these Churches. But for the most part they would be informal. There would be readings and prayers to assist people in the time of anxiety about health and concern about death. In the Free Churches especially, the content would not be standardized and the services no doubt take the same general structure and content of their tradition of free prayer. They would be in accord with the non-sacramental character of most of their services. Thus there would be extemporaneous prayer and comment, exhortations, scripture reading, and psalmody. But this would be parallel to any set rite that the denomination might have. Practices vary. For instance, in the Church of the Brethren the present rite is made up of: reading of scripture, invitation to confession, anointing with oil three times for the three purposes of forgiveness of sins, strengthening in the faith and wholeness as God sees fit.

Many of the Churches make use of free prayer, spontane-

---

[20]For further information regarding the Episcopal rite see Charles P. Price and Louis Weil, *Liturgy for Living* (New York: The Seabury Press, 1979), p. 262.

ous singing and witness, and biblical readings in conjunction with some rites of healing. This is especially true of
Protestant Free Churches. These services tend to be more
charismatic in nature. Usually these gatherings, as well as
the pastor's informal visit to the sick, stand in sharp contrast
to the official rites of the Churches. The findings of psychology and the rejection of an outdated theology of illness have
made it difficult for many Protestant Churches to utilize a
formal ritual in the sickroom.

Protestant Churches are facing the same difficulties
regarding the healing ministry as the Anglican and Roman
Catholic. On the one hand the need to ritualize in such crisis
times as sickness is well founded anthropologically, and yet
the use of anointing in contemporary culture makes it difficult to recover its clear relationship to healing. All the
Churches are still struggling with finding ways to express
concern for the whole person. So much of the language still
presupposes a clear distinction between body and soul.
While on the level of theory few would disagree that the
healing ministry belongs to the whole community and not
just a few, still the way to implement that pastorally and
liturgically has not been notably creative or effective. What
is clear is that care for the sick must flow over into both
public and private worship. Structures are needed whereby
more than just the clergy can be involved in the healing
ministry. And yet those structures must have flexibility so
that sensitivity to the individual and the concreteness of the
situation are not lost. A proper combination of constant
elements as well as those which are personally chosen by the
pastor can effectively maintain connection with the large
parish community while at the same time respecting the
need for rituals which take into consideration the patient
and the situation in which the ministry is taking place.

Protestant and Anglican communions also must deal
with the important area of catechesis. Public worship must
be an opportunity for teaching about the Christian view of
illness in terms of actual experiences of the Church dealing
with sick people. Catechesis outside of the liturgy will be

useless if the liturgy itself confuses. If the rites continue to relate anointing to the dying or do not speak of the whole person as being in need of healing, then catechesis at other times, no matter how theologically informed, will be rendered dysfunctional. Both the liturgy and the pedagogy must be in agreement that God's will is for the wholeness of the human person and that sickness and suffering can contribute to that end. Both must remind the Church that the sick are crucial to the Church and need to be united to the community, that the local community participates in rites which are traditional and in contact with the primitive Church as well as springing from the contemporary culture, that the Church is more itself when it engages in ministry to the sick and elderly.

Since the Second Vatican Council there have been some directives which allow for the possibility of other Christians participating in the rite of anointing in the Roman Catholic Church. For instance, an Orthodox Christian may do so if there is a case of necessity, the person has not been able for a long time to be anointed in his/her own Church, and would be deprived of the benefits of this sacrament (*Directory Concerning Ecumenical Matters, Part One* (May 14, 1967), nos. 40-44).

Members of other Churches may participate in this sacrament in special situations such as danger of death, persecution, or when there is great difficulty in participating in the sacrament in their own Church. Further conditions include: a special need for this sacrament, it is not possible to obtain the services of a minister of his/her Church, the person asks for the sacrament freely, this person professes his/her faith in the sacraments in accord with the faith of the Roman Catholic Church, the person is properly disposed, and there is no danger of disturbance (No. 55 of the *Directory*).

BIBLIOGRAPHY:
THEOLOGY OF THE SACRAMENT
OF ANOINTING

Books

Bishops' Committee on the Liturgy, *Study Text II: Anointing and the Pastoral Care of the Sick*, Washington, D.C.: USCC, 1973.

Brown, Brian, *The Sacramental Ministry to the Sick*, New York: Exposition Press, 1968.

Davis, Charles, *The Study of Theology,* London, Sheed and Ward, 1962.

Knauber, Dr. Adolf,   *Pastoral Theology of the anointing of the Sick* trans. Matthew J. O'Connell, Collegeville: The Liturgical Press, 1975.

Poschmann, Bernard, *Penance and the Anointing of the Sick* trans. Francis Courtney, S.J., New York: Herder and Herder, 1964.

Rahner, Karl, *The Church and the Sacraments*, Montreal: Palm Publishers, 1963.

The Rites, New York: The Pueblo Publishing Co., 1976.

Articles

Alszeghy, Z., "The Bodily Effects of Extreme Unction," *Theology Digest* 9 (1961): 105-110.

Gusmer, C., "Liturgical Traditions of Christian Illness: Rites of the Sick" *Worship* 46 (1972):528-25.

"I Was Sick and You Visited Me: The Revised Rites for the Sick" *Worship* 48 (1974):516-25.

Palmer, Paul, "The Purpose of the Anointing of the Sick: A Reappraisal" *Theological Studies* 19 (1958):309-44.

Stanley, David, "Salvation and Healing" *The Way* 10 (1970):298-317.

The New Catholic Encyclopedia 1967. S.v. "Anointing of the Sick I (Theology of)," by J. P. McClain. Supplement for 1967-1974. S.v. "Anointing of the Sick, Liturgy of," by Charles Gusmer.

CHAPTER THREE:
A THEOLOGY OF ANOINTING FOR PREACHING AND TEACHING

In the previous chapter the theology of anointing was discussed primarily in terms of the official statements of the Church as these were articulated in the solemn gatherings of the teaching Church: Trent and Vatican II. Special consideration was given to the new rite of anointing and the theological presuppositions and implications which are found there. While such a discussion gives an adequate understanding of what the Church holds must be affirmed about this sacrament, this is far from claiming that these official statements represent a full or even balanced theology of anointing. For this more adequate treatment one could refer to the developed systems of some of the major contemporary theologians who have done significant work in the areas of sacramentality and ecclesiology. Rahner and Schillebeeckx are names that come immediately to mind. In systems or perhaps, better, theological frameworks such as these, anointing is seen more comprehensively in terms of a whole sacramental theology. The particular approach that this author presents in the next chapter will hopefully serve to broaden an understanding of anointing that moves beyond any conciliar perspective.

What is proposed in this third chapter is a theology of anointing which is meant to supplement the official teaching in a pastoral way without adopting the viewpoint of any particular systematic theologian. It might be cautiously termed a biblical theology of anointing since it is basically an examination of the James text. This should prove to be pastorally helpful since most instruction and teaching regarding anointing would tend to deal with this text in some way. There is a spirituality found in James which is less obviously found in the necessarily brief affirmations of Trent and Vatican II. In order to unlock this spirituality of anointing, there will first be an exegetical treatment of the text. This will be followed by a discussion of James as a locus for sacramental theology. The exegesis represents the position of more than one exegete. It is rather a summary of much of the biblical reflection on this text that has been taking place over the last several years.[1]

Exegesis of the James Text: James 5:13-16.

Is anyone among you suffering? (13a) *Is any among you sick?* (14a)

The use of the second verb in Greek, *astheneo*, would indicate that the sickness here is physical illness and not merely depression or malaise. The questions are addressed to the recipients of the letter and so for the faithful believers. The fact that the sick person cannot go to the elders but that they must come to him/her indicates that the advice is given for persons who have a sickness which is more than ordinary. Who are these elders of the Church? It refers not to those of advanced age but to those who are associated with the apostles. In other words, James is commanding that sick people summon those in authority in the local Church to perform an act in the name of the Church. This action is to

[1] I wish to express my gratitude and personal indebtedness to Joseph Powers for the use of his personal notes for this section. Those who wish a fuller and/or a different perspective in the matter of exegetical understanding of this text should consult the regular biblical commentaries. See especially: Kevin Condon, C.M., "The Sacrament of Healing (Jas. 5:14-15)," *Sacraments in Scripture*, ed. T. Worden (London: Geoffrey Chapman, 1966), pp. 172-86.

be that of the group and so is a collegial act of the presbyterium to put it in more contemporary terms. It is to be an act done in the name of the Lord and so is an official ministerial act.

And let them pray over him (14b)

These words indicate that the ministers and subjects are in close proximity to each other. This is reinforced by the fact that they anoint the sick with oil. Verses 16-18 indicate that this prayer is efficacious.

Anointing him with oil in the name of the Lord (14c)

Probably the oil used was olive oil, but the real significance is the meaning of the oil and not in the kind. This is not the anointing used in games and baths, that is, the anointings of the pagan world. This would have been abhorrent to the Jews. Nor is it merely medicinal. It is an anointing joined to prayer and performed in the name of the Lord. It designates the healing power and presence of Christ. It is more analogous to an exorcism than it is to anointing after a bath. Both the prayer and anointing are performed by the presbyterium and in the name of the Lord. They are functions of the power which Jesus showed in his ministry of healing. They are symbolic actions of the apostolic ministry, a ministry which the apostles exercised in the name of the Lord.

And the "prayer of faith" will save the sick man (15a)

The basic idea, that prayer with faith is efficacious, is found throughout scripture. In this same chapter five the prayer of Elijah is cited as an example. Verse 18 says: "Then he (Elijah) prayed again and the heaven gave rain, and the earth brought forth its fruit." (See also Mt 7:7-11 and Mk 11:22-24) In Matthew chapter 17 the disciples question Jesus why they could not cast out the demon that possessed a young boy. Here the prayer of faith and healing are seen together in that the disciples could not heal the boy because of their little faith.

But the prayer referred to in the James text is more than one uttered by a person with faith. It is said in *the name of the Lord*. It is not simply a prayer which comes from the faith of the trusting individual, it also comes from the faith of the believing community. The prayer is offered by the elders in the name of the Church. In terms of Roman Catholic theology this is an actualization of the sacramental principle that in baptism, confirmation, and orders the Church is deputed for worship. It can pray in *the name of the Lord*. This is what is happening here. The efficacy of the prayer is due to Christ. The gospel of John also speaks of the prayer of the Church: chapter 14:13-14 states: "Whatever you ask in my name, I will do it, that the Father may be glorified in the Son; if you ask anything in my name, I will do it." (See also 16:23) The words of Jesus in chapter 14 are spoken in the context of the works of power which Christ himself has done.

And the "prayer of faith" will save the sick man (15a)

What does sickness mean here? The meaning is general. Verse 14 indicates that the person is not able to attend the prayer service of the Church but must call the Church to him/her. But the seriousness of the condition is not evident in the text as some would claim.

What is the meaning of "will save" in this text of James? It carries with it all the connotations of biblical salvation including such concepts as grace, justice, freedom from sin, and peace. In the New Testament salvation is tied to faith. Jesus is the Savior who releases people from the power which is inimical to God. This salvation refers to the power of sin, but also includes sin's historical manifestations as found in disease and death. Thus, Christ brings salvation which is both spiritual and corporal. And the disciples' responsibility to carry on this work of salvation includes not only the deliverance from the power of iniquity but also the corporal afflictions which are visible manifestations of the mystery of sin. James uses the verb to mean salvation of the soul. In chapter 1:21, he says: "Therefore put away all filthiness and rank growth of wickedness and receive with meekness the implanted word, which is able to save (*sozein*) your souls." In chapter 2:14 there is the question regarding the person of faith but devoid of works, "Can his faith save him?" Other similar uses of the verb, to save, in James are: 4:12: "There is one lawgiver and judge, he who is able to save and to destroy." 5:20: "Let him know that whoever brings back a sinner from the error of his way will save his soul from death and will cover a multitude of sins."

But James' view of salvation must be placed in the larger context of the gospels. In terms of Christ's healing ministry it means that the efficacy of the healing work is actually conditioned by the faith of those who are healed. For instance, all three synoptics present the healing of the woman with the hemorrhage as a cure which had been conditioned by the woman's faith. "Your faith has made you well" (Mt 9:22; Mk 5:34; Lk 8:48). The healing of the blind man as mentioned in Mk 10:52 was accomplished through faith. The healing of the ten lepers of Le 17:19 is based on faith. The New Testament concept of salvation includes the healing of the body as a sign of Christ's power over illness which in turn is a sign of his power over the kingdom of darkness. The commissioning of the apostles to preach the coming of the kingdom (Mt 10) includes the power to perform the signs of the victorious reign of Christ in the healing of the sick and casting out of demons.

The prayer of faith referred to here has a double meaning: 1) the prayer stressed in James 1:21 and 5:16c-18 and 2) the official prayer which is uttered by the presbyters in their mission of healing. The effect of this prayer (as well as the act of anointing) is to save the sick person, that is, the achieving of victory over sin and its accompanying effects.

And the Lord will raise him up (15b)

The meaning of being raised up is quite wide in the New

Testament, but here it is specified to mean being raised up from the condition of illness that has laid the person low. The drama here is a war between the power of God and the condition of sickness. Jesus as Lord here means not only the Risen Christ but also Christ the sacrament, the visible epiphany of God's power. He himself has received this power (Col 1:15-20) and he exercises it in the name of the Father (Jn 4:34; 5:30-32; 6:38-40). In Jn 17:2 this power is described as the power to give eternal life to all flesh. In Jn 6:40 it is a power that enables Jesus to raise up on the last day the one who believes in him. The ministry of Christ's healing is part of his mission from the Father to reconcile all things to himself in God (Col 1:20). All this is necessary background to understand that the prayer of faith is addressed to Christ and is uttered in his name. As all prayer it is also addressed to the Father who gives whatever is asked in Jesus' name (Jn 16:23).

To raise up in the New Testament can refer to God raising up people to accomplish his designs. "And has raised up a horn of salvation for us" (Lk 1:69). Mt 11:11 says: "among those born of woman there has risen no one greater than John the Baptist." There is some of this feeling in the text of James in so far as through the prayer and anointing Jesus raises up those who believe in him. But the major meaning of raising up in the New Testament is the resurrection of the dead. There are many examples such as Mt 11:5: "and the dead are raised up." Lazarus was raised from the dead by Jesus as John 12:1 notes. Jesus's own resurrection is referred to in Mt 16:21: "and on the third day be raised." The dead are raised up in the eschatological time (Mt 27:52). In the broad sense, then, raising up must be seen in terms of God's saving action: raising up prophets, raising up Jesus, raising up the dead.

Here in the James text the Lord's raising up is directed toward those afflicted with illness. The context is physical healing. This is consistent with other parts of the New Testament, e.g. Mk 1:31 where Jesus raises up Peter's mother-in-law, and Mk 9:27 where Jesus raises up the possessed boy. In Acts 3:7 Peter takes the cripple by the right hand and raises him up. While raising in connection with physical healing is not the usual New Testament meaning, it is not strange to it. Other references that can be consulted are: Mt 8:15; 9:5-7; 9:25; 10:8; Mk 2:9-12; 5:41; Lk 5:23-24; 8:54; Jn 5:8. In sum, in James the sick person is both saved and raised up. The healing that takes place is a total healing. The physical effects of human wickedness as well as the evil itself are overcome in the victorious ministry of Jesus Christ.

And if he has committed sins, he will be forgiven (15c)

As is apparent from the whole context of James' ministry of healing, physical cure and forgiveness of sins are very closely connected. Such total healing is the gift of God to the believer. And as has been noted, in terms of redemption through Christ, sickness is the embodiment of the mystery of evil. Thus, forgiveness of sins is related to the ministry of healing. In Mt 9:2-8 Christ says: "For which is easier to say, 'Your sins are forgiven,' or to say, 'Rise and walk'?" (also: Mk 2:3-12 and Lk 5:20ff) In Jn 5:14 Jesus cures the man by the pool. Afterward, Jesus met the man in the temple and said to him: "See, you are well! Sin no more, that nothing worse may befall you." There is an obvious coupling of the raising up and the forgiveness of sins.

What are these sins that are referred to here? In traditional Roman Catholic theology, they would not be venial sins which all people commit. Otherwise, there would be no sense to a conditional statement about them, "and if he has committed sins." This raises the question for traditional Roman Catholics about the efficacy of this sacrament regarding serious sins. James does not indicate how this remission of sins took place. Was it the normal pattern of the Roman Catholic tradition? Confession of sins to the presbyters?

> *Therefore confess your sins to one another, and pray for one another, that you may be healed. The prayer of a righteous man has great power in its effects.* (16)

Verse 16 places the efficacy of prayer and confession of sins in a broader perspective, that is, the ministry of healing is contextualized in terms of the general utility of prayer and confession for the Christian community. The forgiveness of sins in verse 15 must be seen in terms of this wider notion of confession as can the prayer of faith of verse 16 explain the power of the prayer of the Christian community.

In "Therefore confess your sins to one another," the more generalized idea of confessing in the sense of professing openly takes on the special meaning of the public confession of sinful things one has done. "To one another" means in the assembly. The *Didache* gives some explanation of this public confession because it represents the practice close to this biblical period. Because the *Didache* is often taken as a description of early Church practice, this verse of James is usually cited as the basis of the practice of penance in the Church. In any event, "to one another" here does not imply individual confession, certainly not auricular confession, but the confession of sins in the context of the liturgical assembly. This throws some light on the meaning of the last part of verse 15, "he will be forgiven," regarding the manner in which sins are forgiven in the ministry of the sick and this in terms of the more general Christian practice. In other words, sins (serious) are forgiven in the confession made to the presbyters, presumably in the liturgical assembly. There is no evidence to presume that James is speaking here about a marginal situation, but rather the reasonable assumption is that he is referring to normal practice as in the case of the anointing itself.

The prayer that is referred to in "and pray for one another, that you may be healed," is the prayer of the community, inspired by the gift of the Spirit and "done in the name of the Lord." The purpose of the prayer is healing. Again, the Greek verb used here indicates its closeness in meaning to "being saved" and "being raised up." Physical healing is a "sign" of God's healing power. Thus, it is used in the context of healing human sinfulness. For instance, Isaiah's "Suffering Servant Song" as cited in 1 Pet 2:24 (=Is

53:12), "By his wounds you have been healed," is an example of such usage.

The point is that the healing ministry of Jesus in the light of the Old Testament is directed to redemption from the historical effects of sin on those whom God has called. Jesus announces that he is salvation for the poor, the suffering, and the humble, but this refers to more than those physically sick and deprived. He is bringing the healing and saving power of God to those who are waiting for the justice or righteousness of God. And in this context it makes sense that Jesus's mission to the apostles to heal (Mt 10:1; Lk 9:1-2) has as its result not only physical alleviation but especially the blessings of the kingdom. James 5:16 contains both aspects. And this is accomplished by the prayer of faith made "in the name of the Lord." The prayer of the community through the healing power of God accomplishes the forgiveness of sins for every member of the community. The healing of the sick Christian becomes paradigmatic of the kind of healing that is accomplished in the members through the prayer of the community.

In the second part of verse 16, "The prayer of a righteous man has great power in its effects," states clearly that the source of the power of this prayer is the just person. The justice referred to here must be seen in a larger context, however. The following distinctions can be made.

1) *God is just.* He is the most just of all. He is upright in his saving actions. He is upright according to the promises he made freely and lovingly. God is just because he is true to his promises. Romans 3:25-26 is the clearest statement of his justice:

> whom (Jesus) God put forward as an expiation by his blood, to be received by faith. This was to show God's righteousness, because in his divine forebearance he has passed over former sins; it was to prove at the present time that he himself is righteous and that he justifies him who has faith in Jesus.

Jesus is the end of history. He is the fulfillment of all of

God's saving activity. In sending Jesus God is faithful to his promises. This is God's uprightness.

2) *Jesus is the historical revealer of God's uprightness.* Such revelation takes place through faith and it is for faith (Rom 1:17). Through faith in Jesus, people come to see the righteousness of God. And so in the Christian kerygma Jesus is "the Holy and Righteous One" (Acts 3:14). Acts 7:52 says "Which of the prophets did not your fathers persecute? And they killed those who announced beforehand the coming of the Righteous One, whom you have now betrayed and murdered."

The righteousness of Jesus is clear from the fulfillment of his mission. At his baptism Jesus said to John: "Let it be so now; for thus is it fitting for us to fulfill all righteousness." To fulfill all righteousness here would mean that it is in Jesus that God's saving action reaches its completion in the fulfillment of the promise. God responds to this desire of Jesus to fulfill all righteousness in the manifestation of the Spirit to John and the voice of the Father identifying Jesus as "my beloved Son, with whom I am well pleased" (Acts 3:17). The presentation of Jesus at his baptism is the one sent from heaven to fulfill the saving power of God. He does his work not by his own power, but by that of the Father. Thus, it is Jesus's judgment because he seeks to do the will of God. John 5:30: "I can do nothing on my own authority; as I hear, I judge; and my judgment is just, because I seek not my own will but the will of him who sent me." And Jn 6:40 continues this thought: "For this is the will of my Father, that everyone who sees the Son and believes in him should have eternal life; and I will raise him up at the last day." What John is unambiguously expressing is that the source of the power of Jesus is that he is the fulfillment of the promises of God. This is the guarantee of the truth of what he speaks. Those who see and believe in him are saved and raised up. This being raised up is synonymous with the fulfillment of God's promises. It authenticates the fact that Jesus is the "Son of Man." He speaks not from himself but what he has been taught by the Father. Because Jesus lives his life according to the norm of God's promise, he is called the "just one."

Jesus is the righteous or just one most concretely in his death and glorification. This is the Good News. That is, God has fulfilled his promise in Jesus Christ and this fulfillment manifests the power of God. And this is revealed to those who have faith. The righteousness of God is revealed out of faith. The righteous shall live by faith. Romans 1:17 says: "He who through faith is righteous shall live." And because God has established Christ as the *hilasterion* (the place above the Ark of the Holy of Holies, the throne of mercy, where the blood of Yom Kippur sacrifices was sprinkled in atonement for the forgiveness of sins), he is made manifest by our faith in his blood (Rom 3:25-26).

Thus, the biblical understanding of the Righteous One is very rich. He is the one who because of total commitment to God in faith has righteousness from God. He lives according to this righteousness as the norm of his life. In other words, he is faithful to God because God is faithful to God's own promises. This can serve as the background for understanding the meaning of the verse: "The prayer of a righteous man has great power in its effects."

What is the meaning of "powerful in its effects"? It is not that the prayers should be well-done or fervent. That would be presumed. But that they should be put to work, into operation for the healing of the community is the sense in which they are to be taken. The meaning of "powerful in its effects" is clarified in the example from Elijah (Jas 5:17-18). A person like any other person in his weakness he could, however, open and close heaven with his prayer. The stress is upon the value of prayer uttered in faith. In this sense such power belongs to the prayer of every member of the community. But then why refer to the prayer of the "righteous" person? Because this prayer flows from a person who lives in the context of the fulfillment of God's saving promises precisely because of his/her faith. This prayer done in faith participates in the justice of this righteous person. And sharing in this righteousness is also sharing in the righteousness of God. Thus, the powerful effects of this prayer come from its participation in God's righteousness.

Romans 3:25-26 says that God set up Christ publicly as a throne of mercy to show that he fulfills his promises in righteousness and gives this righteousness to those who believe in Jesus. Prayer which flows from this faith is effective because God is faithful to his promises in answering it. And this prayer uttered in faith is effective because Christ himself is the fulfillment of God's promises. And so the prayer of the righteous is a prayer made in *the name of Christ*. And finally this prayer is one uttered in community as James 5:16 indicates: "Confess your sins to one another, and pray for one another."

In sum, what is found in this text of James is a ministry of healing in the context of effective prayer and anointing in the name of the Lord. The purpose of this ministry is to heal the sick but this is due to the prayer of faith. The one who raises up the sick person is the Lord. This ministry is done in the name of the Lord and it is the Lord himself who is operative in this ministry. He raises up the sick person by means of the prayer of faith and the anointing which are done in his name. This healing of the sick is an act of the Church because it does it in union with Christ, its head. The broader basis for this ministry mentioned by James is the ministry of healing of Jesus which he gives to the Church in the twelve. It is a mission performed by the Church with the power of Christ. It is *not* as if James is announcing a new sacrament to the Christian Church. He is but calling attention to a powerful ministry which already exists in the midst of the Christian community. The paranetic conclusions of the epistles of the New Testament such as the James text tend not to promulgate new practices. This ministry of healing which the Church possesses finds its meaning in its relationship to the proclamation of the Good News. Healing is a "symbol" of the blessings which come to those who have faith in the Lord Jesus.[2]

[2]Cf. David Stanley, "Salvation and Healing," in *The Way* 10 (1970):298-317.

The Sacramental Context of James 5:13-16

It is important to consider the place of James in a general sacramental theology in the New Testament and in the Church. The most fruitful approach to this is: 1) to look at sacramentality in terms of the process of salvation begun by God, 2) to show that this process is sacramental, 3) to see the meaning of sacraments in this light, and then 4) to consider the ministry of healing as found in the ritual of the anointing of the sick. Roman Catholic theology of anointing today would attempt to show the sacramentality of the ministry of healing in the Church in the larger context of the dispensation of salvation as realized in Christ and the Christian community. And only in this larger framework are such elements as matter, form, minister, subject, and effect of the sacrament to be understood.

The basic sacramental principle has been enunciated in the New Testament in Eph 1:9-10: "For he has made known to us in all wisdom and insight the mystery of his will, according to his purpose which he set forth in Christ as a plan for the fullness of time, to unite all things in him, things in heaven and things on earth." The basic mystery (mysterion) or *sacramentum* is the hidden plan of God which comes to visibility historically and which is fulfilled in Jesus Christ. Such revelation is *the* sacrament. People know of God's hidden power and love when they know the course of human history. History itself reveals the saving dispensation of salvation. God is working in human history in a visible way and so men and women can know God in and through history. Romans 1:19-20 refers to this idea that what is hidden and invisible in God is available to human beings because it is manifested in God's creation. As E. Schillebeeckx has put it "every supernatural reality which is realized historically in our lives is sacramental."[3] The content of sacramentality is the mystery of God's saving love,

[3]E. Schillebeeckx, O.P., *Christ the Sacrament of Encounter with God* (London: Sheed and Ward, 1963), p. 4.

but the visible manifestation of this mystery is what constitutes its specific sacramental character.

The paradigmatic instance of this visibility is Jesus
Christ. As Col 1:15 says: "He is the image of the invisible God, the first born of all creation." Christ is the
visible manifestation of the unseen God. He is the face of
God which reveals God to humanity in terms of its own
understanding. Jesus is the sacrament because he is effective, visible epiphany of God's loving power. That means
that Jesus as a person is a symbol. In this visible, corporal
person God shows himself and gives himself to humanity.
This is what is meant by the Pauline idea of Jesus as the *first
born*. That is, in Jesus dwells the fullness of God and everything is reconciled in Christ. The reconciliation of the world
is brought about in Christ Jesus (Col 1:15-20).

And so in Jesus one can see the face of God. This glance at
God is not one that kills but one which gives life. The very
mission of Jesus is to be the sacrament of God. He is to
reveal the words and deeds of God to humanity in terms of
his own human, fleshy existence (Jn 4:34; 6:38-39; 9:4).
Because of this mission Jesus can speak and work with the
power which God has given him over the world (Jn 17:2).
The greatest message that Jesus proclaims, the greatest
work that he does, is the work of God. And this work of God
is that people believe in him whom God has sent (Jn 6:29).
In this *belief*, the work of God is achieved. And this work is
salvation. Salvation is a hidden reality, but is made visible in
God's loving power in Jesus (Jn 1:14, 16).

Christ as sacrament, as the one who shows forth the
invisible God, is closely tied to his mission to be a paradigm
of what it means to be a human being. He realizes (in the
sense of making real) God's entrance into human life and
humanity's complete response to God. The human side of
this manifestation is Christ's *worship*. He acknowledges
that all that he is and does comes from God. And in his
living out this conviction, in his worship, he sanctifies
humanity.

Finally, the reality of the Church must be considered in

this general sacramental background for appreciating the significance of the anointing as found in James. The Church, like Christ, is seen as engaging in the mystery of sanctification. It is done by means of its worship in Christ. It is, however, Christ's worship which the Church offers. It is the visible expression of the worship of Christ that he offers at the right hand of God. Christ is continually praying for humanity and because his prayer is effective, the worship of the Church is also effective. The Church as Christ's body is his earthly visibility.

The Church in offering such sanctifying worship is fulfilling the mission given to it by Christ. "As the Father has sent me, even so I sent you" (Jn 20:21). But mission cannot be without authority and so the Church has the power to initiate and carry out this mission of prayer and sanctification in the name of Jesus. It is precisely this mission and delegation to this mission which the classical concept of sacramental character referred to. Baptism, confirmation, and orders are the missions given to the Christians by Christ to worship and sanctify themselves and the world in the name of Christ. In classical theological language character refers to the "intermediate principle of sacramentalization,"[4] that is, the deputation to make historically visible the heavenly worship and sanctification of Christ. Needless to say, this in no way determines how one views the institution of these sacraments by Christ. Nor does this sacramental theology prejudice in any way how one may understand the meaning of "sacramental character."

What has been noted thus far provides the necessary background for understanding the Church's ministry of healing. This ministry is one of the missions of the Church. It is a ministry performed in prayer and sanctification. But it is also a ministry performed in the name of Christ. It is accomplished through Christ in the Spirit in the prayer and sanctifying work of the Church. It is all an instance of God's saving power taking on historical visibility.

[4] I owe this particular phrase to Joseph Powers.

In discussing the particular sacramental context of James 5:13-16, several points need to be made:

1) The sacramental nature of the ministry of healing in biblical terms. The practice of healing which James relates is not original with him. It is related in the latter part of the letter where the paranetic or hortatory sections are usually found. As already noted, these sections do not introduce new practices. Rather, they encourage the reader to an already known practice. Also, it has already been stated that the apostles made use of the Jewish practice of anointing as a sign of the presence and power of God. But they adopted it in terms of the mission they had received from Christ. It was to be practiced in his name. This is a sacramental action because it is a ministry which is visible and which is salvific. It belongs to the Church through Christ's promise and it is practiced in the name of Christ. Furthermore, it is an act of official worship as is clear from James who says that it is performed by the presbyters in the name of the Lord. The effect of the action is ascribed to the Lord performed in and by means of the ritual and prayers. Moreover, this is not an episodic ministry given to the apostles as special privilege. It is part of the larger ministry of preaching the kingdom and so it must be perennially part of the Church's life. Thus, this ministry is fully sacramental.

2) The sacramental sign in the anointing. The basic sacramental principle in Catholic theology is that God freely saves human beings in terms of religious symbolic actions because humans are bound to matter in their journey to personhood. Salvation is not a purely spiritual process. It is linked to the material. But what makes any concrete event a sacramental sign? It would seem to be the positive institution by Christ. But is there a command of Christ to anoint and pray in his name over those who are sick? There appears to be no evidence to support such a possibility. Mainline Catholic theology is content to claim an implicit institution of the sacramental sign. The general Jewish practice of anointing the sick was seen as sign of the power of God at work. The apostles made use of this ritual. This was a part of

their larger ministry of preaching. In that sense there is an implied way of performing this ministry in the concrete. One might draw an analogy with baptism which as a ritual was established in Judaism.

How much of classical understanding of the sacraments is present in the James text? One can find there the matter /form relationship in the anointing and prayer if those concepts are understood broadly. Matter refers to more than the material elements, but means the ability something has for expressing a saving reality in conjunction with prayer and a context which expresses the meaning of an action as a whole. In this case the anointing of sick people has such a capacity because it had a religious significance in Judaism as a specifically symbolic action. It is symbolic of the healing presence of God. For this reason it could easily be assumed into the apostolic ministry in conjunction with the preaching of the kingdom. Anointing's capacity as a religious symbol is fully actualized when it is practiced in the name of the Lord in connection with the prayer of faith. In this context the materiality of oil anointing can express the saving mystery of Christ. The element which expresses the significance of this action is the prayer of faith. In the language of classical sacramental theology, it is the form. This prayer actually determines that this action is an expression of faith in Christ. Anointing and prayer are two elements which make up one symbolic religious action. This action constitutes a profession of faith in the power of Christ to heal, a power which he has given to the Church.

3) The minister of the anointing of the sick. In James the ministers are clearly stated to be the presbyters, those entrusted to care for the communities. The term, *presbyteroi*, is not clearly defined in the New Testament. It probably refers to a body or group which includes bishops, deacons, and even lay leaders. They perform this religious action in the name of the Lord. That is, what they do is done in terms of the mission given to the Church by Christ, a mission which really belongs to everyone in the Church although participated in differently. In Mark the healing ministry is

part of the prophetic ministry of the apostles. In James it belongs to the leaders of the community who are also the leaders of worship. It is an action performed by those whose task it is to serve the Church. It is a ministry which flows from the general ministry of preaching the kingdom. But as already noted, with every service there is a corresponding power. They have the power to act in the Church, to act in the name of Christ. Such action flows from the ministerial power of the Church, Thus, the James presentation of this ritual deals not with something marginal to the life of the Church but which touches upon the central ministry of the Church. Those who perform this ministry act in the name of the Lord and he raises up the sick person and this person is healed.

4) The subject of the anointing of the sick. It is the whole person. This is important to keep in mind in determining the effects of this sacrament. It is not solely for the body or only for the soul. Nor is anointing addressed to sickness as a medical phenomenon. The sick person is dealt with from the point of view of being sick "in the Church." The point of view is not medical, it is salvific.

5) The effects of the ritual. These are listed variously as salvation, "raising up," forgiveness of sins, and healing. As described in James and proposed by the Church, the ministry of healing is seen to be efficacious. That is to say, the power of Jesus is actualized in ministry. When the elders are brought in, it is expected that something effective will be done. It is more than a pious hope. The words are: "And the prayer of faith will save the sick man, and the Lord will raise him up." The meaning of healing in the verbs, "sozein" (save), or "egeirein" (raise up), includes both spiritual and corporal effects. The person is here understood as a spirit who lives in the world in and by means of the body. The bodily healing is further contextualized by the reference to forgiveness of sins in addition to the saving and raising up which the Lord does through the ritual. From all this it is clear that the healing ministry here means that the person is healed from his/her illness in a total and salvific sense. In

other words, this anointing does not confer immortality. What is of significance is that the sick person shares in the victory of Christ over evil. And this can be manifested either in a physical cure or in the integral way in which the sick persons deal with their condition.

6) Sacramental and charismatic healing. Those who would reject any kind of sacramentality in conjunction with anointing would claim that the James text is referring to charismatic healing since in the beginning the Church was still characterized by a somewhat chaotic manifestation of charisms. Only later did institutionalization set in. In this position office and charism are opposing realities. Institutionalized anointing then cannot make the same claims as may have been verified in the original charismatic experience.

It is well within the Catholic tradition that the grace of redemption can be manifested in two ways: 1) institutionally or 2) charismatically. It is an institutional visibility when it is communicated through the activity of the hierarchy and faithful when they perform certain functions in promoting the mission of the Church. Traditional theology would see this as the actualization of the deputation involved in baptism, confirmation, and orders, in other words, in terms of sacramental character. Each group has been empowered to act in the name of Christ in a specific way. Those baptized and confirmed are officially empowered by Christ and the Spirit to worship and act in the world. They are extensions of Christ in their worship and apostolate. Those in orders have been commissioned to preside over the worship of the community and to teach and rule in the name of Christ. Thus, all have visible missions with a corresponding authority to act and this gives each Christian his/her place in the Church because the structure of the Church is based on these missions.

Grace can also be available charismatically. This means that grace achieves visibility in the lives and activities of those who have a deep inner communion with God. Charismatic does not mean structureless or chaotic. The charismatic Christian life is structured by mission and service in the Church. Charism is not opposed to office; it supports it. Schillebeeckx puts it this way: "Ecclesiologically, according to the inner demand of the Church itself, office (both of the hierarchy and of the ordinary faithful) is borne and supported by charisms."[5] The three sacraments which involve sacramental character not only bring about and celebrate the inner communion of grace, they also involve a visible mission to action in the Church and in the world. But the one depends on the other. Grace is presupposed in the working of the visible mission. The inner reality finds expression in the visible mission.

Charismatic manifestation has nothing to do with semi-hysterical activity. Charism is a gift of the Spirit which makes ministry in the Church a possibility. Paul indicates in 1 Cor 12:7-10 and 27-28 that the Spirit bestows gifts on each in the Church so that the Body can be served by some office. But he also indicates that there is a better way to accomplish the same thing than by the fulfillment of some office, that is, by the ministry of love. Official ministry, then, is based on both power and love. But it is love which is the life-giving principle of the ministry. In one sense, charisms, services, and powers are all the same. As from the Spirit, they are gifts or charisms. As from the Lord, they are services to the Church. And as coming from God, they are manifestations of power. Rather than office and charism being contradictory, they are the two poles around which the Church's interior life is mobilized. They must be kept together for the health of the Church. A separation means either hollow ministry or chaos.

The official ministry of healing as found in James 5 and the Pauline charismatic healings are not in opposition. These latter charisms are given for the needs of the Church. They are free gifts of the Spirit to assist the working out of

---

[5]This is taken from his book, *Christ the Sacrament of Encounter with God*. However, this quotation does not appear in the English translation. I am indebted to Joseph Powers for this quotation.

the design of salvation. They are for the ministry of the Church in order that the Church may be built up (Eph 4:12). The charism of healing also belongs to the Church and corresponds to the office of ministry of healing. It is not clear whether Paul intended this charism to be connected with a distinct office, but it is to be exercised within the institutional structures of the Church. The office of healing as portrayed by James is based on the charism of healing, both physical and spiritual. Its power flows from the gift of the Spirit which is given that the ministry of the Church might manifest the saving power of God who acts through healing prayer and anointing.

Note: In regards to bibliographical references for this chapter, most of the bibliographical listings for Chapter Two would be relevant.

CHAPTER FOUR
ANOINTING: A SACRAMENT
OF VOCATION

Introduction

A way of understanding the sacrament of anointing, one which must be given as much credence and emphasis as the past stress on its being a sacrament of healing, is that it is a vocational sacrament analogous to orders and marriage. Usually anointing is clustered with reconciliation because both are seen in light of Christian healing. However, anointing can also be that sacrament which recognizes that there is a special vocation in the Church of the sick and the aged. Anointing is the ritualization of that vocation. This sacrament is a celebration of the fact that because of Christianity the sick and old person who is fragmented can be brought back together again. It is an articulation of the truth that by dying to oneself, by being the kind of marginal human being a sick and old person is, one opens oneself to a far greater wholeness. In turn, the sick and old person who is anointed, as well as the rite itself, speaks to the Church reminding it that there is a deeper meaning to sickness and old age than what can be explained by the medical and psychological professions. Thus, those anointed minister to the rest of the Church who are well and in the fullness of life. They are called to proclaim that sickness and old age need not be a threat to their fellow Christians whose lives need not be characterized by fragmentation. The sacrament of anointing removes the ambiguity from those endless situations in daily living which bring salvation. The salvational aspect of sickness and old age may be obscure, but it is the liturgy of anointing which can show them for what they are: real events of personal triumph over the past and the present, and representations of growth toward new life. The Introduction of the Rite of Anointing speaks of the vocation of the sick person: "The role of the sick in the Church is to remind others not to lose sight of the essential or higher things and so to show that our mortal life is restored through the mystery of Christ's death and resurrection" (#3).

The vocational aspect of anointing which brings it into a relationship with such sacraments as baptism, orders, and marriage is seen in its character as a rite of passage. Anointing as liturgy remembers the passage of Christ and makes it possible for the sick and elderly person to enter into this same passing over. And just as Christ's own suffering and passage moved in the direction of the kingdom of God, so also those who are sick and old are reminded in anointing that this movement is their own. In anointing this alienation and brokenness is converted into an anticipated experience of the resurrected life.[1]

It is the afflicted or the marginal who are anointed. In that sense the sacrament is not oriented principally toward death. It attempts to give meaning to sickness and old age. Like other liturgical rites its purpose is to remove the ambiguity found in these situations by being a liturgy of passage. Just as liminality (being on the margin) is a way of speaking about liturgy, so this way of being outside the structures that usually delineate people's lives is a helpful way of referring to the sick and elderly. The in-betwixt-and-between character of both worship and these special people in the Church demands that there be such a thing as the liturgy of anointing. Anointing, then, is a liminal rite of passage because that is the character of illness and old age. Being sick or old puts

[1]Thomas Talley, "Healing: Sacrament or Charism?" *Worship* 46:9 (November 1972):525.

one on the threshold between living and dying. Clearly being sick or old involves the three stages of a rite of passage as described by van Gennep: separation, marginality, reintegration.[2] First, the sick and elderly are separated from their usual community and life patterns. Secondly, their present condition involves them in an ambiguous situation prior to reincorporation. This third stage of reintegration has many meanings. It can take the form of a renewed understanding of oneself and one's purpose in life. It can be concretized in a radical conversion. It can also mean union with God preceded by death.[3]

What this sacrament as passage rite raises to visibility is that because of Christ the sick and elderly person and the community wounded because of fragmentation need not lose hope. Rather, there is cause here for celebration. The victory of the cross and the power of the resurrection are manifested through a paradigmatic experience in the Christian body. As in the case of the other sacraments, anointing provides a *Christian* form for living and dying. This form is one that remains continuous through the entire history of the Church. Most Christians shall have to spend all of their lives living with ambiguity. It is hardly necessary to supply proof that sickness and old age are times of confusion. It is anointing which can take that ambiguity and turn it into a promise of new life both in the ways in which the Christian body ministers to the sick and elderly and in the way in which these liminal people witness to the rest of the Church. In order to penetrate more deeply the vocational aspect of anointing, it is now necessary to examine at some length the meaning of sickness and old age that this sacrament can bring to cultic expression.

The Meaning of Sickness

Sickness as a liminal experience.

[2]A. van Gennep, *Les rites de passage* (Paris: Mouton, 1909, repr. 1969).
[3]Talley, "Healing," p. 526.

The liminality of sickness has been most articulately described by M. Jennifer Glen:

> As such, it is one of those privileged intervals which societies have long surrounded with ritual intended to enable both individual and group to negotiate the sometimes treacherous corridor that stretches between the moment of separation from the familiar and that of entry into the world of the new. Whether for the sick that be a world constituted by recovery, by chronic illness, or by death, they themselves enter it transformed by what has taken place in the passage, shaped by its rites.[4]

The revised rites of the sick in the Roman Ritual concentrate on the second stage of passage, the time of liminality itself. Thus it is important to have an understanding of sickness if the rites at this time are to be clear and helpful.

The experience of sickness is one of loss. The future loses much of its possibility. The person is marginalized by alienation and distance. That which is taken for granted when one is healthy, namely, bodily harmony, is now disrupted and the body becomes a focus of concern. It is the loss of personal unity and physical and emotional concord that characterizes the condition of illness. The self has lost control and now the person becomes the battleground between the opposing forces of disease and medicine. No wonder that M. Jennifer Glen can take the now classic stages of dying articulated by Elisabeth Kuebler-Ross and apply them to situations of illness which do not necessarily eventuate in death.[5] Those who are ill, especially seriously ill, will in all likelihood go through stages of denial, anger, bargaining, and depression before they arrive at acceptance.

The ill person suffers from physical separation which confinement to bed, hospital, or nursing home makes clear.

---

[4]M. Jennifer Glen, "Sickness and Symbol: The Promise of the Future," *Worship* 54:5 (September 1980):397. Sister Glen's article is one of the best statements on the meaning of sickness of which I am aware. I have utilized her thoughts on this topic in this section of the chapter. I highly recommend her article.

[5]Ibid., p. 399.

But this is indicative of a deeper separation, that of loneliness and the inability to relate. Often sick people are surrounded by others but they do not have the personal resources to maintain fulfilling contacts. The world for the sick person has changed. This frustrated attempt on the part of these marginal people to relate is poignantly put by Glen: "Nevertheless he may desire to share life with them, only to discover that because illness has shifted his horizons, they no longer share the common universe of discourse which is necessary for genuine communication: he inhabits the restricted world of sickness, they the broader world of health from which he has been banished."[6]

Sickness involves fragmentation through a change in role status. First, the sick person can no longer operate in a specified role which may have given him/her definition and security. Second, there is the need to assume another role, a marginal one which is imposed by society. One must act like a "sick person." This means becoming a passive recipient of the "at times" condescending care of others. One is no longer autonomous and peer relationships tend to disappear in these situations. The purpose of anointing in the Church is to offer the strength of the community to these people so that they do not emotionally regress and simply deliver themselves to paternalistic or maternalistic care.

Thomas Talley, in properly distinguishing the healing of anointing from charismatic healing, raises the question of why the James text explicitly requires the Christian to summon the leaders of the Church. The early Church made great use of blessed oil "but to summon the presbyters of the Church to administer it does not seem to have been a concern of the early Church at all."[7] Why the silence on this command in James for eight to nine centuries? Talley's interpretation appears to be sound; namely, during these centuries the presbyter was not summoned as a healer or as a priest who administers the last rites but as a representative

[6]Ibid., pp. 399-400.
[7]Talley, "Healing," pp. 522-23.

of the community "to protect the sick member from dereliction and separation from the ecclesial body."[8]

Anointing is a vocational sacrament because it speaks to that quality of sickness that makes for a liminal aspect of human life because of separation and alienation. As a rite of passage, anointing of the sick acknowledges the withdrawal and exclusion from community that so many sick people experience. Oftentimes the sick must deal with the limitations and negations that are part of being in an ambiguous relationship to community. But with renewed faith and as more fully integral people they can come back to the community in a restored fashion. It is the rite of anointing which ritualizes this third step in the ritual process, the reintegration after a time of marginality.

As already noted, in the case of sickness this last stage does not necessarily imply the recovery of physical health. It may mean that while the physical conditions remain the same or even worsen, the person can engage in greater sharing with family and friends. For those who are healthy it means that by incorporating the sick person in their own lives they become more comfortable with that person and more open to learn about the mystery of suffering. Although remaining ill, the anointed person professes his/her faith through witness. Anointing, then, is not concerned with curing illness; it focuses on the meaning of being sick. The anointing points to a reconciliation with God and the Church because the anointed person is reconciled with human limitations. Anointing is always a psychosomatic experience. David Power puts it this way:

> Through sickness a person is put in crisis, for it makes his relation to the earth and to the human community an ambiguous one. It is not by coming out of sickness that the crisis is resolved, but by some word that indicates its meaning and reshapes the sick man's relation to the earth and to human community. In Christian sacrament, the word is one of eschatological hope. The sick person who

[8]Ibid.

receives this word in faith and makes it his own becomes in turn a sacrament of meaning for the community.[9]

Power lists four aspects of this third stage of reintegration: reconciliation with the body, solidarity with the material world, integration of finiteness and mortality, and integration of human temporality.[10] Such reintegration is finally ritualized in the eucharistic communion of the sick person, consequent upon the rite of anointing, preferably in the presence of community.

An important aspect that touches on the need to see anointing as a sacrament which recognizes the vocational way of living of the sick and elderly is what happens to these people in a technological and consumeristic society such as one finds in the West. Everything about the value systems of the culture promotes doubt in the sick as regards their self worth. It appears to them that they cannot make any contribution to others according to the going standards. They are reduced to a state of dependency where the emphasis is placed on being a receiver. Often they are made to feel guilty about their present physical state. It may be the result of lifestyle or decisions made or lack of the proper decisions. Is the heart trouble due to overweight, too much smoking, the daily evening cocktail? Often these guilt feelings are augmented by the attitude of the healthy which communicates to the sick persons that they must be responsible for their state in some way.

The kind of fragmentation that takes place for the sick differs from that of the sinner. The sick find themselves reduced to objects and so a personal alienation is always a possibility. They often are forced to concentrate on their physical infirmities to such an extent that they treat their own bodies as objects. Even when the well-meaning community ministers to these people, they become the *objects* of love and concern. And obviously, in the doctor's office or

---

[9]David Power, "Let the Sick Man Call," *The Heythrop Journal* (July 1978):263.
[10]Ibid., p. 268.

hospital, they are very much the object of treatment. Is it not enlightening to notice how the word, patient, is used to describe these people? Patient here is often equivalent to object.[11] This object-oriented approach to health care has been further contributed to by technological society. Dehumanization can only result from such a depersonalized and mechanized approach to the *sick person*. As the year 1984 approaches, one wonders about the intuitive insight of a George Orwell who foretold this kind of attitude in his celebrated book. Such a technological mindset has implications for the use of so-called "extraordinary" means of maintaining life. Fortunately, even the medical profession is addressing the question of the value of sustaining a person in existence as long as there are vital signs. But where such presuppositions remain unquestioned "the sick person may come to see himself through the eyes of others as a machine to be mended or maintained rather than an integral human person. Thus is his alienation from the community of humanity complete."[12]

What the sacrament of anointing attempts to deal with specifically is the feeling and experience of distance from God that the sick have because they no longer have their accustomed relationship with themselves and others. Gone is a sense of self-reliance which may have been a strong factor in their faith. Also gone are the supports of family, friends, peers, employees, students or whatever, which make up the structure of their lives when they are healthy. Their ordinary life context has disappeared and has been replaced by so many alienating components. For many this makes it quite difficult to maintain communication with God because just as there had been an accustomed way of living so there had been an accustomed way of praying. Both have dissolved together. Many people cannot transfer their life of prayer from one context to another and so become convinced that they cannot pray. If it is true that the

---

[11]Glen, "Sickness and Symbol," p. 401.
[12]Ibid.

sick go through the stages described by Kuebler-Ross, then anger and guilt will be very much a part of the experience. Someone must be blamed for this condition about which the person is angry and so it is projected on God. But this induces further anger and then the ability to pray is further inhibited. This may well lead to a crisis of faith. Self-doubt occurs because the usual support props have been removed. It is only one step further to turn self-doubt into doubt about God.

The greatest threat to the sick is also the source of greatest possibility for contact with God, namely, the experience of limit. Alienated from others and from God because of their situation, they are alone in vulnerable solitude. Whether death is to come in the near future or not, they find themselves closed in by their own finiteness. The fact is that they will die, and the present separation is not only a reminder of that fact but is also an experience in anticipation of that final event. Although anointing is not the sacrament of the dying and hopefully will be administered normatively to those sick who are able to participate and who are not burdened down as in the final hours of one's life, it must assist the anointed to deal with the mystery which confronts all; namely, the significance of one's life in terms of human limits, the greatest being that of death. It should be anointing which is able to raise to symbolic perceptibility the fact that it is the limit-experience which is the experience of transcendence.[13] It is precisely because there is a transcendent dimension to the limit-experience that it is possible to speak of sickness as a liminal experience. If death were the end, if there were no passage-way through death, then one could hardly make sense of passing through sickness. And without such passage liminality is impossible. As Glen puts it: "If, on the other hand, death represents the definitive opening out in time into the absolute future, the eschaton of the Christian vision, then every intervening limit is subject

---

[13]An analysis of the limit experience as a sign of transcendence is found in David Tracy's *A Blessed Rage for Order* (New York: The Seabury Press, 1975).

to transcendence. The passage of sickness, integral to the passage of life, assumes meaning in the light of the goal to which it leads."[14]

The sacrament of anointing provides a ritual for the passage of sickness. What it affirms is that in the suffering and sickness of the Christian Christ becomes incarnate. Such enfleshment is possible because in sickness and suffering the Christian shares in the reality of Christ's own redemptive suffering. In the words of Leonard Bowman:

> To suffer with faith in Christ, abandoning the too-human measure of earthly goods and evils and entrusting oneself into the hands of Christ's father, is to reproduce the pattern of Christ's death. Suffering in that spirit is filled with hope, for it bears the sure promise of resurrection. If we copy Christ's suffering, "he will transfigure these wretched bodies of ours into copies of his glorious body" (Philippians 3:21). The Christian in suffering becomes an imitation and an image of Christ—and "if in union with Christ we have imitated his death, we shall also imitate him in his resurrection" (Rom 6:5).[15]

Anointing is one of the ways that the Church celebrates the event of Christ's own loving concern for those who "are sick in the Church." It is a ritual which recognizes that human beings are one in their physical, emotional, mental, and spiritual experiences. Through the symbol of anointing the Christian community hopes to make it possible for the fragmented person to deal with the presence of disorder and weakness at whatever level these are experienced. In baptism the person was commissioned to offer praise in the assembly and to fulfill the mission given to the Church by Christ. It becomes the purpose of anointing to help the sick persons to continue to function as people *baptized.* What the liturgy of the sick is proclaiming is that:

[14]Glen, "Sickness and Symbol," p. 403.

[15]Leonard Bowman, *The Importance of Being Sick* (Wilmington: Consortium Books, 1976), p. 36.

the risen Christ is greatly concerned that illness not turn members of his priestly people away from their sharing in his redemptive mission. He wants them to have peace of heart and a vigorous confidence in God, so they can turn to God in worshipful submission and praise. They need the help of his healing grace, that they may suffer in union with Christ and pass with him into new life—whether still in this world or beyond death.

Therefore anointing is the sacrament of the seriously ill which offers a grace of healing, so that the members of the priestly people may grow through their sickness. Anointing consecrates them for suffering in a dedicated manner with Christ and offers restorative graces that counteract the myriad debilities of sickness. To receive sacramental anointing is a striking act of faith in the risen Christ, who became "a life-giving spirit" (1 Cor 15:45), and continues his redemptive and compassionate service of men and women in need.[16]

The Relationship of Sickness to Sin and Suffering

One of the earliest religious interpretations of illness found in the bible is that God afflicts people with sickness as a form of punishment. Today an unqualified acceptance of this retribution theory would be rejected. It hardly corresponds with the image of a loving God. Also, contemporary theology of the human person sees more than moral failure as the cause of disease. This is not to say that there is no connection between sickness and sin. There are the obvious examples of illness due to human carelessness and indiscretion. Much of modern psychology would affirm the position that often people bring sickness upon themselves. There is enough connection between illness and personal responsibility to make a ritual of self-examination and repentance in this matter meaningful. It appears indisputable that the acceptance of God's mercy in one's life can have positive physical effects.

[16]*An American Catechism: Chicago Studies* 12:3 (Fall 1973):337.

Another religious interpretation of illness would claim that to be sick is to be disciplined by God. It is suffering which assists one in holding on to God with a tenacious faith. While this theory is applicable in many instances, one can only wonder about situations of prolonged and serious illness. The New Testament approach is to move beyond either illness as punishment or as discipline to discover in it an occasion of the manifestation of God's power over sin and evil. God can counteract this world's hostile powers. One can be more certain about that than about the origin of sickness itself. This is not to be understood as rendering medical means of healing superfluous. Medical science and the person's prayer life join together to bring about human health. And in the case of incurable sickness, the Christian must find meaning primarily in the sharing in the sufferings of Christ.

Social scientists more and more see sickness as a time when a person cannot act in society in accepted ways, and so illness is a social condition. Because society defines the sick person in a certain way, that is, in terms of incapacity, the feeling response on the part of the people affected is guilt. Although it may be clear that there are no moral causes for the sick conditions, the feelings persist. The Christian can see that there is some relationship of sickness to the reality of evil and so there is the need for anointing to counteract any ascription of the sick condition to personal sin. In fact, however, as chapter one demonstrates, the forgiveness of sin has often been associated with anointing. In the heavy penitential aspect that has characterized this sacrament in the past there has been at least an implied relationship between sickness and sin. As already noted, often today there is a rejection of any attempts to make this relationship. But this is due more to a specific view of sinfulness than to a particular understanding of sickness. If sin is seen primarily as an individual action for which the person is deserving punishment, then surely, attaching it to sickness imposes a heavy and dehumanizing burden on people already weighted down by their physical infirmities.

But it is also possible that seeing the intimate connection of the two will bring out more saliently the spiritual meaning of sickness. Sin in this context would refer more to the situation of alienation characteristic of the human condition than to individual offenses. Because there is such a close affinity of the material and spiritual in any sickness, the psychosomatic dimension if you will, the person can well ask the question what part she/he played in the separation which sickness brings in terms of a loss of community and human relationships. In dealing with the anthropological considerations of the relationship between sin and sickness, it is important to note that the James text does not seem to make much of a distinction between the two. Perhaps, this text has anticipated some of the contemporary insights of psychosomatic medicine. However one speaks of the relationship of sin and sickness, the human person as an historical whole must always be prominent. The point is that sickness is that kind of marginal situation in which a person feels more deeply the existential guilt before God which is not the result of individual immoral actions. This guilt is concretized in the obvious alienation of being confined to one's room or bed, of being cut off from future planning or past enjoyments. The sick person is confined by and in the present moment.

The rite of anointing deals with the kind of separation and fragmentation that results from this disorder of this imperfect world. People actively create this disorder when they sin and the sacrament of reconciliation addresses that kind of personal excommunication. But not all dehumanizing disorder is caused by individual immorality. It is anointing which takes the separation people experience in sickness and raises it to a meaningfulness which can be found in Christ. All humans are guilty before God; all people participate in the alienation of humanity. And what anointing can do is proclaim loudly in the Church that the heightened suffering of those who are sick carries a special meaning regarding Christ's triumph over the sin of the world not only for them but for the whole community. Anointing says that the partial and fragmented stories of the sick person and of the healthy community must be caught up into the larger incorporating story of Jesus Christ, a story, in short, which is entitled: the Paschal Mystery.

Anointing is the liturgy which clarifies that suffering and sickness are not the symbols of sin but of grace, not of testing and purification, but of a more intimate relationship with God. It is true that the human experience of sickness and suffering is still ambiguous for many, perhaps most, people. For those without God they are meaningless catastrophes. For many without Christ, they are meaningless and signs of the realm of death. The ritual of anointing contradicts all of that when it says that "for one who follows Christ, sickness is no longer a punishment. It is no longer the unwelcome embrace of the realm of sin and death. It is no longer even a solitary training for spiritual purification. And it is no longer a lonely sacrifice for the good of unknown others."[17]

When the New Testament speaks of Jesus referring to his own Messiahship in terms of certain discernible facts: the blind see, the lame walk, the deaf hear, and so forth; it is expressing a meaning which is deeper than physical healing. Jesus is talking about those who cannot hear the Word of God, who cannot see the manifestation of God in this world, who are burdened with sin and so are not in union with God. What Jesus claims for these events is not so much that they are miraculous physical healings but rather eschatological signs of his kingdom. This kingdom which was the primary focus of Jesus' preaching is a kingdom where there will be no more sin and suffering, no evil or disabilities. Thus, what has taken place in these miracles points to what will happen to all at the end of time. They are a foreshadowing of that aspect of the kingdom which must yet come. But they also speak to that dimension of the kingdom already present: the physical healings and the inner life of grace they symbolize. Needless to say, these healings did not (as the sacraments do

[17]Bowman, *The Importance of Being Sick*, p. 35.

not) automatically usher in this kingdom. They demanded a faith response.

This kingdom of God is built up through suffering. The paradox of Christianity is that Christ overcomes sin and evil and death through *suffering*. Christians participate in this passage of Christ, this Paschal mystery, most significantly in baptism in which the most important death for Christians is ritualized. It is death to selfishness and sin. It is conversion. All of life is involvement in this paschal mystery but especially in the case of sickness is this identification highlighted. Sick people are images of Christ himself. Anointing is the proclamation that there is triumph over suffering through suffering itself. Bowman puts it this way:

> For the Christian, suffering and sickness are permeated and transformed by a clear hope: the expectation of the completion of Christ's Kingdom and his final coming in glory, a glory that the Christian shares now as a promise, then as fulfillment. . . . All suffering and sickness must be a share in the whole world's longing for the day of Christ's triumphant return—the glorious fulfillment of the hope of every Christian. . . . The Christian's hope is for the transformation of the entire world, the saving, the restoration, the transfiguration of all men who accept this grace of Christ. And no matter how agonizing or disfiguring the sickness the Christian suffers, he can realize that this very suffering helps bring forth the day of triumph, and his own suffering body will share that triumph.[18]

The Christian community as healthy and full of life is delegated to visit the sick person. The presence of the community in the rite of anointing is intended to be healing for the person caught in the framework of weakness and ineptitude. But the sick and often tormented Christian is also delegated to witness to the larger community that Christians will never be able to make sense out of sickness unless they are willing to be liminal people by passing through sickness

[18]Ibid., p. 37.

and suffering so that the darkness of their lives is dispelled in the light of the resurrected Christ. These sick people have a special vocation in the Church because through their sufferings they become public people whose lives sum up the way in which the kingdom of God is being established in the present time.

There is even a greater significance to the state of sickness than being one with Christ in suffering. Sick persons belong to the privileged group within the Church singled out for participating in the building up of the kingdom of God. While in principle this kingdom was begun in the death and resurrection of Christ, its penetration into this world is a slow process. And this process is often very ambiguous and riddled with conflicts. But, because "being sick in the Church" signalizes not defeat or death but Christ's own victory over death, the Christian who is sick removes much of the ambiguity that surrounds the gradual establishment of the reign of God. The liturgy of anointing celebrates the event of "being sick in the Church" for in it

> the Church recognizes the very great contribution which the sick person makes to the coming of the Kingdom. And so the Church senses that her sick are in a way specially *present* in the congregation, vital participants, though they may be physically absent. They participate intensely in everything that the Eucharist embodies and signifies—the Christian's participation in the saving death and resurrection of Christ.[19]

"Being sick in the Church" is one of Christianity's contradictions. On the one hand it is a challenge to life in the Church because of isolation and boredom. It may prove to be a crisis of faith as the person vacillates between denial and acceptance. It may render the Christian dysfunctional through fears of inadequacy. It may be a temptation to despair in the face of the overwhelming reality of one's own limit. Dependency, despondency, irritability, and indiffer-

[19]Ibid., p. 39.

ence may be as debilitating as the actual physical disease. And yet in the midst of all this negativity and social stigma, the sacrament of anointing speaks of the *vocation* of being sick.

The paradox is that at the heart of the ambiguity of being ill is found the call of God to the Church. The sick in the Church are the ones who bring that call to the rest. They occupy a place in the Church which challenges the comfort and security of those who call themselves followers of Christ. They relativize the pretensions of those who have been untouched by physical illness. They testify to the fact that the redemptive power of God is more operative in the hidden areas of personal suffering than in ecclesiastic display or public social work. Their mission to the Church at large is to call all back to an honest contact with reality: that God is renewing humankind by overcoming suffering not by abolishing it but through suffering itself. The vocation of "being sick in the Church" contradicts the message of every get-well card which expresses or implies that sickness is an evil to be avoided, a pure negation to be passed through.

Ironically, contemporary society is less healthy than it thinks. It is precisely the way that it treats its sick through abandonment and concealment that is symptomatic of the disease which is eating away at what should be a genuinely healthy society. This attempt to ignore the presence of sickness and the person who is ill forces society to distort its perception of reality. People live as in a dream in which life is always getting better and better and suffering and death is what happens "to the other guy." What anointing the sick can make the Church aware of is that Christians cannot afford to live so superficially. Life also contains struggles, conflicts, darkness, and pain. These are constitutive of the *Christian* reality. Bowman points out:

> Sickness can have the prophet's role of jarring the dreamer awake. Sickness is a collision with human limitation, a harsh and uncompromising reminder of the reality of man's finiteness and of the emptiness of the pursuit of an earthly paradise. Sickness forces the sick person to come

to terms with the reality of the human condition, and through him confronts our society with a sign of contradiction, a challenge to truth.[20]

The sick person as prophet to the Church is called to a deeper faith in Christ's own death and resurrection by discerning the movement of God in the mystery of suffering, the anonymity of the experience of illness, the emptying of oneself so that one might more fully embrace the suffering Christ. In the midst of loss of control of their lives, sick people can accept their lives as they are now because they can see beyond the surface dreams of those around them and because they can dismantle their own defenses because their faith provides enough light in their darkness to allow themselves to let go of their fears.

The sacrament of anointing is in a unique way a sacrament of Christian hope. Despite all the unpleasantness of the sick situation, the person who is "ill in the Church" has a new vision. Sickness adds to the significance of his/her life because it destroys the contemporary person's idol of good health and puts in its place authentic health where every part of one's life, even sickness and suffering, has meaning. And so sick persons hope more realistically. They are living examples that sorrow and brokenness are part of life, that suffering cannot and should not be avoided, and that death is part of everyone's personal story. But their lives at the same time proclaim in the Christian Church that amidst all the harshness of sickness and suffering renewal and growth are being accomplished. By living on the margin of the community, these ill people are advancing the kingdom of God in their own lives and in the lives of each community member.

And so the vocation that is symbolically actualized in the liturgy of anointing is one that points to Christian hope. By giving substance to Christian hope for those in the Church who are well, the anointed person is participating in the establishment of the kingdom of God. The mission of the

[20]Ibid., p. 212.

sick and the suffering Christian is to lift up what God is doing in her/his life to the rest of the Church so that all can see the power of God working in what appears to faithless eyes as absurdity at worst or as an unanswered question at best.

The Meaning of Old Age

Being Old Today

The sacrament of anointing is not only for those who are seriously ill. It is also for the elderly. It is the thesis of this section of the chapter that in the present transitional situation, when Christians are moving away from viewing this sacrament as the primary preparation for death, an extreme unction or an anointing unto glory in the life to come, that it is in the case of the elderly that this sacrament functions with its greatest clarity. In this case anointing is removed from a context where death is relatively imminent, where the emphasis is placed on the final moments of one's life, where little can be expected physically or better psychosomatically, barring a miracle. Anointing the elderly, rather, is to say something sacramentally about a group of people who in many cases are alive and well in terms oo the usual medical categories. Some recent surveys of people who in many cases are over the age of sixty have shown that the majority of these people do not consider themselves as "old" or "elderly," but as middle-aged or late middle-aged. While these over sixty people have had to make adjustments in their work and lifestyle, they do not see themselves pondering the final moments before death.

It is important that old age be addressed sacramentally. It is a relatively new experience for the human race. Since the beginning of the century, the average age for the American has increased from forty-five to seventy-five. Growing old is a difficult task and often men and women deny this advance in years. In a society where worth is measured by productivity, the elderly are often ignored and are experienced as objects of shame. Much of the bitterness and cynicism of old people is a mask for their own self hatred.[21] From a Christian point of view, society's attitude to the aged is reprehensible. But even from a secular point of view such treatment of the elderly is destructive and unprofitable. Martin Heinecken puts it this way:

> The aged should be loved for the sake of the rich satisfaction they give to others, filling the want of others out of their plenty. Their wisdom, their experience, their patience born out of years of self-giving constitute an inestimable treasure. It is one of the tragedies of our culture that with the loss of the extended family so many people are deprived of this treasure trove. The same is true in public life and in employment where the aged are too readily discarded and hid away—out of sight, out of mind. Our culture is too often blind to the beauty of old age—wrinkles, white hair, halting gait, crackled voice, trembling hands, all—that deserves better than the designation of "old crone" or "old codger." Out of sheer self-interest society should give the aged their proper place.[22]

And, of course, the Church's attitude toward the aged can be no less. Its care for the aged must be done in light of the kind of love God has for his people, the self-giving, self-sacrificing love that seeks no return.

> There is no question that the aged can become a burden with no longer anything to offer, requiring nothing so much as "tender, loving care."...It is then that *agape* must rule, even when they are not the kindly, gentle, loving beings we want them to be but instead veritable demons of irritability, obstinacy, and querulous self-centeredness. No matter how helpless or senile, wheel-

[21]Christopher Mooney, *Man Without Tears* (New York: Harper and Row, 1973), p. 82.

[22]Martin J. Heinecken, "Christian Theology and Aging: Basic Affirmations," in *Ministry With the Aging*, ed. William M. Clements (San Francisco: Harper and Row, 1981), p. 83.

chair patients cannot be run through the showers as though you were running dirty platters through the dishwasher; and they cannot be kept under constant sedation, just to keep them out of your hair. And when meals-on-wheels are brought to a lonely person who wants nothing so much as to have you stay and talk or listen, this is when Christ-like love is needed.[23]

In 1900 almost no one retired. But now everyone makes some kind of provision for old age. The national concern in the United States regarding the viability of the social security systems attests to the fact that life is being experienced differently than a few generations ago. Life at seventy or eighty is qualitatively different from life at forty or fifty. Studies are only beginning to address the meaning of humanity in these final years. One example would be the work of Don Browning who has developed a phenomenological approach to aging. He says: "The word, 'aging,' refers primarily to perceivable evidence of physical and mental decline."[24] One does not usually refer to a person as aging until there are certain physical manifestations such as gnarled hands, wrinkles, slow movement, and forgetfulness. There is no simple correlation between these physiological manifestations and sociological and psychological aging. Some people are at their prime but have lost their hair and have discernible changes in their skin appearance.

Browning states that an important reason that the presence of the elderly is denied in modern cultures is that all people deny their aging. What is significant is that their knowledge of their aging comes from external sources such as the view of themselves in the mirror, the fact that they cannot run as fast as they used to, and the realization that they cannot work as hard as they formerly did. Many of these signs are ambiguous and more or less easily denied. One that is more difficult to prescind from is that their

[23]Ibid.

[24]Don S. Browning, "Preface to a Practical Theology of Aging," *Pastoral Psychology* 24 (229) (Winter 1975):154.

neighbors are growing older and that the presence of elderly relatives is real.

The phenomenon of aging provokes concerns that cause anxiety. The person in middle life concerned about aging sees the possibility that life will be narrowed and will eventually end. There is also the worry that the world the person relates to will disappear: all the people, institutions, and values. The person can refuse to accept the inevitability of aging and death or try to make the best use of the possibilities present. Browning suggests one way to do this is to become a caring person for oneself and one's world rather than succumbing to a narrowing self-preoccupation. Maintaining oneself in the aging process is the renewal of one's own world in the face of self-diminishment. Fortunately, contemporary psychology is approaching the subject matter of aging with a more positive attitude than was previously the case. The study of the later years of human life is less shrouded in an aura of pathology and terminal decline and is seen more as another period of personal adaptation. Psychological, physiological, and sociological changes are studied in an attempt to promote the best adaptations for those who move into old age.

What must be kept in mind in making the decision between care or self-preoccupation is the point made by Erikson that the past cannot be changed and that the future is more limited in what is possible. Don Browning has expanded on Erikson's idea of generativity as a way of avoiding narcissistic self-preoccupation. This concern for guiding the next generation helps one to escape stagnation and eventuates in the virtue of care.[25] This growth in generativity is what makes it possible for old age to be a time of integrity, a time when one need have no regrets about the development of one's life. Browning says: "The presupposition of integrity is a prior attitude of generativity; it makes it possible for a person to live with what he has been and what he has brought into this world that is likely to survive

[25]Erik H. Erikson, *Insight and Responsibility* (New York: W. W. Norton and Co., 1964), p. 130.

him."[26] Death for the elderly is not only a threat in terms of their personal histories, but also their continuity with the larger world and succeeding generations.

Although during the time of old age there are increasing forms of disengagement from what constituted the source of value in human living, a need to achieve a sense of continuity must be recognized. Even the very elderly must be able to feel that they are caring for others in some way, that even in their old age there is usefulness. The sacrament of anointing can point to the importance of transcending individual life cycles. This is done through care which has lasting significance. It is the sacrament of anointing which can articulate the hope that one's caring efforts are caught up in the activity of God and so transcend their human origin. Christian anointing speaking of salvation means that human values are preserved in God. One need not sink back into a dysfunctional self-preservation but can have hope since renewal of the world is not dependent on one's activities alone. One's caring efforts will go beyond one's labors. What any individual has done has been taken up into God and has become a participant in God's continual urging of the world to renewal.

Browning points to the forces which are aggravating the situation for the elderly in this culture, forces which are militating against the possibility of generativity for the old. These are: 1) earlier retirement, 2) a longer healthy life after retirement, and 3) isolation of the elderly from the rest of society.[27] If earlier retirement continues, it means that people will have less opportunity to express care in their formal vocation. Society is so mobile and the family so nuclear that the aged are easily compartmentalized from other segments of society. The point is that many of the aged are still healthy and their number is on the rise. This means that any theology of anointing must stimulate the Church to support programs, civil and religious, which would not only give

[26]Browning, "Preface to a Practical Theology of Aging," p. 159.
[27]Ibid., p. 165.

support to the aged in personal and financial ways, but which would also offer possible vocational alternatives and which would break down the isolation to which these people have been banished. The sacrament of anointing, if properly practiced among the elderly in the Church, can encourage such a theology by making it clear that while old people need more relaxation and distance from former occupations, they also need to extend themselves in the lines of those who live after them.

But the meaning of old age is not only the concern of pastoral theology, it has now become a question for the speculative theologian.[28] Understanding the meaning of being old must be placed in the context of people being historical and temporal beings. The process of aging, of which being elderly is part, is the concrete expression of time. It seems that Christian theology will have to understand time as more of a process than a series of disconnected moments if it intends to find significance for the aging process. The Christian understanding cannot accept any kind of escape from time or history. Being human is to be in time. Temporality is constitutive of human existence. If aging is only a series of atomic moments, then one can pick and choose which ones will be meaningful and the final period of old age will be pointless. Contemporary understanding and experience give human temporality a much more positive interpretation.

Biblical and theological studies affirm that religious meaning has its locus in history and time. "Therefore, we may clearly give a fully positive interpretation to the process of aging as the clearest existential expression of the process of temporality."[29] Systematic theology, then, can challenge those who choose only a part of their lives as meaningful by arguing for a fully positive understanding of the process of time itself and thus also for the process of aging. In other

[28]One good example of a systematic theologian's reflections on aging is found in David Tracy's "Eschatological Perspectives on Aging," *Pastoral Psychology* 24 (229) (Winter 1975):119-134.

[29]Ibid., p. 124.

words, the three modalities of human time: past, present, and future, make up the human experience of time. No one can decide which mode of temporality is to be the sole source of meaning of their existence. The constant threat both for the theologian as well as for the person in the street, is to declare that all of life's meaning comes from the present. To relativize the present as the only way of understanding human growth will aid in avoiding consigning the past mode (and therefore, the aged) to the margin of society and in avoiding an idealization in terms of the dreams of the future (in fact, usually the youth of society). David Tracy makes this point when he says:

> But by means of the present understanding of temporality we should be able to liberate our imaginations and our experience from the temptation to declare the aging process a cruel fate and the plight of the aged a seemingly cruel reminder of that fate. We may learn instead to respect the natural process of aging and the ever fluctuating sources (past, present, and future) of our temporal meaning.[30]

Christopher Mooney in his book, *Man Without Tears*, makes an initial foray into what might be called a theology of old age. He starts with an insight from Simone de Beauvoir: "The whole meaning of life is in question in the future that is waiting for us: if we do not know what we are going to be, then we cannot know what we are."[31] He stresses that growing old is not simply that which happens to people. Humans are not simply the victims of old age. It is not a purely passive experience. Rather, growing old requires as much self-possession and integration as any other stage in one's life, such as adolescence or middle age. The usual denial of the aging process at this time is as detrimental as the refusal to deal with entering adulthood or the "middle age crisis." Often this denial continues until some affliction

[30]Ibid., p. 126.
[31]Simone de Beauvoir, *The Coming of Age* (New York: Putnam, 1972), p. 5.

demands that one recognizes this stage in one's life. This author recalls the traumatic experience for his own mother when she became physically inhibited due to arthritis, although her mental faculties remained unimpaired. It was then that she had to acknowledge that she was an old person.

This refusal to accept old age as part of one's salvation history is only reinforced by the prevailing American value system which does not cherish this penultimate period of human life as such. Americans are ashamed of their elderly and treat them as something to be avoided. They pretend old people do not exist. And thus they culturally pre-condition themselves for what old age will mean for them. Simone de Beauvoir maintains that people define the significance of their closing years by the way they lead their lives. Thus, old age can be a freeing time and not something which is necessarily culturally conditioned. Those who have worked with the elderly know the variety of ways in which they meet this stage of life with a sense of freedom. Some enter old age as a time of blessing without fear or remorse. Others relax into those closing years without any particular sense of direction. Some settle into this final period by creating new roles for themselves and by entering into different kinds of meaningful activities. Some, of course, find these years less freeing and so suffer through the ravages of being elderly. Hopefully, even these will not simply capitulate to increasing weakness, being content to define themselves as a burden.

A counter-cultural approach to old age articulated in the sacrament of anointing would see this final stage in life as a time of growth and not the end of one's process of development. As Mooney observes, many old people do not do things, they just *are*. But meaning must be found in that. He quotes Erikson who speaks of the task of old age from a psychological point of view. It is worth reproducing that quotation here. This task according to Erikson is:

> The acceptance of one's one and only life cycle as something that had to be and that, by necessity, permitted no

substitutions. It thus means a new, a different love of one's parents, free of the wish that they should have been different, and an acceptance of the fact that one's life is one's own responsibility. . . . Although aware of the relativity of all the various life styles which have given meaning to human striving, the possessor of integrity is ready to defend the dignity of his own style against all physical and economic threats. For he knows that an individual life is the accidental coincidence of but one life cycle with but one segment of history; and that for him all human dignity stands or falls with the one style of integrity of which he partakes.[32]

The point is that people unfortunately do not accept their own one life as the ultimate for them. Many of them either hope for another or try to rid themselves of theirs in midstream. Again, Mooney refers to Erikson:

Despair expresses the feeling that the time is short, too short for the attempt to start another life and to try out alternate roads to integrity. Such a despair is often hidden behind a show of disgust, a misanthropy, or a chronic contemptuous displeasure with particular institutions and particular people—a disgust and a displeasure which...only signifies the individual's contempt of himself.[33]

One can find a similar observation in the writings of Carl Jung:

A human being would certainly not grow to be seventy or eighty years old if this longevity had no meaning for the species. The afternoon of human life must also have a significance of its own and cannot be merely a pitiful

[32]Erik H. Erikson, *Identity and the Life Cycle* (New York: International Universities Press, 1959), p. 98.
[33]Ibid.

> appendage to life's morning... Whoever carries over into
> the afternoon the law of the morning... must pay for it
> with damage to his soul, just as surely as a growing youth
> who tries to carry over his childish egoism into adult life
> must pay for his mistake with moral failure...

> It is particularly fatal for such people to look back. For
> them a prospect and goal in the future are absolutely
> necessary. This is why all great religions hold out the
> promise of life beyond... which makes it possible for
> mortal men to live the second half of life with as much
> purpose and aim as the first.[34]

Jung's point is that the repressions that took place in the
first half of one's life as part of the growth process as an
individual cannot be maintained into old age. Jungian scho-
lar, Edward C. Whitmont, puts it this way:

> The bill will now be presented for what was by-passed in
> the earlier years. Whatever was left behind, indeed had to
> be left behind because it was not suitable for external
> adaptation, for success and practical use, demands now
> to be heard and realized. The questions present them-
> selves: Who am I? What am I here for? What is the
> meaning of my existence? What am I moving toward?
> What is my own story—that is, what is the meaning and
> myth behind what appears as the conflict or (all too
> often) the seeming chaos of my existence.[35]

Those who cannot accept their lives and make frantic
attempts to achieve some other identity will surely have
painful and disruptive times. They lack a sense of self-
acceptance and trust in themselves. They lack what Erikson
calls "wisdom." Wisdom is "a detached concern with life

---

[34]C. G. Jung, *The Collected Works of C. G. Jung*, vol. 8: *The Structures and Dynamics of the Psyche* (Princeton: Princeton University Press, 1960), paragraphs 787, 790.

[35]Edward C. Whitmont, *The Symbolic Quest* (New York: Harper and Row, 1969), p. 283.

itself in the face of death itself."[36] Wisdom is the quality that enables old men and women to finish off life well. They become living exemplars of the integrated life. It is not a question of achieving total integration in this life. It is that there must be some wisdom of this kind in one's life, if it is to end well and be freed from the despair that often characterizes those who experience the conclusion of their lives with a sense of helplessness. This wisdom is made evident in the strength of the elderly who know how to close life well and can be generative by bequeathing this wisdom to the next generation.

The Ministry of the Elderly: To Close Life Well

The sacrament of anointing can help the elderly and those who minister to them, and therefore the entire Church, to view old age as a time which is more than an empty waiting for death. It is a time of growth and fulfillment because it is the very continuation of life. Anointing points out that old age should be viewed as closing life well. This life style in the elderly can help all Christians to realize that they must accept the totality of their lives as the only one that they have. No part of it can be rejected without detriment to their present identity and happiness. People have middle age crises, or crises at any time in their lives, because they try to pick and choose what part of their personal history they are going to accept. There is an implicit rejection in such a choice and their rejection will cause fragmentation. Anointing, then, is the sacrament in the Church which attempts to deal with that kind of fragmentation.

The special vocation in the Church which belongs to the elderly is not an easy one. These people must also be courageous witnesses. No longer spurred on by the enthusiasm of youth or the expectancy of the inexperienced, these

---

[36] Mooney, *Man Without Tears*, p. 87. In this section on aging I have made use of many of the insights of Christopher Mooney. I found his section on old age in his book not only perceptive in understanding the meaning of "to be old in the Church," but I also found it personally moving. I wish to acknowledge my debt to him. He gave voice to my own experience with my elderly parents.

elderly have been sobered through the years by their own limitations and failures. What precisely can they offer the young for whom success is seemingly near at hand and for whom all is still possible? The message appears to be one of sadness more than hope. Modern society protects itself against any kind of discouraging word from the elderly by dismissing their experience of years as something that has gone out of date.[37] But it is precisely in the limitations and the lack of success of the lives of these people, that they become sacramental for the Christian community. What they articulate, what their lives are living paradigms of is that *life is worthwhile*; life is worth closing well not because of what has been achieved by an individual but because one's very being is of *worth*. It is the often quoted but little accepted dictum that it is not what you do but what you are that is of ultimate significance. Anointing can put in a Christian perspective that the value of old age springs from the meaning of life itself. It can bring to ritual expression the faith one can have in life. As Christopher Mooney puts it:

> There is such a thing as faith in life itself, in the worth of one's own lived life, which must now be seen to the end because it is somehow valuable for its own sake and not for what it can usefully do.[38]

Faith can transform human trust. One can say that human trust as a secular reality finds its ultimate significance in faith. It is this faith that gives the old people the courage they need to overcome the loneliness, abandonment, and sense of loss that accompanies this period of life. The search for meaning, which is the human life task, takes on its own special cogency at this time. Crises at other times in human life, especially the much discussed middle age crisis, arise out of a suspicion that the purpose of life may be questionable or even absent. The crisis of old age comes from the inability to retrieve the past of one's own history.

[37]Ibid.
[38]Ibid., p. 88.

Such a crisis can only be met adequately when the person accepts what has been done and does not attempt to do away with any aspect of the past by some form of repression.

Different theologians address the question of the meaning of life in terms of time. For process theologians all that is of value is not lost. In faith the elderly can be assured that nothing of their lives needs be taken away. What they have been and what they continue to be are all part of a process that finds its meaning in God. This process of living contributes to God's own life. Catholic theologian, Karl Rahner, puts it in a less process-oriented perspective when he says that while the becoming passes away, what one has become does not. "What perishes is not the secret extract of life but the process of its preparation."[39] The past is not simply a collection of inert material now stored in one's personal museum. It is alive and well in one's present existence. It has been preserved in one's life in a generative way giving persons their present identities. People sum up their lives in old age in a total way bringing their pasts with them. Mooney says this is what Rahner calls the comfort of time: "the belief that to close life well is also to attain oneself completely, with all that one has been and done, in strength as well as weakness."[40]

But what makes it possible for the elderly to close life well when they are confronted with the failures and weaknesses of the past? What in the faith perspective assists the elderly to deal with the fact that not only their limitations but even their sins accompany them into these final years? How is it possible that both growth and fulfillment can be the result of moral failure? It is the courage that comes from the wisdom of those gifted with such insight and understanding. As Mooney puts it: "The life hidden in the guilty deed must be embraced; only what was death in it need be rejected.... Through repentance and wisdom losses of the time of guilt

---

[39]Karl Rahner, "The Comfort of Time," in his *Theological Investigations III* (Baltimore: Helicon Press, 1967):145.

[40]Mooney, *Man Without Tears*, p. 90.

can be made up."[41] Urban Holmes makes the same point when he refers to the proclivity of old people to tell stories about the past.

> There is no profit in being bitter about the past longing for a fantasized potency lost in our despair over an unappreciated aging. The wisdom that graces the older person can be defined as the willingness to acknowledge what the past has made us and yet forgive the past that we might be open to the future. Hope, humor, and vision are three gifts of one who grows old not only gracefully, but with purpose.[42]

The sacrament of anointing should proclaim clearly that the meaning of old age is that life is worth closing well, just as any other part of life is worth living well. To grow old, then, is to believe in the worth of one's life. But this is not an easy task. Courage is the desired virtue for the elderly and only a courageous faith can deal with the sense of loss and diminishment, the lack of self-esteem, the suppressed guilt and feeling of abandonment which are the temptations at this time of life. Anointing is the celebration that in Christ and his Church one need not let such experiences control one's life. Through anointing the community visits elderly persons to assure them of the power of old age. Liturgically, the Church is saying that it needs these old people if the incarnation is to make sense on the human level. How can the Christian life be significant in this world, if one's total individual history cannot be accepted? If old age becomes meaningless, then all of life is called into question and the Christian must take refuge in an other-worldly spirituality, waiting out this life in desperation and fear until the time of that everlasting city shall have arrived. God's word in Jesus Christ is that this life is not just an unpleasant and annoying interval but that this human life is the arena of salvation.

[41]Ibid., p. 91.

[42]Urban T. Holmes, "Worship and Aging: Memory and Repentance," in *Ministry With the Aging*, ed. Clements (San Francisco: Harper and Row, 1981), p. 96.

What anointing can bring out is that the faith perspective supports belief in the worth of one's own life. In times past, because of the emphasis on this sacrament as a last rite, anointing did not necessarily point to the value of human life. In some cases because of the stress on this being an anointing for the next life or as a source of forgiveness of sins, anointing reinforced people's lack of appreciation of the positive values of this world. It tended to lead one out of this world to a life *after* this life. However, anointing can manifest that to believe in one's present life can be a way of believing in God.

Often old people find themselves possessing attitudes which the people with whom they live do not share. They no longer feel the need to do, to achieve, to accomplish. There is no longer any sense of urgency to define themselves in terms of their productivity. Such experiences are part of their stage of life and are not the kinds of things that they can control. This throws them back into faith in the transcendent dimension of their lives. For Christians this transcendence is mediated through Christ. What Christians believe is that God cares for them. What Christ reveals is that God finds their human lives worthwhile. The elderly can especially appreciate such loving concern. Maggie Kuhn, the vital leader of the Gray Panthers, sums it up so very well:

> It might just be one of God's surprises for us, that he may use those closest to death—nearer to that other life—to show the Church how to break with self-centered purposes and goals and look to the good of all and serve that good.[43]

The loss of so much of one's powers and achievements and the sufferings which inevitably are found in the closing years of one's life receive their ultimate meaning in Christ. Teilhard de Chardin put this well when he said "as a result of

[43]Quoted in Heinecken, "Christian Theology and Aging," in *Ministry With the Aging*, p. 89.

his (Christ) omnipotence impinging on our faith, events which show themselves experimentally in our lives as pure loss become an immediate factor in the union we dream of establishing with him."[44] Loss and gain go together as anyone who defines his/her life in terms of the death/resurrection of Christ knows. To use the words of Teilhard again: "In spite of the fundamental, prime, importance I've always been led to attribute to human effort and development, I realize that the soul begins to know God only when it is forced *really* to suffer diminishment within him."[45] Clearly for Teilhard old age would be a forceful example of this kind of redemptive diminishment.

For the elderly, anointing can assure them that in their weakness they can find their strength. They can now accept each moment of their lives as gift. They need no longer try to control the lives of others. They can be free from the expectations to fulfill certain societal roles. No longer is there any imperative to spend time and energy on plans for a better tomorrow. They are achieving their purposes, they are fulfilling their vocation by being old and by being old in a Christian integral way. Old people have less time but more space. They can now explore the space of their inner worlds. Holmes says:

> We move into what some have called a receptive mode of consciousness—as opposed to an action mode—where images and free association within space take precedence over temporal, logical thinking, with its desire for prediction and control. We become like the little child, not in the literal foolishness of pretending to be one, but in the graceful wisdom of one who has recovered the capacity of wonder and surprise.[46]

Resignation is one of the required and hoped for virtues of this time of life. But such resignation must be more than

[44]*The Divine Milieu* (New York: Harper and Row, 1960), p. 88.

[45]*The Making of a Mind* (New York: Harper and Row, 1965), p. 275.

[46]Holmes, "Worship and Aging," pp. 96-97.

mere passivity in the face of physical and moral evil. The attitude which calls for a "giving up and letting all in God's hands" may turn out to be another form of cowardice. The sacrament of anointing calls the elderly to move beyond this kind of misguided "virtue." God is not simply present in human passivities, but where people choose to grow in the face of opposition. There is no time in one's declining years when the human growth process is at an end. Christian resignation means accepting one's life as it is in faith and struggling with that life so that any given moment is not absolutized or perhaps better put, "finalized." There is always a future. There is always movement.

What every good therapist and spiritual director knows is that what lies behind the meaning of old age is that these declining years inevitably come. What is inevitable is that there is both an advance in years, a growing old as well as a decline, a loss of powers, a diminishment of talents and capabilities. But that is not all. There must be a new sense of life to sustain this experience. This new life springs from the conviction and appropriation that one's life is so important, so worthwhile, so significant, so loveable, that it is worth closing well. Mooney has summed it up succinctly:

> Such belief can be based upon the love of family and friends as well as upon remembered achievements, but for the Christian it must ultimately rest upon the religious convictions that one's life has been and still is important to God. Old age will make sense in the end only if life makes sense.[47]

Too often Christians understand old age as directed towards death. This is surely true. But it is also directed to growth. If it is psychologically true that growth takes place through clarification, then there is a kind of growth which may have to wait upon old age for it to occur. For many, it is only old age which makes it possible for them to see life as a whole. Now they must lay aside many of the distractions,

[47]Mooney, *Man Without Tears*, p. 95.

pre-occupations, and support systems which prevented them from dealing with the totality of their lives. Whether it be money, position, status, passion, relationships, or the many forms of service, these structures and people can no longer serve to dilute the experience of self-understanding. Definition no longer depends on projection outside of oneself. Old age can leave one standing alone peering into a personal history of success and failure in a disinterested and unbiased way which permits greater clarification than previously possible. And such clarification is what leads to growth.

Old people continue to grow when they appreciate and perceive the symbolic reality of their lives. By leading their natural lives they become symbols in the Christian Church. Jung emphasizes the importance of the natural life as a symbol of a deeper reality:

> Natural life is the nourishing soil of the soul. Anyone who fails to go along with life remains suspended, stiff and rigid in midair. That is why so many people get wooden in old age; they look back and cling to the past with a secret fear of death in their hearts. They withdraw from the life-process, at least psychologically, and consequently remain fixed like nostalgic pillars of salt, with vivid recollections of youth but no longer living in the present.... The negation of life's fulfillment is synonymous with the refusal to accept its ending. Both mean not wanting to live, and not wanting to live is identical with not wanting to die. Waxing and waning make one curve.[48]

But the natural life of old age need not be that. Rather it can be that period of life characterized by the gifts of sharing, toleration, and affirming others, all with no need to prove oneself. This is what it means to live with a symbolic consciousness. It is the opposite of an institutional definition of the self. Holmes says that successful aging "perceives that consciousness is more than logical thought, and that possi-

---

[48]Jung, *The Structures and Dynamics of the Psyche*, paragraph 800.

bilities for a significant aging lie in an awareness of the archaic power of symbol and myth."[49]

The sacrament of anointing can speak to the challenge to grow as an old person, to this privileged time for clarification. In a faith perspective, anointing can allow the elderly to experience the giftedness in the present moment. No need to regret the passing of time, no necessity to try to hold on or recapture what has been lost. Anointing should bring the community's acceptance for this time of life. It should prevent the panic that often seizes people at the loss of their future. This sacrament brings the courage needed at this time by removing the terror that many people capitulate to when confronted with their weaknesses. Perhaps, Paul's words to the Corinthians would make an appropriate reading at an anointing service for the elderly. 2 Corinthians 12:9-11:

> But he said to me, "My grace is sufficient for you, for my power is made perfect in weakness." I will all the more gladly boast of my weaknesses, that the power of Christ may rest upon me. For the sake of Christ, then, I am content with weaknesses, insults, hardships, persecutions, and calamities; for when I am weak, then I am strong.

An even better selection would be 2 Corinthians 4:7-12:

> But we have this treasure in earthen vessels, to show that the transcendent power belongs to God and not to us. We are afflicted in every way, but not crushed; perplexed, but not driven to despair; persecuted, but not forsaken; struck down, but not destroyed; always carrying in the body the death of Jesus, so that the life of Jesus may also be manifested in our bodies. For while we live we are always being given up to death for Jesus' sake, so that the life of Jesus may be manifested in our mortal flesh. So death is at work in us, but life in you.

[49]Holmes, "Worship and Aging," p. 98.

Anointing must speak to the elderly and how they are to accept their lives. It also speaks to the young and healthy Church. It is the community's reminder that much that affects the elderly is not in their own control and that the larger Church must deal with these issues. Economic difficulties, public health, social security and the like, while affecting the old very intimately are precisely the areas which can only be effectively dealt with on the larger parochial and national scenes. Nevertheless, they constitute the large ambitus in which anointing takes on its meaning. Mooney sums up the problem very well when he emphasizes that the old themselves cannot deal with these larger problems:

> Old people themselves cannot solve problems that are financial or medical. They cannot go on strike. They cannot help it if the young and healthy see them as disagreeable reminders of mankind's common end. Neither can they remedy their invisibility: the fault is not theirs that people do not see them in the same way that one sees a pretty girl or the driver at the wheel of a shiny car.[50]

However, the point of the sacrament of anointing is not medicare and social security programs, although there is a connection. Anointing's primary focus is what old people are to do with their lives and what they say to the Church at large. What anointing reminds both the elderly and those who have not reached that stage is that human growth does not take place automatically. Full humanity is not a quality that comes to people if they but survive. It is something all men and women are constantly choosing. Often it is only when the physical dimension of their lives is slowing down that they look seriously at their potential to become good human beings. What anointing reminds the young is that there is no part of their lives which they can prefer over any other lest all of life be diminished. What anointing calls the

---

[50]Mooney, *Man Without Tears*, p. 98.

middle-aged to is to simplify their lives, to streamline their involvements so that the inner life can be more fully developed. Both are achievements which require explicit decisions. When anointing works in the Church, Christians are assisted in making such choices.

Anointing is a vocational sacrament because "being old in the Church" is a ministry. Those who have the calling of being old in the Christian community challenge society's presupposition that there is something bad about growing old. Like good wine, life should improve with age. One may retire from work, but not from living, and it is one's living, not one's work, that is one's ministry in the Church. Old people are forced by the limitations of their bodies to live in a different way. But that very different way, while less productive according to secular standards, has an apostolic character in the Christian Church. Anointing as a sacrament of vocation affirms that the old in the Church are fulfilling their vocation by growing old. They are responding to their call from God by serving and praising this God by being more honest, more free from the demands of technological society, more self-affirming, and more willing to face the real questions of human existence. Anointing celebrates old age as a way of life which is to be pursued and not merely passed through or regretted. Holmes puts it well when he says that worship (and anointing is worship!) should be for the aging:

> the evocation of a memory that calls them to repentance, and consequently makes them a source of wisdom. The aging are to us a witness of a "cleaner" set of values, purged of the clutter of egocentric striving and open to the whisper of God calling us into being. It is a deeply satisfying prospect for which to long.[51]

One of the major ways in which anointing the elderly challenges the Church, and these old people thereby exercise their ministry to the Church at large, is the way in which

---

[51] Holmes, "Worship and Aging," pp. 105-6.

they call into question the culturally accepted values of the worshippers. The fact is that people who are initiated as infants, formed in a family, educated in the school system, and taken into the job status, are not asked to undergo any kind of conversion. Our liturgical rites are really celebrations "of our values and goals as Americans-with-a-Christian-tinge. They ask for no conversion. They simply lend an aura of respectability to what we have been, are and always will be."[52] A culture which is money and success oriented will find it almost impossible to have much appreciation for old age. The elderly are offensive to such a culture because they contradict its own value system. Thus, along with the poor, American society attempts to hide these people. It is precisely the sacrament of anointing which can call for a conversion of values in this area on the part of Christians. Anointing becomes the symbolic call for depth and spiritual sensibility which are part of the Christian maturing process so that when the time of diminishing powers and dependence on others arrives, these Christians will have learned how to find their significance in that attitude which runs contrary to prevailing cultural perspectives.

It is precisely because of this conversion process that one can speak of the wealth of experience, the wisdom of old age. It is not simply that these people have lived longer. There are old people who are not wise. It is not simply the accumulation of knowledge or information. Much of that may no longer be relevant. But, they have gone through the conversion process. They have made or are in the concluding time of a rite of passage that all who wish to be fully human must pass through. In that sense they are truly wise. They can really be generative. Old people have gone through the life cycle as a whole. They have felt its rhythm. They have evolved from birth through maturation to obsolescence and death. The end result of this evolution is not merely that they "feel old." Rather, it can bestow a deep

---

[52]Robert Hovda, "Old Age, Ministry to Dying Person, Planning for Death and Funerals," in *Living Worship* 8:9 (November 1972).

understanding of what it means to be human.

But if the only time contemporary society allows the old to become visible is when they entertain the grandchildren with stories, the witness of their constant conversion will not be available to the community which is young and healthy. It is anointing which raises these people up and allows them to become a living judgment on the worship of money and youth. Anointing, as any good liturgy, removes the ambiguity from what could be a confusing situation. It makes it clear that all have limits, old age and death being part of that limitation. And it is in dealing with these limits that Christians find God in ordinary human living.

Anointing and Social Justice

A particular aspect of sacramental life that is a focus of contemporary times is the relationship of the worshipping community and social justice. Anointing as a sacrament of vocation takes up this theme of Christian liberation in a particularly poignant way. This sacrament can concretize with its own specificity the characteristics of the liturgical assembly which must be rooted in a sense of social justice. Such characteristics are:[53]

1) The just community has Jesus as the center of its life and the members of the community relate to Jesus in a personal way. As Segundo puts it: "Before we encounter sacraments in the Gospel, we meet an authentic community which is creating its own distinctive signs under Christ's direction."[54] In a community which is moving toward greater justice for itself and the world, Jesus is viewed as the paradigmatic liberator. He makes it possible for humankind to live in communion, free of injustice and oppression

[53]These characteristics have been analyzed in a Master of Theology thesis by one of my own students: Rev. Anthony F. Krisak, "Sacraments for Human Justice: A thesis presented to the Jesuit School of Theology at Berkeley." The thesis is unpublished. I wish to acknowledge my debt to Father Krisak for his insights in the matter of liturgy and social justice.

[54]Juan Luis Segundo, S.J., *The Sacraments Today* (Maryknoll: Orbis Books, 1974), p. 32.

because he demolishes sin which is the source of injustice. Christ is the paradigm because in the man, Jesus, people discover what God wants for the world. Christ is the liberator for secular society as well as for the Christian community and so even in the political field the incarnation of God's salvation is taking place when political endeavors become the means whereby humankind moves forward to its completion.

Christ's whole life was a negation of everything oppressive. His gospel is one of healing and humanization. He is the vindicator of the poor calling upon those who possess this world's goods to transcend the inhibiting tyranny of private property and to live by an economy of giving. With Jesus and his community, the Church, a new spirit has entered human history. It is a spirit that calls for humanizing love and mutual concern. It is a spirit that overcomes fragmentation by creating new bonds. It is this spirit that gives meaning to the Church whose mission it is to release this new energy in the world.

Anointing's relationship to a community of liberation is based on seeing Jesus' mission of healing as an instance of God's victory over evil. On the level of human experience this is equivalent to freedom from injustice. Anointing is the sacrament that makes clear that human beings have the capacity to overcome destructive forces and situations that are associated with sickness and old age.[55] The stress in the new rite on the pastoral care that must surround any ritual celebration is an instance of social justice in so far as it helps overcome the distance between Christian action and the celebration of the sacraments. A community which lives under the aegis of Christ the Liberator must be just to those members who are in special need of God's justice.

The justice of God is experienced in many different ways. In anointing, the elderly and the ill experience it when they are treated with dignity within the community, when the community communicates to them that they are still impor-

[55]Krisak, "Sacraments for Human Justice," p. 49.

tant members, when the community acts as Jesus did. Jesus did not treat the sick and those possessed of evil spirits as if they were less human. They experienced his justice in his healing, in his enabling them to live humanly.

2) The community that worships justly has a liminal character or an anti-structural quality. It is a community of critical reflection. It is open to change and evaluation. It is one which relativizes its own local institutional gods and is prepared to focus on more global concerns. To be just the Church must be a community of believers who discern the signs of the times. It must promote that which humanizes life for all; it must bring about the unification of the global community in Christ; it must enable its members to work for these goals. It should inspire concrete initiatives for the transformation of human society.

Although liminal, the Church is not an institution alongside worldly structures. It is a community within the world which recognizes God's work for humanity, confirms the importance of people to fashion their futures in freedom, protests the pretensions to ultimacy in any human organization, and suffers with people in the combat against the power of evil. The primary end of the Church is not confessional proclamation or cultic celebration, but a discerning reflection on God's presence and promise in the midst of history. As a result the Church must renounce its claims to honor and power. It must be part of the renovation of this world. This means that the lines between the Church and the world will be less distinct. It is not that the Church summons all people to itself. Rather it moves toward the world to embrace it.

Anointing celebrates the paschal mystery as an experience of justice when because of the Word proclaimed and because of the compassion of the community, the sick and elderly become aware of a new meaning in their lives. As Krisak puts it: "Whenever a time of sickness is experienced as such, persons move beyond a dreary kind of existence into a liminal state where there is genuine hope, despite the stark fact of disability."[56] If the Christian community is to minister to the liminally sick and old, it itself must step outside of societal structures. This should take place in terms of its ministry whether it be the actual rite of anointing or whether it be in something seemingly more pedestrian such as supplying worship space which is barrier free and comfortable for everyone.

The sacrament of anointing is counter-cultural, or liminal, when it relativizes the presuppositions of the members of the community not only about the place of the sick and elderly in society but also when it challenges the quality of the lives of its members both in terms of the mission of the Church and in regard to personal holiness. Anointing, in calling the larger Church to be a bringer of justice to its own members, can be a motivating force for the renewal of unjust structures and debilitating systems outside of the Church because it smashes the idols of power and restricting self-fulfillment. If Christians can discover what justice is required for the good human life of the sick and elderly, then there is greater assurance that these same people will recognize the means that they must take to deal with more national and international needs. Anointing, as a vocational sacrament, however, also emphasizes that social justice presupposes individual justice. The young and middle-aged Christians must experience themselves as just or they cannot bring justice to the sick and elderly and so to the rest of the world. Often those who attempt to work for social justice are motivated by a sense of guilt and self-depreciation. Sexual conflict, unresolved anger, and self-hatred can be as much the reason that some people work for others as the desire to be with one's brothers and sisters out of love for them. In anointing, those anointed can minister to those who are seemingly alive and well, although in need of their own kind of healing.

3) The worshipping community as an incarnate reality lives with the tension of existing in history and yet being a

---

[56]Ibid., p. 51.

manifestation of God in that history. The symbols which give identity to the community point to transcendence, but only because they grow naturally out of their cultural context. Sacramental worship in the Church has a paradigmatic quality about it that points to salvation by indicating what it means to live a truly human life. Sacramental reality lives in the dialectical tension between history and revelation. Because the Church lives in this tension it must proclaim that all are called to build up the kingdom of God, but not all are called to be members of the Church. What it brings out of concealment is that salvation is taking place wherever human beings enter into the process of liberation, but what it must also accept is the fact that not all are called to belong to that sacrament which is the servant of that kingdom being born in the course of human history.

Segundo says:

> In order to make its own specific and divine contribution to universal salvation, the visible Church qua community must be a sign, a sign of the universal salvific plan, of the recapitulation for which the whole universe is waiting, of a message that God sends through his Church in order to contribute toward solutions of (people's) historical problems that are truly human.[57]

It is basic to the various forms of liberation theology that the kingdom of God is now growing in this world and that if Christians are to participate in the founding of that kingdom they must struggle against the various forms of institutionalized injustice. This is not done through some form of enlightened legalism or choosing a substitute ideology, but by personal commitment to God by means of a covenant of love in Jesus Christ. This signifies that the Christian as a spiritual person is one who is building up the kingdom of God in this world rather than preparing for the enjoyment of that kingdom which comes only at the end of life. A "kingdom spirituality" is characterized by the conscientiza-

[57]Segundo, *The Sacraments Today*, p. 9.

tion whereby Christians recognize any part they have played in delaying or destroying the kingdom, by the covenant whereby they are responsible to each other to live in community in such a way as to make the kingdom more visible, and by the mission which calls for the completion of this Christian spirituality by moving beyond the Church itself.

Christians, while maintaining that the reign of God which has begun is not yet fully realized, must accept a real responsibility for working for the completion of this kingdom. This responsibility points to the mission of the Church which is one of gratuitous and unrestricted sharing. The eschatological dimension of this mission, however, reminds believers that the freedoms they have won are not definitive. From these freedoms comes the possibility of both new freedoms and new oppressions. But what must be stressed is that there is something "already," and this grounds Christian hope and makes liturgy a possibility in the midst of so much violence, hatred, destruction, and oppression. It is precisely in worship, where God is recognized as the one who gives meaning to all human projects, that Christians are designated missionaries to live in such a way as to liberate people from their oppressors. In liturgical celebrations new freedoms can burst forth into ordinary life in the world.

One of the liturgical celebrations which speaks to the eschatological tension of the justice-bearing community is anointing. When this sacrament is celebrated in a fully human way, it can become that kind of experience of the paschal event that makes it possible for people to live life more fully without leaving the arena of their personal histories. Anointing is one of the gestures of the Church whereby it manifests to those outside of its community that salvation is phenomenologically found wherever the process of freedom is promoted. As noted earlier in this chapter, there is much institutionalized injustice surrounding the sick and the elderly today. Anointing sits in judgment upon such evil.

A raised awareness that anointing is no longer the sacrament of entrance into a heavenly life, but is the recognition of the salvific aspect of sickness and old age will do much to call all Christians to examine their consciences on how they have inhibited the kingdom of God *in this life*. Anointing should not allow the community of Christ to postpone his mission until the end of time. The kingdom of God achieves some fulfillment here whenever liberation is brought to the sick and elderly and when these people become the models of how the healthy Church is to minister to the world.

4) The community that does justice is not turned in on itself. It promotes the kingdom of God in *this* world. Therefore, it must be a community of prophecy. The faith of the community demands it. It requires active commitment. Its worship calls for the type of living which asks for an active response for others. Members of the Church must go forth and preach the gospel and this in terms of direct action for justice and participation in the advance toward greater freedom for those who are enslaved by economic, political, and social structures. This does not mean that the Christian community can provide remedies for social evils. Rather, the Church's competence is to keep alive the hope and inspiration for the kingdom and its values. Through its critical stance the Church becomes the herald and catalyst of these kingdom values. But it must personalize these values. It cannot be identified with abstractions whether they be peace, justice, reconciliation or affluence, power, and authority.

The ministry of those who are old and ill is a just ministry because of its prophetic quality. Suffering for any prophet can be a growing experience for that person. One thinks of the deepening of insight and faith of Jeremiah through the sufferings due to his prophetic role. There is a challenge to grow in being a prophet because such a way of life is a form of ministry. The sick and elderly are answering a call from God through a particular community to minister to that community. This mutual ministry that anointing raises to visibility has been well expressed by Krisak. He is speaking explicitly of the sick but his remarks are also relevant to the ministry of the elderly:

> The sick person, hearing the word of God in scriptures and in prayer, is asked to reflect on that word and evalu-

ate his/her relation to the community. The sick person
does not participate in the ritual of anointing only for
his/her own personal salvation but as an expression of
faith which the community needs if it is to be a truly
human community. The personal-social dialectic takes
concrete form as the individual and community have a
humanizing effect on each other which is articulated in
the sacrament of anointing.[58]

But the ministry of the old and the ill to the community
does not end with that community. It is a reminder that
salvation is for all and that this must be witnessed to in the
concrete. The community is urged to take up its task to
become active in those areas of society where the sick and
aged are considered to be without value. Members of the
community join the poor in their struggle for medical aid
and proper treatment. They seek justice in that quality care
applies to all regardless of their status or position. In cases
where death is imminent, they try to provide for death with
dignity.

5) The liturgical assembly that celebrates justly experiences solidarity with the victims of injustice. Those marginal
people: the poor, the oppressed, the humiliated, the dispos-
sessed must be able to experience liberation in the sacramental worship of the Christian Church. This is the ultimate
test of the authenticity of the community's public worship.
The presupposition is that the community that hopes to
celebrate in a just manner must be made up of those who are
in a covenantal relationship with God. This covenant is a
commitment which permeates all levels of their lives, especially the area of human relationships. This will be concretized in their ethical stance towards their brothers and
sisters which will lead to a sharing that is based on need and
not on merit. It is a sharing which is unlimited; it is not
merely the sharing of material goods, but also faith and
whatever personal charismatic gifts may be involved. To
have solidarity with one's neighbor means conversion to

[58]Krisak, "Sacraments for Human Justice," p. 53.

one's neighbor. It is a conversion which also demands that Christians try to convert the oppressors from their oppressive ways. It means challenging these people, but it also means caring not only for the victims of oppression but for the personhood of the oppressors themselves.

Those who are liminal because of injustice and dehumanization will not experience the needed liberation in the Church's liturgy, if those special marginal people in the Church, the sick and the elderly, do not also have the experience of justice in the liturgy. They are the paradigms of what solidarity with all oppressed brothers and sisters means. A community justly worships when it experiences solidarity with those who are sick, aged, and dying and when this solidarity with these people is reflected in the ritual. This kind of liturgy, then, articulates a spirituality which calls all to participate in the suffering, hope, and healing of these liminal people. The community which is lacking in justice here will anoint with the intention of a speedy eternal union so they will be free of these who often are a burden to them. The true meaning of anointing is the negation of such an attitude.

Justice is obtained when the community does not relegate its ministry only to those moments when ritual is called for. The ministry of the sick and elderly is a continual process of conscientization for all in the Church. And so the Church must be constantly present to these people. It is present when it has members who are free enough to suffer with others and who can deal with those who are ill or superannuated. These people are ideally those who celebrate the ritual of anointing. It is important to keep a close connection between sacramental and pastoral ministry here to avoid the situation which is still very much present; namely, the pastoral care speaks more loudly of the justice of God than does the actual sacramental liturgy. And yet it is liturgy which is supposed to be clear and umambiguous about the kingdom of God. Where it is not possible to have those ministering to the sick and elderly celebrate anointing, an effort should be made to make them very visible in any anointing rite. They can perhaps be ministers of the eucharist for those being anointed. The laying on of hands might well be highlighted as their form of ritual contact with the sick and old. The elderly's presence at the regular parish eucharist should be felt. Their physical presence and the concern of the community's representatives (the ushers, for instance) can be most effective. Although the sick most probably could not be present at the celebrations, the texts of the prayers can call the community's attention to these people. The point is that the practical ministry should be motivated by the conviction that these people are special sacraments of the kingdom preached by Christ, a kingdom of justice as well as of peace.

Finally, the attitude of the ministering Church is important here. Both sickness and old age can be obstacles to the full experience that one is worthwhile, that is, that one is lovable, that one is just. If those who minister to these people reinforce those feelings and convictions, a situation of injustice is created despite the good intentions and concern. If the liturgy emphasizes union with the suffering Christ in such a way as to make people content with suffering rather than be challenged to free people from the weakness and hurt of sickness and old age, then the liturgy is unjust. What such a liturgy would say to those oppressed in other ways and on a broader scale than sickness and old age is obvious.

Anointing's relationship to the mission of the Church to bring about the justice of God in the world is seen in terms of the vocational aspect of this sacrament. As in the case of all liturgical celebrations, the rite of anointing is the place where the focus for the justice for which Christ died are released. The interaction between the community and the people anointed, their mutual ministry to each other, keeps a proper balance between the emphasis on the individual and the call to the wider mission of the Church. It is the vocation of the sick and elderly to sharpen continually the consciousness of the worshipping community about all the dehumanizing components found in contemporary society.

Sensitivity to the sick and the old in the Church can only support an actualizing concern for the poor, the weak, and the oppressed. In that sense the sacrament of anointing proclaims to the larger Church more than the salvific value of being "sick or old in the Church." It also says that to be a Christian is to be on the way to freedom. More must go on in the anointing than comfort and care for those who cannot take care of themselves. In this rite, the community should experience liberation and receive the courage and motivation to keep alive the hope of freedom. Just as those who minister to the sick and elderly assist them to deal with the limitations which flow from their condition, so these people in turn call into question the limitations that the young and healthy in the Church allow in their lives which impede their engaging actively in bringing about justice in society. The celebration of anointing should be a liturgy which induces liberation in the Church and beyond its confines. In this sense, anointing is vocational.

Anointing and the Body

An important anthropological consideration from a Christian perspective which anointing can affirm is the more semitic concept of the body. If anointing is to speak effectively in the situations of illness and old age, it must move away from a dualistic understanding of the human person. As Charles Gusmer has pointed out:

> If in the first eight hundred years of anointing physical healing was at times overplayed, and if the Scholastic Period could recognize only the spiritual effects of the sacrament, today we need a theology of healing which includes anointing and regards the sacrament as effecting the whole man.[59]

For the Hebrews the person is not divided into body and soul. The person is a body, an external manifestation, a

---

[59]Charles Gusmer, "Liturgical Traditions of Christian Illness: Rites of the Sick," *Worship* 46 (1972):537.

symbol whereby the person can communicate and share with others. The person is a body-person or a body-alive.[60] Persons are related to God through this body symbol. In sickness and old age the body symbol is not working well and so there is some loss of existence and meaning. In these liminal situations it may be more difficult to relate to God and so this may bring about alienation from God and others. Anointing can be a way of overcoming the brokenness which results from these situations. It may be a way of experiencing one's unity. Both scripture and modern psychology are one in asserting that the entire person is sick. This is even more obvious in the case of old age. The total person is elderly and suffering from such a state. It is not only the body (as opposed to soul) which is affected. The whole person must be ministered to.

Since it is the entire person who is sick or old, it is not possible to separate medicine and visitation from the sacrament of anointing. They are part of the same ministry of human caring. The purpose of this ministry is to bring about human wholeness, an integral body-person. This can only take place if the entire community takes an active part in dealing with the sick or aged, the isolated or the suffering. Visitation with prayers and imposition of hands or some form of touch may be the ordinary way most members of the community will exercise their ministry in regard to these people. More professional ministers should take care of more specialized needs.

Anointing as a vocational sacrament is dependent on the more holistic approach to the human person. This view which sees the body as the source of meaning, which views the body as a way of being in the world, and which holds that because of the body one can be in dialectical relationship with one's humanity must find expression on the level of pastoral care. Two rituals which might be ways of raising to visibility the significance of sickness and old age as bodily

---

[60]Francis Ryan, *The Body as Symbol: Merleau-Ponty and Incarnational Theology* (New York: Corpus Publications, 1970).

and vocational ways of existing in the world (and, of course, the Church) are the laying on of hands and the anointing *with oil.*

The Laying on of Hands[61]

This liturgical action in the rite of anointing is a particularly human gesture. It is a physical symbol of relationship. It carries with it both proclamation and response of personal presence. It is not only that a person imposes hands on another, but that a human being is accepting this touch from another human being. Because in this sacrament the minister represents the community, she/he cannot really act as an individual only. She/he brings the presence of that community to the sick and elderly. Such a touch can claim these people from a state of isolation. What is so significant for those receiving this laying on of hands is that it is a way that the community proclaims to them that they are acceptable—a much needed experience for such liminal people. Such an expression of solidarity becomes the human way in which the faith conviction that God first loves his creatures and so they are lovable can be ritualized.[62]

In an article entitled: "The Laying on of Hands in Healing,"[63] Godfrey Diekmann shows that in both the Old and New Testaments touch and the laying on of hands are synonymous. The proof is found not only in the explicit situations of imposition of hands but in other references to touch such as Mk 10:13: "And they were bringing children to him, that he might touch them," or Mk 5:23 which gives the incident of the daughter of Jairus when Jesus took her hand, touched her, and told her to rise. There are other

---

[61]In this section dealing with the laying on of hands as well as the following one dealing with anointing with oil I have made use of the valuable insights of M. Jennifer Glen.

[62]Glen, "Sickness and Symbol," p. 404.

[63]*Liturgy: The Sick and the Dying* 25:2 (March/April 1980):7ff. See also: Michael Moynahan, S.J., "The Sacramentality of Touch," *Modern Liturgy* 5:3 (April 1978).

instances such as Acts 3:7 where Peter cured a lame man by taking him by the right hand and pulling him up. These instances of touch are also symbols of the conferring of the power of God either through Christ or his followers. As Diekmann puts it:

> Nor should this be at all surprising. For touching some-
> one is a sign of transferring something of oneself to
> another...When trying to comfort someone bereaved
> and all words fail, we touch that person, perhaps place
> our hands on his or her shoulder as a sign that we deeply
> care, we share our love. On the part of the person who
> touches, the gesture often implies gentle affection, pro-
> tection or communication of strength. To allow another
> person to touch me is an act of openness, of acceptance
> on my part of what that person wishes to communicate or
> to give to me in love. Or again, we shake hands, that is we
> touch each other firmly, to seal a contract. In doing so we
> pledge ourselves, our most precious possession, our
> honor.[64]

Diekmann makes the point that preaching and healing are tied together by Jesus. And from the way the two worked together in biblical times he concludes that the word, "healing," can apply to all the sacraments. Since in Patristic times the laying on of hands was the basic sacra-mental gesture, healing and imposition of hands are to be part of each of the sacraments, one enlightening the other. This but emphasizes the importance of touch in the special sacrament of anointing. It can be highly effective pastorally when not only the priest but also others such as friends and relatives place their hands on the sick or elderly person.

In effect what is happening is that a human gesture which signalizes presence and human bonding to community speaks also of the God that transcends this human relation-ship. In a sacrament such as anointing, the laying on of hands still addresses the person precisely as human in

---

[64]Diekmann, "The Laying on of Hands in Healing," p. 9.

manifesting acceptance and acceptability, but now it also makes visible the power of the Spirit that resides in this human community. Moreover, the further signification of the laying on of hands, namely, the commissioning to some form of ministry, brings out clearly the ministerial position of the sick and the aged. In this sense, the vocational aspect of these liminal people is brought to liturgical expression.

In the faith context, the imposition of hands means the communication of the Spirit as one who heals, however health might be understood. The liturgical texts speak of life and new health. But this rite also speaks to the relationship of sin and sickness, as ambiguous as it may be, in that it is associated with rites of exorcism. And if exorcism is seen primarily as a way of claiming one for God, much of the negativity and questionable theology of the past regarding this ritual can be alleviated. Because the laying on of hands has such a wealth of meaning, it can be the symbol of the relationship of the marginal person to the community on several different levels. It can be an apt symbol of the overcoming of fragmentation that can be suffered by someone who is already situated in the community through baptism and reconciliation. It is precisely this multiple relationship to community which from a faith perspective becomes the basis for hope in the future. Because the community assists the sick and elderly through their rites of passage, it is possible for these people to experience God in terms of re-integration and human reciprocity. Glen says:

> In laying on hands in the Christian rites for the sick, the community offers not merely communion with itself but, in and through it, with the all transcending God; inherent in that relationship is the faith that it will perdure not only in time but beyond it into the eschaton of which the Spirit is both pledge and power. Against that horizon, the sick person is invited to stand before his own mortality, perceiving it not as enclosure but as threshold to life transformed.[65]

[65]Glen, "Sickness and Symbol," p. 406.

Laying on of hands points up very well the meaning of sickness and old age in a Christian context. Laying on of hands, because it is a commissioning in the Spirit, is concerned more with the restoration of the significance of life through invitation back into community, than it is with the restoration of one's former health and social role the person had prior to illness. Imposition of hands with its multivalent meanings becomes an appropriate symbol of the vocational aspect of the sick and elderly because rather than treating these people as dependent and recipients of the community's benefactions, it deals with them as adults, not as healthy or productive (according to the present culture's values) adults, but as peers who make a contribution to the community in terms of meaning. These liminal people are human acts of faith for the community regarding mortality and human limits. They are credal incarnations of Jesus' own passage into life.

And so what this sacrament, and in the particular the laying on of hands, is celebrating or raising to ritual visibility is 1) that these marginal people will make it through the passage in which they are involved with the assistance of the community and 2) that sickness and old age transcend the life of any individual Christian to effect the quality of life of the larger community so that the Christian Church can make its own final passage into the kingdom of God. In a very real sense laying on of hands means that what is done for the sick and elderly is done for the community.

While this more holistic view of the meaning of sickness and old age and the sacramental care for those who are "sick or ill in the Church" restores a balance to the theology of anointing, the question of physical healing cannot simply be dismissed. There is the possibility that physical recovery will be one of the results of this sacrament and that the imposition of hands is the obvious ritualizing to be connected with that process. The difficulty today, although not limited only to the contemporary scene, is that when the culture seeks to deny death as an accepted reality, human healing through touch can very easily be co-opted into that frame of mind.

Anointing and touch are then directed to the production of some spectacular effects. But any physical healing that takes place in a sacrament or in some sacramental situation is only temporary. Thus, there is the concern not to focus too narrowly on physical healing as the result of this sacrament as well as the attempt on the part of theologians to broaden the meaning of health. Health is more than physical well-being; it is the wholeness of the whole person, of which sickness and old age are components. The restored health that is proper to anointing is the enabling of the person to accept his/her state and in such acceptance to find peace and reconciliation with God and community. The future health which is offered to the sick and elderly in this sacrament has been brilliantly described in the words of Glen:

> If the sick person finds himself at the end of his passage whether it be recovery, chronic illness or death, reintegrated with himself as human person, with his community and his God, transformed by a confrontation with mortality which has been opened out into a future enriched and extended, surely he has been healed, for the humanity which was disrupted has, in the most profound sense, been made whole, whatever the physical condition of the body.[66]

The Anointing with Oil

The anointing with oil, which is central symbol of this sacrament, has the same foundational meaning as the laying on of hands. This is logical because the imposition of hands is the basic sacramental gesture and anointing is a form of laying on of hands. Thus, historically both gestures have been related, sometimes acting in complementary fashion, and at other times being merged together into a single action. But anointing has some further connotations for the sick and the elderly as it is employed in this rite.

An analysis of oil as such is ambiguous. It is used in

[66]Ibid., p. 408.

cooking, massage, machinery, the hospital room, the fuel station, and the locker room. But in the Judeo-Christian tradition anointing has taken on the meaning of the blessings that God gives his people. Healing is one of those blessings. Like the imposition of hands, anointing symbolizes the bringing of the life of the Spirit to someone. Oil makes it clear that the Spirit is concretized in the blessings of God. But while it is true that healing is counted among these Spirit-filled blessings, it is not simply physical healing according to gross medical categories, but health in the fuller eschatological sense.

Much of the religious understanding of anointing in the Old Testament took on concrete form in the case of the consecration of kings, priests, and prophets. In a New Testament context this eschatological expectation was brought to expression in the personhood of Jesus Christ whose name literally means, "the anointed one." He is anointed by the Spirit to be Lord and Redeemer: *the* king, priest, and prophet. Thus, it is consistent that the Christian community through the ages has continued to use anointing in conjunction with the ministerial sacraments of baptism, confirmation, and orders since these deal with the structuring of what is supposed to be a priestly, kingly, and prophetic community.

Anointing in regard to the sick and elderly need not be seen, then, in terms of the healing aspect of oil only. In this sacrament it also speaks of commissioning. It is also delegation for ministry in the Church. It may not be articulating that which permanently structures the community, but it is still publicly recognizing a group of people in the Church who fulfill a ministerial function. In this sense anointing and laying on of hands are identical. However, there may be some differentiation in anointing's added meaning of bearing witness. Such witnessing is brought about because the anointing in this sacrament recapitulates that of baptism and confirmation where the Christian has been ritually conformed to the Anointed One, the Christ. Through the suffering and marginality of sickness and old age the person now participates more fully in Christ's own confrontation with human limit and mortality. Anointing in this sacrament is a more explicit identification with the paschal mystery. And this union with Christ is where the promise of a saving future, the eschatological dimension, emerges. What the community is promising to the anointed person is that death is not the final word. Anointing is the experience of the resurrection both concretely and in anticipation.

Conclusion

Anointing, as liturgy, is the celebration of the significance of sickness and old age, or better, of the ill and aged Christians who live in the midst of the Church. It is a ritual recognition of their ministry to the young and healthy Church and is the articulation of the community's recognition of the paschal mystery as concretized in sickness and old age. Through this act of worship the Church offers to its marginal members in symbolic expression its own commitment to the Anointed One who has conquered death. Because of the community's faith there is new meaning to be found in their present condition. In the words of Glen:

> He who has been separated from his own person, from his fellow human beings and from his conception of God by the diagnosis of illness need not despair: all that has been lost shall be restored, renewed, within the horizon of a future that is partial now in pledge that it will be absolute.[67]

Ultimately, anointing is a sacrament because it speaks to the Church in which the sick and elderly live. Sacraments are always primarily expressions of the Church and are its attempts to define and realize itself. Anointing is a major form of proclamation to the Christian community. And while it surely proclaims to the sick and elderly that they can transcend the debilitating confines of the present because it promises a future as something which is human, it voices

[67]Ibid., p. 411.

even more loudly to the believers once anointed in baptism, that there is freedom from the suffocating attitude which capitulates to the present with its brokenness and loss of integrity.

Anointing promises no pie-in-the-sky, whether to the sick and the old Christians or to those who are alive and healthy in the Church. But what hope it conveys, is a communal hope which forms the parameters in which the fragmented and alienated life can recover its significance. It is the contention of this author that today the sick and perhaps especially, the elderly witness to this hope more effectively than any other single group of Christians. And for that reason anointing is to be affirmed as a sacrament of vocation.

It seems fitting to conclude this chapter with some references which give support to the idea of the ministerial dimension of the sick and the old and of anointing as a vocational sacrament:

> I consider that the sufferings of this present time are not worth comparing with the glory that is to be revealed to us. For the creation waits with eager longing for the revealing of the sons of God;. . . . . because creation itself will be set free from its bondage to decay and obtain the glorious liberty of the children of God. We know that the whole creation has been groaning in travail together until now; and not only the creation, but we ourselves, who have the first fruits of the Spirit, groan inwardly as we wait for adoption as sons, the redemption of our bodies.[68]

> By the sacred-anointing of the sick and the prayer of the priests the whole Church commends those who are ill to the suffering and glorified Lord that he may raise them up and save them. And indeed she exhorts them to contribute to the good of the People of God by freely uniting themselves to the passion and death of Christ.[69]

[68]Romans 8:18-23.
[69]*Lumen Gentium*, 11.

The Sacramental Rite of Christening (anointing) should open for the patient the widest perspective of Christian discipleship, the privilege of unwarranted suffering along with our Lord on behalf of a fallen world, with the prospect of redemption that this makes possible.[70]

So maybe, after all, there are old men and women hidden from our troubled vision, whom we have to bring into the midst of our assembly so that they can cast away the darkness of our confusing existence and tell us top from bottom.[71]

[70]Brian Brown, *The Sacramental Ministry to the Sick* (New York: Exposition Press, 1968), p. 63.

[71]Nouwen, Henri and Gaggney, Walter J., *Aging* (Garden City: Doubleday and Co., 1974), p. 51.

BIBLIOGRAPHY:
ANOINTING: A SACRAMENT OF VOCATION

Books:

de Beauvoir, Simone, *The Coming of Age*. New York: Putnam, 1972.

Bowman, Leonard, *The Importance of Being Sick*. Wilmington: Consortium Books, 1976.

Clements, William M., ed., *Ministry With the Aging*. San Francisco: Harper and Row, 1981.

Erikson, Erik H., *Identity and the Life Cycle*. New York: International Universities Press, 1959.

McCauley, George, *Sacraments for Secular Man*. New York: Herder and Herder, 1969.

Mooney, Christopher, *Man Without Tears*. New York: Harper and Row, 1973.

Nouwen, Henri and Gaggney, Walter J., *Aging*. Garden City: Doubleday and Co., 1974.

Rahner, Karl, *Meditations on the Sacraments*. New York: The Seabury Press, 1977.

Liturgy: The Sick and the Dying. Vol. 25:2. Washington, D.C.: The Liturgical Conference, March/April 1980.

Sontag, Susan, *Illness as Metaphor*. New York: Farrar, Straus and Giroux, 1977.

Articles

Browning, Don S., "Preface to a Practical Theology of Aging." *Pastoral Psychology* 24 (229) (Winter 1975):151-167.

Glen, M. Jennifer, "Sickness and Symbol: The Promise of the Future." *Worship* 54:5 (November 1980):397-411.

Power, David, "Let the Sick Man Call." *The Heythrop Journal* 9 (July 1978):256-270.

Tracy, David, "Eschatological Perspectives on Aging." *Pastoral Psychology* 24 (229) (Winter 1975):119-134.

U.S. Bishops', "Pastoral Letter on Health and Health Care." *Origins* 11:25 (Dec. 8, 1981): 396-402.

CHAPTER FIVE: PASTORAL PERSPECTIVES ON THE RITES OF THE SICK AND THE ELDERLY.

In this chapter some pastoral reflections are offered on the rites for the sick and the elderly. This is done by means of analysis of Part One of the revised ritual as proposed by ICEL. This first part which is entitled the *Pastoral Care of the Sick* contains four chapters which deal with the visitation and anointing of the sick. The comments on these chapters which are offered here are intended to assist the pastoral implementation of this revised rite in the life of the Church. These observations are preceded by some detailing of the pastoral imperatives that are demanded by the implementation of the revised rite and by some points for catechesis which must come before an adequate celebration of the sacrament can be expected. This chapter concludes with some suggestions for future possibilities for the administration of this sacrament in the life of the Church.

Pastoral Imperatives

The major pastoral consideration is that the sacrament of anointing will only be effective if it is experienced in the broad perspective of a total ministry to the sick, aged, and dying. From the time of Trent, as well as before, because of the narrowing of theological understanding regarding anointing, the concern for the sick has been restricted to the act of the priest anointing the patient. Such a practice, unchallenged until the renewal of the Second Vatican Council, reflected the cultural attitude of neglect of those who are marginal in society: the sick, the elderly, and the dying. Often such people were effectively abandoned by society. And anointing had become equated with priests slipping into hospital rooms to perform an act with oil which was more noted for its mechanical efficiency than it was the proclamation of the Good News. Charles Gusmer has written:

> The sacramental ministry to the sick and dying is the most liturgically deprived of all the sacramental ministrations in the Church. Consider the frequent impersonal, mechanistic and hurried attitude in the sacramental ministry to the sick, and even to the dead. At times a misplaced *opus operatum* mentality prevails, as if the sacraments were almost a kind of magical rite, which produces grace without any action on the person who is celebrating or receiving them.[1]

It is easy to see that such practices produced a quasi-magical understanding of the sacrament whose purpose was to get one into heaven. Such a view individualized anointing as well as engendered destructive guilt and anxiety for persons dying without the "last rites."

Pastorally, more, not less, is being asked of all, whether the priest, the community or the persons to be anointed. Anointing cannot be seen as an isolated ritual action but must mirror the acts of concern which precede and follow the anointing. As in the case of the other sacraments, the authenticity of the anointing depends on the quality of religious experience being articulated. Anointing must have its reality enkindled through the lives of the members of the community who show their concern for the sick, elderly, and dying that Christ is the Lord of their lives. If sacra-

[1]Charles Gusmer, "The Sacramental Role in the Department of Pastoral Care," *Rite for the Anointing and Pastoral Care of the Sick* (Washington, D.C.: Federation of Diocesan Liturgical Commissions, 1973), p. 24.

ments, including anointing, are not lived realities in the community, they become empty forms, structures without life.

Concretely, what will restore life to anointing as a ritual would include frequent visitations, distribution of communion, and the sacrament of reconciliation. The presence of lay persons can make anointing an affirmation of the worth of the Christian to be anointed. Deacons and ministers of communion can visit and bring the eucharist. Prayer services to be used during visits need to be developed. And the restoration of the communal service in the life of the parish so that it operates normatively in the lives of all Christians must receive top priority.

Since anointing represents more than itself, it should promote the Church's awareness of the ecclesial dimension of the sacraments. It should be an obvious experience that sacraments are celebrated by the Church as well as in the Church. Anointing without the presence of a community, at least family and friends, is as anomalous as is the private celebration of the eucharist. The reformed rite of anointing calls for an end to the private anointing as the norm. Rather it challenges the community to experience itself as Church in terms of drawing people together who face liminal situations through sickness, old age, and death. The rite itself clearly states that the ministry to the sick, elderly, and dying belongs to all the members of the Church:

> It is thus fitting that all baptized Christians share in this ministry of mutual charity within the body of Christ: by fighting against disease, by love shown to the sick, and by celebrating the sacraments of the sick. Like the other sacraments, these too have a communal aspect, which should be brought out as much as possible when they are celebrated.[2]

[2] *Rite of Anointing and Pastoral Care of the Sick*, no. 33. Since at the time of the publication of this book the revised rite as proposed by ICEL has not yet received final approval by the American bishops, it is not possible to quote directly from it. All direct quotations come from the 1974 *Rite of Anointing and Pastoral Care of the Sick*. While many of the pastoral notes have been rewritten in ICEL's revision

This more ecclesial approach to anointing should assist people in taking a less paternalistic posture towards the sick, elderly, and dying. In the long run such paternalism can emphasize the separation rather than the union between the individual Christian and the community. Paternalism flows from an attitude that the sick or elderly person is the highly favored recipient of the great gifts that the community has to offer. It does not consider what the sick, aged, and dying have to offer to the community or the local Church.

That anointing should be seen in the context of the pastoral care of the sick and old implies that these people need more than purely spiritual assistance. They may need food, transportation, and clerical help in filling out forms. The poor who cannot afford a lawyer can be assisted by the parish. And even beyond these ministries of visiting and social service, the Church should be pastorally involved in the active support of social justice for the sick and elderly. This may mean supporting programs dealing with public facilities for the handicapped, with improving the quality of health care, supporting the moral rights of the seriously ill to refuse painful and expensive life-support systems with little realistic hope of recovery, helping families to avoid excessive burial costs, and curbing morticians who take advantage of the emotional state of the mourners. The Church must practice what it preaches in providing adequate health insurance and pension plans for its employees.[3]

Since one of the most severe burdens of the sick and elderly is the feeling that they are no longer of any use, ways should be found whereby they can continue to be constructive. Those who are not seriously incapacitated can be employed by the parish as a concrete sign of care for the sick and elderly. Programs should be provided for those in retirement so that they can continue to be creative in their final years. At the very minimum the parish can pray for the

entitled: *Pastoral Care of the Sick — Rites of Anointing and Viaticum,* there has been no major theological change. The wording of the pastoral notes of the 1974 rite are still relevant and useable.

[3]Krisak, *Sacraments for Human Justice,* p. 132.

sick, elderly, and dying (by name) in the Universal Interces-
sions of the liturgy. More traditional parish societies such as
the St. Vincent de Paul Society or the Legion of Mary can
find renewed meaning in a ministry to the sick, elderly, and
dying. Since sub-groups in the parish should be prayer
groups rather than collections of people who are primarily
task oriented, this ministry can take the form of small
communities that pray with others. Young people are often
inspiring in their generous response to the sick, elderly, and
dying if the official Church will but call upon them.

Besides this more comprehensive ministerial context for
anointing, a second major pastoral imperative is the meaning of sickness, old age, and death. A ministry of anointing,
no matter how broadened in terms of the care of these
people, will be weakened if the ministry, the community,
and the person anointed have a superficial understanding of
sickness and healing. There are still too many Catholics who
define the sick and old person in terms of neurophysical and
clinical categories. Such a view of sickness and old age will
foster either a disregard for anointing as an ineffective
superstitious custom or lead to an approach which hopes for
charismatic results. This flows from a purely physical
understanding of sickness as something that can be grafted
on hospital charts, traced by sophisticated machinery, and
solved through the right pill if it can be found. To see
sickness in grossly medical categories will mean viewing
healing as something that can be mitigated by men and
women graduates of the medical schools or something that
takes place through a miraculous seizure by the Holy Spirit.
Rather anointing as a sacrament must be grasped and pastorally experienced in a faith dimension in which there are
diseases deeper than cancer and healings more marvelous
than those that take place at a pentecostal service.

Thus, both those who anoint and those who are to be
anointed must know what it means to be sick and old. A
large part of the total ministry to the ill and aged here will be
the challenge to see sickness and old age as a severing of one
from the past and future, as an experience of being isolated

in the present, and of being unable to do those things which once were the source of pleasure and personal fulfillment. The sick and elderly are separated from those closest to them; they are faced with the possibility of becoming excessively preoccupied with themselves; they have lost their sense of community; they feel alienated through medical advice or human neglect. A variety of weaknesses accompany sickness and old age and one can find oneself overwhelmed by them. There is the monotony of medicines and doctors. There is the imperceptibility of recuperation. There is more than clinical disease in all of this. There is the possibility of fragmentation.

Sickness and old age are distinctly psychosomatic experiences. The human person is experienced as one. What might be separated clearly on the level of theory, e.g. the spiritual and the physical, becomes blurred at such times. Not only is it difficult to treat either sickness or old age as purely spiritual or purely physical, it is also impossible to ascribe the cause of sickness to either an outside or an inside cause. While the physician may have to distinguish between spiritual and physical illnesses for medical purposes, no such separation can be made in the case of the Church's ministry to the sick and aged. The sacrament of anointing deals with the whole sick person, the entire aged and dying person. It is rarely clear that the cause of sickness is simply something that comes from outside the person or is the result of human freedom in some way.

Because sickness does not allow for clear identification of its causes, people at this time experience themselves as a mystery. There is an obscurity in their self-understanding that is more obvious at this time. The full depths of themselves exceed their powers of penetration. They become a question to which they have no adequate answer. Thus, in sickness (and also, in old age) people experience themselves in a special way. They are no longer in control, at least not to the same point as in the case of health. Clearly sickness and old age are more than medical phenomena. The whole person is sick or old. And because sickness and old age move beyond the physical dimension, they can, in a Christian perspective, constitute a threat to the person's salvation, that is, to life in Christ. The separation from friends and loved ones at that time is more than mere social isolation. It is the experience of the paschal mystery. It is the passage into death for which there must be a corresponding passage into new life. Anointing is an invitation to such an experience.

Put in existential language, this paschal passing over is described as the overcoming of fragmentation. If sickness and old age are symbols of the possible destructive disunity in the human person and of separation from community and from God, then the purpose of the sacrament of anointing is to provide the experience of the death/resurrection of Christ precisely in terms of this kind of alienation and fragmentation. Any pastoral care on the concrete level should emphasize that the plight of the sick and elderly is not senseless and cruel suffering. Rather, it can be a time of growth for these people as human beings and as Christians. Ministry to them must stress their ministry to the larger Church. Pastoral care will highlight the witness value of those who suffer. They remind the rest of the Church of the importance of life, health, death, and salvation as compared to the many trivial things which preoccupy people. The Church needs the sick and the elderly.

A third major pastoral imperative is that anointing must be experienced as liturgy, that is, as worshipful praise, as prayer, and celebration. Its primary purpose, like all liturgy, is itself. It is not a means to an end. The pragmatic emphasis in the past in regard to this sacrament is no longer appropriate. Such an approach which sees anointing as productive of something, whether it be the forgiveness of sins or physical healing, depreciates anointing as liturgy. It also causes an excessive preoccupation with the question: what does this sacrament do?

The listing of effects of this sacrament not only stresses a consumeristic approach to anointing, it also is confusing. There have been so many effects ascribed to anointing that it appears that more is claimed for it than it can accomplish. Some of these effects are: the grace of the Holy Spirit, restoration of the health of the person, trust in God, strength to resist temptations, alleviation of the anxiety about dying, etc. But does anointing always produce these effects? Must not a sacrament always be effective?

If the pragmatic cause/effect approach to anointing is taken in which it is experienced primarily in terms of the prayer of petition, the theology of this sacrament can only be bewildering. If anointing is kept as an experience of worship, however, there is a sense in which it always works. Praise to God is always given when two or three gather in Jesus' name around the sick, the old, and the dying to proclaim their love and trust in the goodness of God. The sacrament works, that is, is a sacrifice of praise and thanks, if those gathered around the one to be anointed commend that person to Christ in explicit reference to the paschal mystery. Anointing is clearly a sacrament of praise when it moves the sick and elderly to contribute to the welfare of the people of God by associating themselves freely with the larger community in such a way as to minister to it about the mystery of sickness and old age.

To say that anointing is praise does not exclude the petitionary aspect of the sacramental rite. It is quite legitimate to pray for the lightening of the sufferings of the sick and old. It is in place to pray for both spiritual and physical healing. But if these prayers are seen to be effective in their results because of the rite, a sense of inauthenticity can result. Anointing as intercession is like any other kind of petitionary prayer in the liturgy. It is the form whereby the community attempts to open itself to God by being conscious of some of its concrete concerns. It is not attempting to persuade God to change his mind or to intervene in this world's affairs.

Anointing is a ritual, that is, a pattern of repetitive behavior, which expresses and celebrates something already present in the participants. If this ritualizing is authentic, then it can facilitate growth in the strength and hope for life for those performing the ritual. But the question about what does anointing do and does it always do it points up the limitations of scholastic theology's approach on the pastoral level. The medieval cause and effect model can seriously depreciate the experience of anointing for the sick and elderly because it reduces the many-layered and richly textured liturgical experience to a moment narrowly defined in terms of the production of an effect. Theologians and pastors need to be more cautious about what they claim for this sacrament. What can be claimed for it is that it should be authentic praise and the celebration of "being sick and old in the Church."

Catechesis for
the Sacrament of Anointing

The sacrament of anointing will not be pastorally effective if attention is given only to those who are already ill and old. Catechesis must be directed to those in the Church who are well and not in their declining years. It is the healthy Church which cares for those to be anointed. Those who are ill and aged cannot be expected to experience their situation as salvific or ministerial if the healthy Church does not so experience it. Especially in the United States the culture routinely disguises the realities of sickness, old age, and death. The administration of a single rite cannot successfully combat this cultural mind-set. It is important that the Christian community be countercultural in this area. Until there is a change of thinking and feeling regarding anointing on the part of the healthy Catholics, any change for those who are sick or old will be less than what it can or should be.

In contemporary culture the healthy, because of denial and escape, pretend that sickness is what happens to someone else and that old age is still in the distant future. The reason that the Church expresses itself through this sacramental symbol is to remind itself that life does entail suffering, sickness, and death. The believer is one who can and does recognize and embrace these realities. In attending to the plight of the sick and elderly, the healthy Christian acknowledges these liminal situations. Those who have supported and cared for these people in the Church will be able to celebrate those times in their own personal histories with more authenticity and belief.

Since the sacrament must be contextualized to be effective, catechesis must be directed to enabling the community to experience anointing of the sick and the elderly as a real sign of the community's concern for these people who perform a vocational function in the Church. An important part of the understanding of this sacrament is the way in which this concern is prolonged in the community. There must be a mutual giving and sharing between those who are healthy and those in need of healing. There is much more demanded than an understanding of the theology and liturgy of the rite. Both the problems of the sick, elderly, and dying and the problems of those who care for them must be dealt within the community.[4]

Catechesis, then, is the keystone to the success of this sacrament in parish life. Points which should be covered in any catechetical program would include the following:

1) The rites are part of a larger context. The anointing cannot take place as an isolated phenomenon. This proper context consists of:

a) The Christian perspective on sickness. The Christian does not view sickness as a punishment for personal sin but as part of the fragmented human condition. This is that part of the human experience referred to as original sin. The Christian wishes to give meaning to such suffering by making an explicit connection with the suffering of Christ. "Now I rejoice in my sufferings for your sake, and in my flesh I complete what is lacking in Christ's afflictions for the sake of his body, that is, the church" (Col 1:24; cf. also: Introduction: nos. 2-4, 34).

b) The Church's pastoral concern for the sick and old.

---

[4]For much in this section I am indebted to the catechetical booklet, *Rite for the Anointing and Pastoral Care of the Sick*, published by FDLC.

Not only does this mean that the Church commends the sick and old to Christ, but that they are encouraged to contribute to the whole Church. They are the paschal mystery in the concrete for the healing Church. If the local community gives some indication of its interest in the sick and elderly, praying for their recovery as well as assisting them on the way, then, those anointed can experience more authentically the meaning of the prayers for their recovery and strengthening. Thus the catechesis should be made real through pastoral visitation (40 b), public celebrations in the church (80-99), and home liturgies with the family present (34, 37).

If people are to learn about the meaning of sickness and old age, they will need to be taught when they are well. There is a limit to the amount of instruction that the ill can absorb and the mystery of old age cannot be understood through a few Sunday homilies. People need to have spent time reflecting on this for years. Nor should the Sunday homily be seen as the most effective tool for such communication. An occasional essay in the parish bulletin that people can keep, and perhaps, best of all, some experience of actual ministry to the sick and elderly, will prove to be more effective. One should not discount the importance of the parish's experience of the public rite of anointing.

2) The priest as the representative of the community. The priest is not present to the sick, aged, and dying as the Grand Inquisitor or death personified but he is there to ritualize the Christian understanding of sickness, old age, and death. He is there so that the whole Church may heal this person. He is there to ensure that this person experiences the community in the concrete. For this reason there is not only the rite of anointing, but a series of rites which constitute this sacrament: visits to the sick; visits to a sick child; communion of the sick both in ordinary circumstances and in a hospital or institution; anointing of the sick outside Mass, during Mass, and in a hospital or institution; viaticum during and outside Mass; commendational of the dying; and rites for exceptional circumstances such as in the case of emergencies and

the Christian initiation for the dying. A fine statement about the duties of the parish priest to raise the consciousness of the whole parish regarding the sick is this one of Brian Newns:

> Besides concerning himself with the care of the individual sick person, the priest will need to think of the parish as a whole. He will want to make his parishioners aware of the sick among them, and encourage them to feel some responsibility towards them. He will wish to make the sick aware that they are not alone, especially the permanently sick, and besides seeing that they are visited he may be able to bring them into contact with each other, even if this is only by telephone. From time to time he may be able to arrange services, such as the anointing of the sick, in the parish church, for those who can be taken to church.[5]

3) Who may be anointed? The points which should be brought to the attention of the parish whether through announcements or bulletins would include: (1) This sacrament cannot be repeated except in the case of recovery or changes for the worse in the same illness, or in the case of a protracted illness (no. 9). (2) The elderly may be anointed because of the weakness of old age. They need not be seriously ill (no. 11). (3) Children may be anointed if they are old enough to understand and participate in this sacrament. But infants and small children are not anointed, no matter how sick. They are not in need of such inner healing. But at such times, as in the case of the dead, the priest should pray for them and pray with the families.

4) When to call the priest? People must be encouraged to seek anointing at the beginning of a serious illness. This will be difficult to communicate if the practice continues whereby anointing is delayed until the final hours before death or even shortly after death. Instruction on when to call the

[5]Brian Newns, "The Anointing and Pastoral Care of the Sick," in *Pastoral Liturgy*, ed. Harold Winstone (London: Collins Liturgical Publications, 1975), p. 219.

priest should take place from time to time in any parish. With such volatile congregations today, it is necessary continually to inform people on this matter if the fear of summoning the priest is to be dispelled. The catechesis on this matter might follow these five points:

(1) It may be that someone is at home convalescing from a disease or surgery. While the person is improving, their state is such that they cannot get out. There may be no need for anointing, but a visit by one of the staff of the parish is much in order. These people should have the opportunity to receive the sacraments of reconciliation and eucharist.

(2) A second situation is one where the person is confined to the home because of serious illness such as a debilitating heart disease or a lingering cancer. It refers also to a person who is elderly and weak. It may be a crippling arthritis which renders the person less mobile. Anointing is very much in order. It is not necessary that the situation be either critical or terminal. Because of the isolation and fragmentation of these weakening conditions, the priest should be called to provide sacramental assistance.

(3) This is the well-known emergency situation. If someone has been rushed to a hospital because of a heart attack or stroke, it may be that the hospital chaplain will take care of the person. If that is not probable, the parish priest should be informed. Information such as whether the person is unconscious or not could help the priest to make the proper preparations such as bringing the eucharist. Calling the priest at this time is important so that he can be physically present to the family of the stricken person.

(4) A more usual situation for the parish priest is the case where a person is dying, probably from old age or an extended illness. Perhaps the person has been previously anointed. This is an emergency situation because the dying person should have the opportunity to receive viaticum. Also, it is important that the priest be present with the family at this time.

(5) If someone dies, the priest can still be called although it is good to find out the local pastor's practice. The priest is

not to anoint a dead body. However, it is appropriate for him to bless the body and his presence to the family at this time is of major importance. If the priest is called more readily in the other cases, thus removing the idea that anointing is a last rite, the priest's visitation on the occasion of death can be an opportunity of consolation and enlightenment for the family itself.[6]

5) Anointing takes place in a faith context. Anything that implies a magical result to this sacrament must be avoided. It is primarily prayer. It is liturgy, an act of thanksgiving for God's love at work in this person through the Christian community. It is also petition for healing on many different levels in the human person. Such healing includes the petition for hope and strength. But there is no cause/effect relationship between the person's faith and the recovery of physical health.

This may well be the most difficult area of catechesis regarding anointing. It will take courage on the part of the parish staff to keep insisting that this sacrament is directed to the whole person and that the salvation that is being celebrated in this rite is not productive of effects which put it in competition with the medical profession. Yet with patient understanding and constant catechesis a change of view on the part of the ordinary parishioner is possible. More difficult will be convincing people whose experience of anointing has been exclusively associated with the hospital room, the sickbed, or the dying person that anointing is really worship. Communal celebrations and prayerful individual anointings will remove some of the blocks to such understanding. But as in the case of reconciliation, the recovery of the idea that sacraments are before all else the way in which the liturgical community expresses itself will prove to be the herculean task of the sacramental renewal of the Church in the future.

---

[6]For these points on when to summon a priest the author is indebted to the comments of Father Michael Ahlstrom which appeared in *Liturgy* 70 5:4-5.

Part One: Pastoral Care
of the Sick

CHAPTER ONE: VISITS TO THE SICK.
CHAPTER TWO: VISITS TO A SICK CHILD[7]

How this sacrament assists the sick and elderly to be healed in terms of their fragmentation needs to be made clear to the Church, both healthy and sick. Surely, it is not accomplished through a fixed prayer formula and the dabbing of some oil on someone's forehead and hands. An important way, if not the central way, that such ministry takes place is through visiting those most in danger of this fragmentation while living in the midst of the Christian community. The pastoral ministry of the sacrament of anointing can be epitomized in these words of Christ: "I was sick and you visited me." Such visiting is what makes the sacrament effective in the language of ordinary experience. The ritual states:

> All Christians should share in the concern and love of Christ and the Church for the sick and show their concern for them, as each one is able, by visiting them and strengthening them in the Lord, and by offering help as brothers and sisters do. (42)

Priests are to be with and pray with the sick and elderly and speak in an encouraging way about their situation (43).

Visiting sick people, and even more, aged persons, is healing them in the very process of reaffirming them that they are not alone and abandoned. Others might leave the ill and aged to such abandonment, but Christians come

---

[7]The recently revised *Pastoral Care of the Sick: Rites of Anointing and Viaticum* is divided into three parts. Part I deals with the pastoral care of the sick, part II with the pastoral care of the dying, and part III consists of readings, responses, and verses from sacred scripture. The pastoral suggestions in this chapter of the book refer to part I of the revised rite. The final chapter of the book takes up part II of the new ritual.

together to assure the sick and aged of wholeness and integration within the community. They do this before, during, and after the liturgical rite. It should be noted that such visiting may be an opportunity for more lay involvement. Visits from lay persons convey the reality of the caring Church. They can enhance the occasional visits of the priests.

Because sickness and healing have a deeper significance in the life of the Church and to the person of faith, the sacrament of anointing takes on a more flexible role in the life of the community. It becomes the occasion of bringing separated people together. It allows the alienated and fragmented to celebrate their life held together in Christ. Anointing helps them to understand that to die to self does not mean negating part of themselves; rather, it demands opening oneself up to great wholeness. The rite asks Christians to believe that new life results when one's horizons are expanded by dying to one's marginal existence of fragmentation. Anointing is the act of praise thanking God that because of integration into the community, what could be dispiriting, disruptive, and dehumanizing, namely, sickness and old age and death, can now be joyful realities. To be specific, the pastoral care of the sick must deal with the loneliness that accompanies the physical and psychological isolation of illness. Part of any care here is the Church encouraging the visitation of the sick and elderly by relatives, friends, neighbors, and the clergy as well as other ministers in the parish. In some places organizations have been formed to link permanent invalids to each other by telephone.

Another obviously human reason why visiting is such an essential aspect of this sacrament, if not in fact its primary description, is that still today hospitals are understaffed and underequipped. Health insurance still leaves much to be desired. And visiting the sick is not a common practice except in rural and ethnic communities. Humanly speaking, the Church must take over much that society neglects to do and religiously speaking, just as the bread and wine of the eucharist cannot be separated from the meal context, so the act of anointing cannot be isolated from the visitation of the sick and elderly.

An important part of the ministry is the attitude of those who visit the sick, elderly, and dying. They may have feelings of fear, anger, being threatened, frustration, hopelessness, and the like at such a time which reminds them of their own mortality. It will be crucial for them not to deny or repress these feelings lest in so doing they render themselves less effective as ministers. Often the priest is seen as the only one who can do anything in these extreme and liminal situations. But unless he is dealing with his own feelings about sickness and old age and death, he will not be able to assist others in dealing with theirs. The stages of dying as articulated by Elizabeth Kuebler-Ross can serve as a form of examination of conscience for those who engage in the ministry of visitation.

(1) *Denial.* It is understandable how those who are ill, especially seriously so, and those who face their declining years can refuse to recognize their situation. However, if anointing and visitation are to become a ritualized way of entering into this process, those who minister to these people must not be the ones engaging in the denying. The patients should not have to deny their serious state because of confusing signals from the ministers. This is especialy true at the beginning of a serious illness.

(2) *Rage and Anger.* The reaction of those who minister must be honest. They should communicate that the acceptance of anger is an opportunity for growth. Avoidance or excessive kindness by the ministers in this situation is counterproductive. Those who visit need to put themselves in the sick or old person's position, both to recognize and own that person's anger as well as their own. For this, ministers and visitors will need to listen to the patient and to themselves.

(3) *Bargaining with God.* Often this stage results from a religious background based upon duties and merit. Such attempts at postponement are usually done in secret. But when they are shared, it is usually with the priest or other

ministers. It is at this point that anointing and visiting can raise up the idea that one's faith in God is primarily concerned with praise and thanksgiving. Those who visit, when they pray with the sick, aged, and dying, should witness to a belief in God in which bargaining makes no sense.

(4) *Depression.* The visitation of the sick, elderly, and dying must be a ministry of comfort. Self-consciousness and a sense of unease will pervade the person and the circumstances if the representatives of the community are ill at ease in this situation. And this is especially true since probably the most helpful thing any minister can do when a person is depressed is to be non-verbal. Touching the person, stroking the person's hair, and being quietly present to the person are some of the more effective ways of ministering at this time.

(5) *Acceptance.* This is the final redeeming state about which visitation and anointing in the Church are supposed to speak loudly. Kuebler-Ross' conclusion that those who talked about religion had more trouble in acceptance than others indicates that anointing and visiting the sick and dying cannot bring about this acceptance easily. What is presupposed, as in any sacrament, is a deeply religious commitment. It is incumbent upon those who minister to the sick and elderly, as well as the dying, to compensate for this lack of religious conviction to whatever degree possible. But when the dying person has reached the accepting stage, the family will need more support than the person. Often the minister will need to look at the kind of acceptance he/she has of the dying person who has already achieved this stage.

It is not out of place to note here that many, perhaps even most, priests find work with the sick and elderly distasteful. Frequently, it is the first thing avoided and the last thing done. Ministry to these people represents one of the great contemporary challenges to ministry. A priest must be willing to celebrate the sacraments with these people, whether reconciliation, communion, anointing, or viaticum. It is even better if he involves the person to whom he is ministering and the family of that person in the planning of whatever liturgical celebration there may be. At the very least the whole group present should be made to feel included through the explanations that the priest would normally give in the course of the rite. The priest must do more than the rite itself. He is the one to pray with others, to read the scriptures if necessary, and to bless all the people present. The sick and elderly minister to the official minister to the degree that they assist him in getting in contact with his own feelings about sickness, his defense mechanisms regarding old age, and his denial of the reality of death.

The ICEL revision is wisely concerned to give the visitation of the sick its own integrity. Thus, it provides for a rite for the visit to the sick and an additional rite for the visit to a sick child. The visit to the sick is a simple structure which can be readily adapted by the minister. It has the following pattern:

> Reading
> Response
> Lord's Prayer
> Concluding Prayer

Part Three of the ritual contains a considerable amount of material so that it should be relatively easy to arrange a brief liturgy of the word following the above outline. Because visitation is a very personal experience, spontaneous prayer seems to be very much in order. The ministers should pray *with* the people rather than pray *over* them. The word can be proclaimed by one of those present. The minister may give a brief explanation after the reading. After the blessing the priest may lay hands on the sick person or other ministers may trace the sign of the cross. It is important to note here that the revised ritual uses the words, "priest" or "deacon," only when the rites must be celebrated by a priest or a deacon in his absence. Whenever another minister is permitted to celebrate the rite, the word, "minister," is employed in the rubrics. Often, of course, this minister will be a priest or deacon.

The pattern for the visit to a sick child is identical in

structure to the above rite with the expected adaptations in language and attention to the age of the child. In conjunction with the final blessing the priest may impose hands and *all others present* may trace the sign of the cross in silence.

Any visitation will depend upon the circumstances of the old and ill. Those who visit must always adapt. In a situation of a hospital visitation the parish team might come as a group or individually at different times. Members of the hospital staff might be mobilized in such a way as to participate effectively in "visiting" the patient. In any event, visiting must be very flexible. At times it may mean conversation with the person; it may be a matter of reading to them or praying along with them. In other situations the most appropriate thing might be to hold the person's hand in a reassuring way. As already noted one of the most effective ways to visit is to listen. Listening is especially necessary in the case of liminal people. And at the end of the visit, the laying on of hands can be most healing. It is a gesture that all Christians can use and it need not be reserved to the clergy. But if it is to be a significant experience, it must be more than a token gesture. It means the firm placing of both hands on the person. Through this action the whole community is present.

CHAPTER THREE:
COMMUNION OF THE SICK

Much can be taught in the local parish about the pastoral care of the sick in terms of the eucharist. The eucharist is the sacrament of unity for Christians and this includes those members of the parish who are sick, aged, and dying. Just as the early Christians brought the eucharist from the Sunday celebration to those confined in their homes, so today the same practice can be most effective for concretizing the community's ministry to these people as well as the latter's ministry to the healthy community. Communion of the sick and elderly, then, apart from the sacrament of anointing is one way in which the larger pastoral context for this sacrament can be supplied. Efforts for frequency of the eucharist for the sick and elderly should not be viewed as promoting "special services" for individual members of the congregation, but as ways in which to make the entire parish more aware of its ministry to these people. Often it is communion of the sick which will make the anointing more meaningful at some later date. More frequent communion may be significant for those who when younger and well did not receive so often. The practice of reception of the eucharist for the sick and elderly may and need not be the same as their previous practice.

The use of extraordinary ministers of the eucharist not only heightens the ecclesial dimension of the eucharist itself, but also "catechizes" the parish regarding anointing. It calls to mind those who have received or will receive this sacrament at some time. In some places a full corps of special ministers brings communion to the sick and old after the Sunday celebration. The connection with the worshipping assembly which this practice highlights can be even more intensified if these ministers would make use of one of the Sunday readings, perhaps giving the gist of the priest's homily. The significance of having a friend or a member of the family act as minister of communion to the sick and elderly is obvious. In any event, the important point is that the sense of isolation can be overcome and links with the parish can be strengthened because those who bring communion are representatives of the community to these sick and elderly, although there is at this time no question of administering the sacrament of anointing. But the sacrament of the sick, administered in a parish where this continual concern for the sick and elderly has been manifested eucharistically, will be a clear example of what anointing in the Church is supposed to be.

The ordinary rite of communion of the sick is simple. It has this structure:

> *Introductory Rites*
> Greeting
> Sprinkling with Holy Water
> Penitential Rite

> *Liturgy of the Word*
>   Reading
>   Response
>   General Intercessions
>
> *Liturgy of Holy Communion*
>   Lord's Prayer
>   Communion
>   Silent Prayer
>   Prayer after Communion
>
> *Concluding Rite*
>   Blessing

The structure of the rite is the familiar form for a liturgy of the word followed by a sacramental action. It places the emphasis immediately on the centrality of the paschal mystery in the life of the Christian through the sprinkling with holy water as a reminder of baptism. Such a remembering is necessary at this time since most people have been baptized as infants. But more than this, this memorial of the baptismal moment also helps all present to reclaim the unity they have in Christ. The use of holy water can be the occasion of the kind of reflection on the part of all present that every Christian must pass through various rites of passage of which being sick or old are the more obvious examples. This ritual action is found in the Sunday eucharist and so can all the more effectively tie communion of the sick and elderly to the larger assembly.

Penitential reconciliation as part of any sacramental process takes on many meanings. As a distinct sacrament it should take place apart from the communion service if possible. But some kind of reconciliation in the communion rite itself can help the sick and old to see meaning in their present situation. It assists them to remain in the present and to look at the doubts, feelings of guilt, and paralyzing fears with which they must deal. For those present with the sick and elderly, such a liturgical experience may trigger a necessary reconciliation between family and friends.

More and more liturgists are favoring the positioning of

the penitential rite after the biblical reading since God speaks first and then people respond. A penitential response follows the purifying Word of God. While the ICEL format continues to place the penitential rite before the scriptural reading, the general introduction to the rite indicates under adaptations which can be made by the minister that the penitential rite may be placed after the reading from scripture. The penitential rite can be omitted when sacramental confession takes place. But since there will usually be others present, the sacrament of penance will usually take place earlier and so the penitential rite will have to be included.

Communion to the sick and old is in the nature of a response. The proclamation is constituted by the reading of the Word which precedes the actual communion. This is in accord with what the liturgical movement has recovered for the contemporary Church, namely, that sacramental action is a response to God's proclamation in the Christian assembly. But the eucharist in this context is not only a response on the part of the person receiving the sacrament. It is also the community's response in that it is a sign of its concern for the sick and elderly. Sharing in the communion of the sick and old is a communal manifestation of belief in the healing power of the paschal Christ. And when the bread and wine (ideally) are brought to these people on Sunday in conjunction with the parish liturgy, this action can make all aware of the belief which is expressed in the eucharistic prayer, the kiss of peace, and the sacramental sharing in the parish church.

The rite requires the priest to wear appropriate vestments. In the United States this usually means clerical dress with a stole. While clerical dress may well be apt apparel for this situation and what is expected by the people, the use of a stole (usually a puny one) over a shirt does not seem to have much meaning. Stoles go with albs, as ties go with shirts. Perhaps, it would be best simply to omit the use of the stole, clerical dress being sufficient. The idea that the stole symbolizes priestly authority appears to be a meaning read into that garment rather than a connotation which springs from it intrinsically. If Robert Hovda's suggestion that the stole resemble a shawl was implemented, this would change matters considerably.

What is asked of the stole in terms of having a full sign value applies to all the material elements of the rite, especially the bread and wine. When possible both elements should be used. It is possible to obtain containers to transport the wine. The endeavor to recover the full symbolism of the meal should apply to these situations as well as the Sunday liturgical assembly. When the person cannot receive under the form of bread, the use of wine is permitted. Other points to be considered to make this service as fully human as possible would include: (1) The family should be encouraged to create as much of a prayerful atmosphere as possible by the use of candles, cross, or family devotional objects. (2) When the person receiving communion is lying in bed, the minister may fittingly remain seated during the cememony. (3) The greeting of peace could be appropriately used sometimes in the liturgy such as at the conclusion of the penitential rite. It should be omitted if it would be redundant because of other forms of greeting that have taken place.

Besides the liturgy for communion in ordinary circumstances, the rite also provides for communion in a hospital or institution. It has a simple structure:

> *Introductory Rite*
> Antiphon
>
> *Liturgy of Holy Communion*
> Greeting
> Lord's Prayer
> Communion
>
> *Concluding Rite*
> Concluding Prayer

The antiphon is prayed in the hospital chapel or the first room. It is recommended that the minister proclaim a scripture reading after the greeting in the room. When possible the minister is to lead the sick in the Lord's Prayer. The concluding prayer is said in the last room or the chapel. If time does not allow the reading of even a brief scripture text, then in each room the minister of communion could amplify the invitation to communion with a brief scriptural quotation or paraphrase. Perhaps, an informal comment before the invitation which would recall some biblical image would serve to keep the element of the proclamation of the Word present in this case. This would also make for more personal contact between the minister and the one receiving. The danger of the brief rite is that it can become mechanical very easily.

CHAPTER FOUR:
ANOINTING OF THE SICK

There are three major subheadings to this chapter indicating the various ways in which anointing may be administered: anointing outside mass, anointing during mass, and anointing in a hospital or institution.[8] While in many ways, the least important part of the pastoral care of the sick and elderly is the actual anointing, nevertheless, this rite requires as much careful planning as any other liturgical service. And this despite the fact that the rite is relatively simple and straightforward. Full participation in the liturgy by all concerned is to be encouraged and the ritual itself should be a humanly attractive celebration.

The most fundamental principle underlying the pastoral approach to the liturgy itself is that the communal celebration is the norm and that emergency room occurrences are the exception (nos. 34, 37, 83-92, 99). Although individual anointings may be more frequent in any given pastoral situation, the communal liturgy should always be the guide for the way in which the anointing of an individual is planned and celebrated. Even when individuals are anointed without the community context, efforts should be

---

[8]The ritual first presents the rite of anointing in its own setting. Then it presents it with the necessary adaptations when celebrated in a eucharistic context. Finally, it presents the rite in the less normative setting of a hospital or institution.

made to have some others present in the room. On some occasions, the priest can prevail upon some members of the hospital staff to participate. The experience of the communal dimension of this sacrament must become more usual in the life of the Church. Individual anointings in extreme circumstances take their meaning from the ordinary, full liturgical expression.

The most effective way to bring back the sacrament of anointing as an act of community worship is through the experience of a celebration which is well done. When both communal and individual anointing services make use of the liturgical symbols to their fullest extent, the community will be providing a pattern for understanding anointing in those necessarily truncated rituals performed under emergency conditions. A parish will need to find ways to supplement the usual catechesis which is required to reinstate the sacrament of anointing in the context of the pastoral ministry of the sick. Services of healing or ritual celebrations dealing with the theme of healing will be one way to enhance the understanding of anointing as a ritualization of the salvific character of human healing and wholeness. If the sacrament of anointing is to be taken out of the hospital emergency room and put in the context of ministry to the sick and elderly, the Church must experience it as the place where people find the holy in themselves and in their total lives. *Environment and Art in Catholic Worship* states:

> Like a covenant itself, the liturgical celebrations of the faith community involve the whole person. They are not purely religious or merely rational and intellectual exercises, but also human experiences calling on all human faculties: body, mind, sense, imagination, emotions, memory. Attention to these is one of the urgent needs of contemporary liturgical renewal.[9]

Like the other liturgical rites, anointing must again become a healing art. One of the reasons that anointing

[9]Bishops' Committee on the Liturgy, *Environment and Art in Catholic Worship* (Washington, D.C.: National Conference of Catholic Bishops, 1978), no. 5.

became the sacrament for "extreme situations" is that it was treated too conceptually. The symbols of the rite were suffocated in the theology dominated by causality. They did not speak as artistic symbols. They were not allowed to put people in touch with their feelings, their doubts and fears, their moments of joyful exuberance. A section from *Environment and Art in Catholic Worship* is pertinent here:

> Liturgy is total, and therefore must be much more than a merely rational or intellectual exercise...it is critically important for the Church to reemphasize a more total approach to the human person by opening up the non-rational elements of liturgical celebration: the concerns for feelings of conversion, support, joy, repentance, trust, love, memory, movement, gesture, wonder.[10]

It is ironic that often in the past the symbols of the sacrament of healing-anointing have not been permitted to function in a healing way. Perhaps, parish services of healing will do much to restore this symbolic quality to anointing. Such a service could be a simple liturgy of the word which concludes with a communal laying on of hands.[11]

Individual Anointings

The liturgy of the anointing of an individual takes place either outside or inside Mass. Schematically it looks like this:

ANOINTING OUTSIDE MASS	ANOINTING DURING MASS
Introductory Rites	*Introductory Rites*
Greeting	Greeting
Sprinkling with Holy Water	Reception of the Sick
Instruction	Penitential Rite
Penitential Rite	Opening Prayer

---

[10]Ibid., no. 35.

[11]A sample service of healing can be found in *Liturgy* 18:4 (April 1973): 24. The author of the service is Charles Gusmer.

Liturgy of the Word Reading Response	*Liturgy of the Word*
Liturgy of Anointing Litany Laying on of Hands Prayer over the Oil Anointing Prayer after Anointing Lord's Prayer	*Liturgy of Anointing* Litany Laying on of Hands Prayer over the Oil Anointing Prayer after Anointing
Liturgy of Holy Communion Communion Silent Prayer Prayer After Communion	*Liturgy of the Eucharist*
Concluding Rite Blessing	*Concluding Rites* Blessing Dismissal

The rite of anointing in a hospital or institution is an abbreviated one. There are introductory rites of greeting and instruction. The liturgy of anointing consists of the laying on of hands, the anointing, the Lord's Prayer, and the prayer after the anointing. There is no litany or prayer over the oil.

Individual anointings will usually take place in a home, some room in a hospital or other institution, and chapels. This would be true when the anointing is set in a eucharistic celebration.

In this setting the opening greeting would best be informal in order to establish the human parameters of the rite. What was said about the use of vestments in the rite for communion for the sick would apply here. If full vestments are inappropriate in this setting, so is the tiny reversible stole. However, at the present time eucharistic vestments are required when the anointing is during Mass. The address in the beginning of the rite is important for stressing the religious nature of the ceremony. If helpful comments are made at other places in the liturgy, this address should be brief. It should clearly establish the salvific value of being sick or old in the Church. And the vocational character of anointing can be emphasized at the same time. Both notions can be expressed in terms of the James text.

The sick or old person may receive the sacrament of reconciliation at this time. In anointings outside Mass it takes the place of the penitential rite and in anointings in a hospital or institution it is part of the introductory rites. The meaning of the two sacraments of reconciliation and anointing emerges most concretely at the time of the individual anointing. The revised rite still sees the sacrament as connected with the remission of sin and speaks of it as "the consummation of Christian penance." However, anointing is not primarily a sacrament of reconciliation and the Church has abandoned the notion that its primary effect is the forgiveness of sins. If reconciliation is appropriate in any individual situation, it should be celebrated before anointing. Anointing is not some kind of substitute for reconciliation, nor an easier way which requires less conversion on the part of the person. Anointing does not relate to reconciliation as confirmation completes baptism. Anointing does not address the sinner as such. It deals with the paschal meaning of sickness and old age. It is a "consummation of the life of penance" in so far as both sickness and old age are liminal experiences open to Christians at this time in their lives by means of which they can enter more deeply into the passing-over of Christ.

In the anointing outside Mass a short scripture text is proclaimed either by the priest or preferably by someone present in the room. Ideally, the family bible should be used. If the sick or old person's condition permits it, a short homily should be given. The reason for the word proclaimed and explained at this time is so that the action of anointing can be more clearly experienced as a response to a proclamation. The sick and elderly can hear their condition being interpreted and set in the context of the biblical message. As in all liturgy word and sacrament are intimately related. The word read and preached should place sickness and old age in a salvational context. Topics that could be included in a homily (or expressed at other times in the rite) would be: 1) the healing power of the presence of Christ in the lives of the people present, 2) the Church as the bringer of this healing to its members, 3) the meaning and acceptance of sickness and old age, 4) the need to change one's understanding of this sacrament, 5) the significance of the main actions of laying on of hands, blessing the oil, and the anointing, and 6) how through the eucharist people can commit themselves to provide for the sick and elderly in the Church.

The litany is the communal prayer of faith in response to the word. Here especially, the Christian community is praying in the name of the sick or old person who may not have the psychological energy to do so. The 1974 version of the rite contained three forms for the litany. The ICEL revision has only a single litany in both the anointings outside and during Mass. These do not differ in emphasis.

The rite of anointing proper begins with the laying on of hands, a gesture which recalls Christ's act of healing. Since the imposition of hands is the basic sacramental action, the way in which it is experienced will affect the communicative value of the anointing with oil which follows. It is an expression of love for the person. It should be done in a fully human way reminiscent of a caress. The laying on of hands expresses the community's care for the person and so hopefully in the future all those present will be invited to touch the person in this way. At the present time this communal aspect to the laying on of hands is acknowledged in the fact that all the clergy present may lay on hands. Silence can enhance this community expression. It is the one completely non-verbal part of this liturgy.

Based upon the relationship of the laying on of hands and healing, Godfrey Diekmann offers some suggestions for pastoral practice: 1) Compassion for the sick.[12] One here

---

[12]Godfrey Diekmann, "The Laying on of Hands in Healing," *Liturgy* 25:2 (March/April 1980):36.

can recall the dramatic situation of Jesus touching the forbidden leper and what that must have meant for that person. The adulterous woman who not only touched Jesus but also anointed and kissed his feet must have been overwhelmed. 2) Faith and healing are mutual realities. Real healing takes place in a faith context. Jesus often said: "Your faith has made you whole." Jesus could work no miracles in Nazareth because of the lack of faith. Anointing, as the other sacraments, is a "sign" of faith. Sacraments are faith made visible. 3) At times Jesus healed someone because of the faith of others. Diekmann refers to Mk 2:4ff and the story of the paralytic let down through the roof. "Seeing *their* faith, Jesus said: 'Take up your pallet and walk.'" Jesus does not refer to the faith of the paralytic. Pastorally, this indicates the importance of the communal nature of anointing. It is the faith of the Christian community which is of significance here. Anointing should not be an individualistic faith experience. Also, Diekmann suggests that in those cases where the person to be anointed seems to be hostile or indifferent and for some reason cannot be responsive, the ministry of healing can be brought to this person in terms of those present and the larger Christian Church.

Usually the oil used in this rite will have been previously blessed at the Chrism Mass. In that case a responsorial prayer of thanksgiving is said over it. Structurally, this prayer is similar to the second and third forms for the blessing of the baptismal water. The other option is that the oil is blessed by the priest who is doing the anointing. This is the usual practice in the Eastern Churches. It may be that blessing the oil on any specific occasion would be more pastorally helpful or be an opportunity for personal instruction on the meaning of the oil. At times this consideration will supercede the ordinary value of retaining the connection with the bishop who is the pre-eminent minister of this blessing. When the anointing takes place during Mass, the blessing of the oil by the priest seems to be especially appropriate. Usually olive oil will be used, although any plant oil will do. If the priest is to bless the oil, the family of the person to be anointed might provide it. Oil which is left over after the celebration can be absorbed in cotton and burned.

To the degree possible it would be better to move away from the use of the small oil stock for anointing. Oil is the primary symbol here and its full value should be expressed. One should not have to guess at what is in the container. Today, often the words of the blessing are clearer than what is being blessed. If the family supplies the oil, it can be placed in an appropriate container and enough can be blessed so that it can be applied in a liberal fashion. The parish should be catechized in such a way that families would have readily available a beautiful vessel for the oil. Ordinarily, it should be a vessel that is designed for pouring.

At the time of the actual anointing, enough oil should be used to make all aware that something is being applied in more than a mechanistic way. It is also important not to apply so much that the person becomes uncomfortable. Pouring the oil into a flat container or in the cupped hand of the minister can bring out the fullness of the sign since oil should not only be felt and smelled, but also seen. The minister should anoint the entire palms or the backs of the hands and not merely mark them with the sign of the cross. The same holds for the anointing of the forehead. The form of the cross is neither required nor desirable in this instance. This does not mean that anointing in this sacrament is to be equated with the experience of massage. It is primarily a signing and so it should be perceived by all concerned. Oil should remain on the forehead and hands until the entire ceremony is completed. If the person is to receive the eucharist in the hand, the backs rather than the palms should be anointed.

Reference to the number of anointings in special circumstances and the meaning of the prayers accompanying the anointings have been treated in other chapters of this book. The ICEL revision indicates that the priest may anoint other parts of the body especially the area of pain or injury. What is of supreme importance to note is the absence of any penitential character to the formula that is considered the form of the sacrament. Even in case of extreme necessity when only the one anointing on the forehead is possible, the entire formula should be said. People will need to be instructed and encouraged to respond to the prayer formula with "Amen."

If the number of anointings has been reduced in the revised rite, the number of prayers after the anointing has been increased. Now prayers are available which correspond to the conditions of the person to be anointed. There are general prayers for the person who is sick, for the one about to die, for the case when illness is the result of old age, for before surgery, for a child, and for a young person. This possibility of choices makes the rite more real and concrete. No longer need people pray that God restore good health to the very old and dying. The individual rite outside Mass concludes with the Lord's Prayer, communion (if it is to be given), and the blessing. The blessing provides the necessary conclusion to the rite, although hopefully a sense of warmth and hospitality will continue to exist after the bestowal of this blessing.

Most individual anointings outside Mass will require that the priest adapt according to the circumstances and the condition of the person to be anointed. The most important consideration is that it be a fully human and prayerful experience. In this liturgy it is especially important not to be too verbal. The embarrassment and self-consciousness of the minister may be a temptation to be talkative. Non-verbal symbols work best with the sick and old people. The personal experience of the meaning of life and suffering in terms of Christian hope is what the minister has to give. He/she can call the person to minister to the larger Church at this time. Without these realities, the use of oil will be meaningless.

The ICEL revision contains a special preface and other additions for use in the eucharistic prayer. When the rite of individual anointing takes place during Mass, it may be celebrated in the church or in the home of the sick person or the hospital. Such a celebration can make the sick and old feel that they are still part of the larger community. If the eucharistic celebration is the votive mass for the sick, the vestments are white. The readings for the mass for the sick are chosen from either the lectionary (871-875) or from the anointing rite (Part III). However, different readings may be chosen by those involved. On Sundays of Advent, Lent, and the Easter season, on solemnities, Ash Wednesday, and Holy Week, the scriptural readings are proper to the day. One of the readings for the sick may be allowed on the above mentioned days when the votive mass is not permitted except Christmas, Epiphany, Ascension, Pentecost, Corpus Christi, holy days of obligation, and the Easter Triduum (81). In the homily the preacher should speak of the meaning of sickness and old age and place them in a salvation history context. He should stress that the effect of the sacrament is the healing of the whole person.

Apart from following the liturgical norm that specific sacramental celebrations be within a eucharistic context, anointing inside the Mass emphasizes that it is not primarily for those in imminent danger of death. Anointings during Mass as well as the community anointing service move toward the more ecclesial dimension of the sacrament. They also have an ecumenical flavor in that in the Eastern Churches the sacrament of the sick is administered within a full liturgical ceremony.

Communal Anointings

Although the anointing of more than one individual sick or elderly person either during or outside Mass is strictly speaking communal in nature, what is envisaged here is the celebration in a large assembly such as on the occasion of a pilgrimage and diocesan, city-wide, and parish gatherings. It is to take place in a church or some suitable place such as a hospital. Suitable pastoral preparation and full participation are requisite to make communal anointing an experience of the Easter joy which should characterize Christian life. What follow are 1) some suggestions for planning and preparing the context for the communal celebration, 2) some ways to make communal anointing a fully human and symbolic experience, 3) some points to keep in mind regarding the musical component of the rite, 4) the outline of the communal service both inside and outside the Mass with some detailed suggestions for implementation, and 5) some examples of communal anointing services.

(#1) If the communal celebration is going to be the most significant form of this new rite, it will need planning and preparation. While there is considerable leeway in planning communal celebrations, they should clearly be connected with the pastoral care of the sick and aged and they should convey a respect for the special place these people have in the liturgical assembly. Practically speaking, communal anointings can be done at most two or three times a year in a parish. But at these times the larger pastoral concern can be manifested in many ways. Only a few examples can be listed here. The sick and elderly will need to be transported. A parish can set up a core team which contacts people personally to explain the rite to them. The same core group makes the arrangements for bringing the sick and elderly to Church. The ministry of the Church can be easily identified in such things as the organizing of car pools for the sick and old. Nurses and doctors may need to be present during the liturgy. Hospitals in the parish might be able to assist on these occasions. Some of them welcome opportunities for their student nurses to get experience assisting the sick in such situations. Having nurses in uniform participate in the liturgy itself can be very meaningful. Those who have difficulty moving during the ceremony should be given the opportunity to be anointed in their places. Ushers need to be on hand to assist people in various ways. It would be most reassuring if each person to be anointed were accompanied by a healthy person, such as a friend or relative. It would be helpful to have a first aid kit in the sacristy. One cannot take for granted the need for such things as accessible bathrooms, ramps for wheelchairs, and open spaces.

The presence of the larger community is important at

such anointings. This presence can be brought about by having the anointing at a Sunday eucharist. But the rite will be even more powerful at a situation where the people come for a special anointing service. The proper kind of publicity is important for the success of communal celebrations. Bulletins should contain the time and date of the ceremony, suggestions on who is the proper subject of anointing, invitations to doctors, nurses, and those who work with the sick and elderly to participate in the liturgy, and perhaps, even a detachable registration form for people to return to indicate their plans to be anointed. Such a form could request such needed information as whether transportation for the person is necessary. A request for the visit of a priest for the sacrament of reconciliation might also be on such a form. Advance notices in bulletins are good, but even more effective are a series of homilies on the previous Sundays. Perhaps, a Sunday afternoon service would be more practical, giving some flexibility which would not be available on the busy Sunday morning schedule. Repeated announcements regarding the service are necessary for broader participation on the part of the parish. But many of those who might be anointed also need to be contacted in a special way. Shut-ins are such people. National Shut-In Day, which is usually the third Sunday of October, would be a most appropriate time for a parish to have a communal service. Weather permitting, some outdoor events remembering the sick and elderly could be scheduled. Since this is a national day of remembrance, the entire parish, including the school children, could be involved.

If this ceremony is to be a moment of solidarity for the whole Church, others than those to be anointed must be invited to attend. In other words, the healthy Church should also be present. But being present for the liturgy is insufficient to make this a sacrament of *pastoral* care for the sick and aged. There should be something after the liturgy into which the celebration naturally leads. Refreshments and entertainment afterwards is also part of the desired atmosphere. Such a context is necessary for this rite as well as the other Roman rites which suffer from the handicap of the conceptual being emphasized to the expense of the experiential. This social celebration will help dispell some of the fear and trembling that has been attached to the "last rites."

Catechesis is indispensable for the proper employment of this rite in a communal setting. Methods of catechesis can include discussion groups, filmstrips, slide presentations, fliers, and copies of homilies given on previous Sundays dealing with the sacrament. It is still necessary to remind people that this is not extreme unction, that it is not a last anointing, that it is not a sacrament of the dying. People must be given permission to participate. Some Catholics worry that they are not sick enough or not old enough. Experience has shown that it is required to invite people to this sacrament. Bulletins and announcements are important, but many will still think that they do not qualify. In some situations it might be best to have people who wish to be anointed to sign up ahead of time. It may be possible to provide them some special catechesis. Then, if there appears to be the possibility of some abuse of the sacrament, this may be a way of determining who should be anointed. There should be evidence of some kind of weakening due to sickness or disease, imminent surgery, or old age. Old people who still live a vigorous life should not be anointed. Nor should those who have already been anointed, receive it again during the same illness unless there is a significant change in their state. However, any assessment of who may be anointed must be based on the criterion that this weakness is not only physical, but can be psychological and spiritual as well. Situations where people indiscriminately go from one anointing service to another will most probably be rare and can be dealt with individually. What is more important in this preliminary catechesis is for the parish to find ways to keep some contact with those who have been anointed in this communal ceremony.

The communal rite can be most effective in nursing homes and hospitals. While these celebrations are similar to those sponsored by an individual parish, there are peculiarities that need to be taken into consideration. This simply emphasizes the fact that communal celebrations more than most demand a special environment. Whether in church or retirement home, attention must be paid to such things as the use of banners, the lighting, and the seating arrangement.

(#2) What is of principal importance in the communal anointing is that full use of the community's symbols be employed. These symbols need to be experienced humanly if they are to provide the atmosphere for a prayerful celebration. One easy way to make the communal service, which may involve several hundred people, more personal is by providing name tags so that the names can be used throughout the service. The traditional symbols that the Church has in its repertory must be treated with the sensitivity that allows them to proclaim clearly the meaning of the paschal mystery in the lives of the sick and elderly. For instance, the paschal candle could well play an important part in the liturgy calling to mind the vocational aspects of baptism *and anointing*. However, the primary symbol here as in all liturgy is the human body. It is imperative that the body as a powerful sign of God's presence come through clearly in any anointing celebration.

In this regard, experience has shown that the imposition of hands is a most moving part of this ceremony and special care should be given that it is done publicly and attentively. Hands are the extension of human beings and through hands people communicate compassion and mercy. Through those same hands the community can empower the sick and elderly in their ministry. Silence during the laying on of hands is preferred since it allows the gesture to speak for itself. It should not be trivialized by explanations or accompanying readings. If music is used due to the larger number of people being anointed, it should be the quiet reflective type, preferably instrumental. Whether hands are imposed on each individual or collectively by the concelebrating priests, the gesture must be done in such a way that it speaks of the community's blessing and is a sign of fellowship. If such is to be the meaning of the imposition of hands, it seems necessary to include members of the congregation. Those who minister to the sick, such as the nurses present, should be allowed to lay hands on those to be anointed. To avoid any legal complications one suggestion is to have a global imposition of hands by the priest(s), followed by one in which friends or family members impose hands individually on a sick or old person. Combining the imposition of hands with the actual oil anointing may take away from the significance of the "touching."

Anointing with oil can no longer be a brief sign of the cross made by an oily thumb. The oil must be seen, smelled, and felt. Oil is to be applied so that the person feels massaged in some way. Pouring the oil in several containers from one large one is an action that should be visible to the congregation. The anointing needs to be done with liquid oil rather than oil-impregnated cotton wool. The oil should have a pleasing fragrance and it should not be wiped off the person immediately after anointing. The oil should be prominently displayed. Perhaps, it could be put in a glass container which is then carried in the opening procession. In order that the symbol of oil be more perceptible the anointing should not be done by a brief sign of the cross but by having the oil generously applied to the forehead and the back of the hands of each person. Anointing the palms is inappropriate because it is messy and makes communion in the hand difficult. Another suggestion to heighten the symbolic character of the anointing is to have the person anointed rub the oil in the area where the pain or sickness can be identified. Although it seems obvious, it is important to note that those who have difficulty walking should be anointed in their places. Pews can be reserved in such a way that only every other pew would be used for seating. The priest would then have room to pass through the congregation to anoint these people.

Another way of personalizing the ceremony is to have some of those who were anointed express some words of witness to the congregation. This can be done by means of brief statements or by composed prayers, either of which can be read by the anointed or by substitutes as a form of communion meditation. Some form of memento, such as holy cards, that the anointed person could take home would be a way of keeping the power of the sacrament alive long after the ceremony. Plants, flowers, or candles may well be given to those anointed. The symbolic reference to growth and life will not be missed by these liminal people.

(#3) Music in communal celebrations is of prime importance. It provides the comforting background which assists people in experiencing the anointing ceremony as uplifting and strengthening. Music is part of the proclamation of the Good News that the sick and elderly bring to the healthy Church. The music should be unifying. That is more important than the type or style of music. Music's ability to evoke a prayerful atmosphere is more important than the particular idiom. All styles of music should be employed. Given the situation of the communal anointing ceremony, most of the music should probably be characterized by short, easily sung refrains. A good song leader is indispensable in this situation.

The use of music will have to be judged according to the concrete circumstances.[13] But music can be an aid in any of the three usual situations of anointing: 1) in a sickroom with family and friends present, 2) in a home or church with a small group of worshippers, and 3) in a large place such as a church with a large congregation. The usual places for music would be: 1) the entrance or opening, 2) the response to one or more of the readings, 3) the litany, 4) the laying on of hands, 5) the anointing with oil, 6) the Lord's Prayer, and 7) the closing. The opening hymn whose function is to bring people together could well have a baptismal theme. When there are large numbers of people to be anointed, music can

[13]For specific musical suggestions see: Eileen Freeman, "Music Hath Charms to Heal," *Modern Liturgy* 5:3 (April 1978):26; Marie Roccapriore, *Anointing of the Sick and the Elderly* (Canfield, Ohio: Alba Books, 1980), pp. 85ff; Study Text II: *Anointing and Pastoral Care of the Sick* (Washington, D.C.: USCC Publications, 1973), p. 36.

provide a background for both the imposition of hands and the oil anointing. In both cases, however, the music should not begin until the congregation has experienced some laying on of hands in silence and has heard the words said with the anointing a few times. A joyous recessional is appropriate since this is a sacrament of victory. Hymns that older people would know should be part of the musical program. When the anointing takes place at Mass, there would be the usual musical additions of the acclamations at the gospel and during the eucharistic prayer as well as communion music.

(#4) The ritual provides a general structure for communal anointings. There are two forms: one outside a eucharistic celebration and another within.[14] The most immediate preparation will include decisions such as 1) whether or not the anointing will take place during Mass, 2) the choice of the scripture readings, 3) musical selections, 4) the use of flowers and other decorations, and 5) the preparation of a booklet to be used in the celebration. During the rite itself some points to be noted are: 1) the reception of the sick and elderly in the beginning should show the Church's concern for them, 2) the scriptural readings can be taken from the lectionary (871-75), from Part III of the ritual 229), or be any other appropriate readings, 3) the laying on of hands usually should be done in silence, 4) music during the anointings should allow people to hear the words at least once, 5) communion under both kinds if permitted to all, and 6) if there are several priests involved in the ceremony, each one lays hands on some of the sick and elderly and also anoints them.

(#5) It seems pastorally helpful to include some suggestions for a communal anointing service which would reflect the kind of theological emphasis expressed in Chapter Four of this book. The suggestions given here are more concerned with content than with the structure since it is presumed that

---

[14]For one example of communal anointing during Mass see: Roccapriore, ibid., p. 61.

the celebration will follow the general outline of the rite. There is no attempt here to work out all the areas of the rite in detail, but simply to provide suggestions for parts of the liturgy where a different theological emphasis might be articulated. The following suggestions lay no claim to being the only kind of emphasis appropriate to anointing. However, since anointing as a ritualized way of dealing with fragmentation characteristic of those who hold the vocational roles of being sick and elderly in the Church needs to receive greater publicity, the suggested content will move along those lines.

In a communal anointing liturgy which stresses the vocational role of the sick person in the Christian community the following points are recommended. 1) After the greeting the presider might make comments of this nature:

> Sickness is a very natural part of all of our lives. It is not this sickness that should cause us any grief or worry because it is not the sickness, but, rather our attitude towards this state that we find ourselves in, that is the cause of any unhappiness. Therefore, today we are concerned with this attitude we all have towards those things in all of our lives that are in need of healing. We celebrate today this miracle of healing that is only possible through the grace of God that we experience through one another and which is exemplified in the life of Jesus. Just as good health is a very beautiful gift from God, in which we can experience our physical strength and the beauty of our world, it is through our suffering that we experience the reality of our humanity through the humanity of Christ and the love that God has for us all. Sickness is a period when we take time patiently not only to rejuvenate our bodies but to experience ourselves in our limitations and weaknesses. And it is at this time when we see and admit our weaknesses that we are really strong. So this celebration today is an admission of our limitations, both physical and spiritual, and we pray that in God's loving providence we may be healed of any infirmities that are

preventing us from experiencing the joy and peace that we as Christians are all invited to live in.[15]

2) The following comment could well be made before the first reading at the beginning of the liturgy of the word:

> To be sick means to be overcome by a sense of fragmentation, that is, separation from oneself, from friends, and from loved ones. In the readings today this sense of fragmentation is stressed. Let us then after these readings look at those things in our own lives that cause us to feel separated from ourselves and others and produce an alienation within ourselves from the love of God.[16]

3) What follows is a model homily based upon the Mt 8:5-13 text: The cure of the Centurion's Son:

> Jesus' primary concern was not healing bodily ills. When the servant of the centurion was healed it seemed to Jesus what the centurion really needed was the firm assurance of his relationship with God. "Truly, I say to you, not even in Israel have I found such a faith." Only afterwards and as a sign and proof of this inner healing, did Jesus heal the servant.
>
> What Jesus healed was not so much the particular ailments of the relatively few sick people he encountered, but he healed sickness itself. For one who follows Christ, sickness is no longer a punishment. It is no longer the unwelcome embrace of the realm of sin and death. It is no longer a lonely sacrifice for the good of unknown others.
>
> Christ and those who believe in him form an organic unity, a single reality. In every detail of the Christian's life, Christ is embodied and made real. Through Baptism

---

[15]This paragraph is taken from a liturgy of anointing composed by Larry Gosselin, a former student of the author. The present writer has made come emendations, but the text is that of Father Goselin. His liturgy remains unpublished.

[16]These comments were written by Larry Goselin, although they have been somewhat emended.

and Eucharist a Christian participates in Christ. And with Christ and for all who participate in him, suffering and death are linked irrevocably to resurrection and transfiguration: Good Friday is forever one and the same moment as Easter. For the Christian sickness and suffering mean sharing in the very reality of Christ's own redemptive suffering. Indeed if anyone desires to follow Christ, it is the cross that he/she must expect. But the cross is Christ's cross—and to bear the burden of the cross is to share in the whole mystery of Christ's redemptive death and resurrection. . . . The Christian in suffering becomes an imitation and an image of Christ.

But there is an even greater significance to sickness and suffering in union with Christ. For to suffer with Christ is also to participate in his work of establishing the realm of God on earth. It is true that God's kingdom is definitively established by Christ's death and resurrection. But the incorporation of the world as a whole into the reality of Christ is a slow evolutionary process, as is the gradual purification of the individual person. The penetration of God's kingdom into the whole world makes slow and sometimes ambiguous progress through history, gradually touching and purifying each individual in his/her relationship with God, gradually incorporating all of humankind and all of history into the reality of Christ. There remains much work to be done—and it is to be done through suffering and sickness. This is the vocation of being sick in the Church: to call all healthy Christians to look toward the completion of Christ's kingdom and to help build up that kingdom so that they can share in his glory.

You who are to be anointed today are called to speak to us of God's loving providence. Your vocation is to remind us that we are to be instrument's of God's peace and proclaimers of Good News to those who are in need of healing. We can find light in darkness, strength amidst doubt, joy in sadness, and God's love in time of despair because you witness to us of the meaning of sickness in the Christian Church.

For your vocation and for your lives we give thanks today both when this community anoints you and when we all share at the same table, eating a meal of reconciliation and hope.[17]

In a communal anointing of the elderly the comments and prayers of the rite should establish the meaning of anointing for these people. Here are some suggested ways of implementing the anointing rite along lines that would be especially appropriate for the elderly. In fact, most communal anointing rites will be addressed to the sick and elderly at the same time. Thus, these suggestions would probably be integrated with those which tend to emphasize the meaning of sickness in a Christian perspective.[18]

1) In the liturgy of the word after the greeting, the presider might use words such as the following:

May the love and fellowship of the Father, Son, and Spirit be with us today as we celebrate the anointing of our brothers and sisters, for they bear witness to the words of Jesus: "Come to me, all you who labor and are overburdened and I will give you rest. Shoulder my yoke and learn from me, for I am gentle and humble inheart,

[17]This homily is the construction of Larry Goselin except for the last third which is the author's addition. The entire text has been emended in places. The homily was not intended by Father Goselin nor is it intended by this author to be used in an actual celebration. It should serve as a catalyst for further thought and creativity on the part of the homilist.

[18]These suggestions are taken from a liturgy composed by two former students of this author. This liturgy has been published: Robert Marino and Walter Sidney, S.J., "Communal Anointing of the Elderly," *Modern Liturgy* 5:3 (April 1978):24-25. The following suggestions are a combination of quotations from this liturgy and the author's own interpretation. Those who would like to see the actual text of this liturgy should consult the particular issue of *Modern Liturgy*. This liturgy contains some prayers and meditations which would be appropriate as fraction rite or post communion meditations. This volume of *Modern Liturgy* also contains material appropriate for special situations of anointing such as in the case of those facing serious surgery.

and you will find rest for your souls. My yoke is easy and my burden light." (Mt 11:28-30)

2) Among the possible readings that could be chosen, the following seem especially appropriate: 1 Pet 1:3-9; Mt 5:1-10 or Mk 10:13-16. 3) If the Matthew text recounting the beatitudes is used, the homily should focus on the distinctive "vocation" of the elderly within the total Christian community—a "vocation" which the rite of anointing is celebrating. Poverty of spirit, gentleness, patience, mercy, etc. are especially characteristic of the elderly. These are the ways in which their vocation becomes visible in the Church. Their lives express confidence in the saving death and resurrection of Jesus and they become manifestations of the paschal mystery in the way that they show their gentleness and patience in relationship with other members of the community. If the Markan text is read which describes Jesus' acceptance of little children to whom belongs the kingdom of heaven, the homily can deal with the certain childlikeness, the openness and simplicity, which are characteristic of the elderly. The homily should be developed in such a way as to show the relationship between their anointing and their witnessing these trusting qualities to the Christian assembly. The anointing is thus a commissioning to continue to bear witness to an eschatological reality, the kingdom of God.

Future Possibilities

Before turning to the final section of this chapter and of this book, which deals with the rites of the dying, some reference to the possible future directions in regard to anointing needs to be made. Among the several areas of possible change in the practice of anointing in the future, two are of paramount importance: the extension of the meaning of the minister of the sacrament and the integration of the charismatic renewal in the context of this sacramental ritual.

Deacons, sisters, brothers, and many laypeople involved

in working with the sick and elderly are becoming more aware of the limitations of their pastoral ministry. They can counsel and comfort but in many ways it is still a ministry of preparation for when the priest comes to do the essential sacramental action. More and more they are asking such questions as whether there is any historical precedent for diaconal and lay anointing. They point to the fact that sacramental ministry has not been exclusively limited to those who are in orders as is clear from the example of baptism where in certain circumstances lay people may baptize. The question of the minister of a sacrament is one which is subject to historical development. This is obvious in the case of the sacrament of confirmation. Presbyters in the East became the ordinary minister of confirmation. Even in the West priests became the extraordinary minister of this sacrament, although much later. There is also some evidence that abbots ordained to the priesthood.[19]

Objections to any change in the matter of the minister of the sacraments are usually based on the decrees of the Council of Trent. However, such decrees must be understood in the light of historical analysis and theological insight. Paul Palmer, for instance, offers evidence that "it was not the intent of Trent to deny that presbyters could be delegated or authorized to confirm and possibly to ordain."[20] Many scholars are convinced that it is necessary to relativize the past understanding of this Council in the matter of sacramental discipline. Regarding anointing Trent says that the priest alone is the proper minister of this sacrament (Session XIV, canon 4[DS 1719]). The question that arises for the interpreter of Trent today is: what is the meaning of the word, "proper"? Does it mean that *only* the priest can anoint or that *ordinarily* the priest should anoint?

As the chapter on the history of this sacrament has already indicated, the practice of self-anointing as well as

---

[19]Paul F. Palmer, "Who Can Anoint the Sick?" *Worship* 48:2 (February 1974):82.

[20]Ibid.

lay anointing existed in the Church until the Carolingian reforms of the eighth and ninth centuries. Understandably, Trent did not deal with the question of lay anointing since in the mind of most theologians at that time anointing was the sacrament that prepared for the departure from this life. It was a sacrament tied to the forgiveness of sins. Trent understood anointing to be administered to the dying Christian and so the situation would ordinarily involve sacramental reconciliation for which a priest was clearly required. Thus, when Trent concludes that the priest is the proper minister of this sacrament, it is more a defense of the contemporary practice than it is a denial of the possibility of lay anointing.[21]

It seems that a logical consequence of the Second Vatican Council's move from treating this sacrament as an extreme unction to an anointing of the sick is the reconsideration of who may administer this sacrament. Anointing resembles more a consecration of the state of sickness than an absolution for the forgiveness of sins. This is clear on the level of pastoral practice where the sacrament is now opened up to children and the mentally ill.[22] The surrounding ministries, such as the communion of the sick, no longer require the ministry of an ordained priest. It is now theologically possible and pastorally desirable to extend the ministry of anointing to deacons and lay people, especially to those to whom the care of the sick and elderly is entrusted. If there are special ministers of the eucharist, why can there not be special ministers of anointing? There are already many Catholics: religious sisters and brothers, seminarians and lay people, who are exercising the ministry of the Church to the sick and elderly in every way except the use of the liturgical rite. If liturgy is the celebration of what is already present in Christian living and if liturgy is the ritualization of the spirituality of the Church, then it seems to follow that those who perform this larger ministry should be able to

[21]Ibid., p. 91.
[22]Ibid., p. 92.

preside at the liturgical celebration which brings to visibility the significance of that ministry as an ecclesial reality.

There needs to be room for more charismatic expressions of the ministry to the sick and old in the ritual of anointing. In other words, the place of the Holy Spirit in the life of the Church must be made more visible in terms of liturgical symbolism. In the fullest sense this would mean that certain communal and individual anointing services would be characterized by the charismatic expressions found in the prayer groups that take their inspiration from the Catholic Charismatic Renewal. Such services would be enhanced by the ministries of tongues, prophecy, teaching, healing, miracles, discernment, and practical service which are ways in which the charismatic experience comes to concrete expression.[23] These Pauline gifts would bring about a shared faith-consciousness about what it means to be sick and old in the Church.

All Christians, but especially those who minister to the sick and elderly, should be allowed to ritualize their personal charisms which are part of their relationship with the people they serve. It may not be possible that most instances of sacramental anointing will be situations where the extraordinary gifts of the Spirit are manifested. Unfortunate though it may be, most rites of anointing will probably not be characterized by what should be perceived as the ordinary gifts of tongues, prophecy, and healing. But the charismatic experience can at least be brought to this ritual by permitting those who care for the sick and elderly to lay hands on those to whom they bring their ministry. Perhaps the imposition of hands could be done by all people present and this would be considered part of the sacramental rite. It would be a way of having the larger community concelebrate the sacrament. This communal gesture would make visible that the whole community is anointing in the Spirit so that these liminal people can live out their vocation of

---

[23]Donald L. Gelpi, S.J. *Charism and Sacrament* (New York: Paulist Press, 1976), p. 98. See Gelpi's chapter, "The Charismatic Experience," for a helpful discussion of the charismatic character of the faith experience.

being sick and old in the Church. Although this additional ritualization is minimal, it can help restore to the experience of the sacraments the importance of the Holy Spirit which still needs emphasis.

In the Charismatic Renewal the laying on of hands is often associated with healing, whether it be spiritual, psychical, or physical. In the best of Charismatic theology, there is no sharp distinction between psychical and physical illness. As an experiential approach, Charismatic theology sees the whole person in need of healing and not just the body or the soul taken separately.[24] Nor do Charismatic theologians usually equate healing with miracles. Rather healing is first placed in a context of conversion, then of the transformation of suffering into grace, and then finally this healing which is born of faith may remove suffering and its causes. When this latter kind of healing takes place in an unexplainable way, it is called a miracle. It seems important that the liturgy of anointing be more open to the experience of Charismatic healing of whatever kind in conjunction with the laying on of hands.

Godfrey Diekmann in dealing with the topic of laying on of hands and healing refers to some of the texts in which the two phenomena are connected.[25] Some of the texts he deals with are: "And he (Jesus) went about all Galilee, teaching in their synagogues and preaching the gospel of the kingdom and healing every disease and every infirmity among the people" (Mt 4:23). "So they went out and preached that men should repent. And they cast out many demons, and anointed with oil many that were sick and healed them" (Mk 6:12-13). "Whenever you enter a town and they receive you, eat what is set before you; heal the sick in it and say to them, 'The kingdom of God has come near to you.'" (Lk 10:8-9). Diekmann acknowledges that there is still controversy whether Jesus was communicating this power of preaching and healing to his immediate disciples only or

[24]Ibid., p. 89.
[25]Diekmann, "The Laying on of Hands in Healing," p. 10.

whether it was to be a charismatic gift to anyone who in some way is commissioned to preach, to communicate the gospel. He concludes:

> I am personally convinced that the latter is the case: healing by prayer and laying on of hands, that is, by touching, was to continue through the ages as a sign to the world of the mission of Christ. It is a sign of the presence of the power of Christ's spirit in our midst. It is certain beyond doubt that such was the conviction of the early Christian centuries. Eusebius, in his *History of the Church*, gives a number of instances.[26]

Godfrey Diekmann has pointed to the coupling of preaching and healing. The gospel is proclaimed through healing as well as through preaching. In that sense the word, healing, can be used to describe the total sacramental activity of the Church. Baptism and eucharist are sacraments of healing as well as reconciliation and anointing. Vatican Council II attempted to restore the laying on of hands to all of the sacraments in some form. The form of imposition of hands in connection with healing as found in the prayer groups of the Charistmatic Renewal is in accord with this trend. The communal laying on of hands would do much to stress the place of the Spirit both in liturgy and Christian life.

[26]Ibid.

BIBLIOGRAPHY:
PASTORAL PERSPECTIVES ON THE RITES OF
THE SICK AND THE ELDERLY

Books

Fournier, William, O.M.I. and O'Malley, Sarah, O.S.B., *Age and Grace: Handbook of Programs for the Ministry to the Aging*. Collegeville: The Liturgical Press, 1980.

Gusmer, Charles, *The Rite of Anointing: Pastoral Care of the Sick*. (three cassette tapes) Kansas City: NCR Cassettes, P.O. 281.

Krause, Fred, O.F.M. CAP, *Liturgy in Parish Life*, New York: Alba House, 1979.

Ohanneson, Joan, *Anointing of the Sick: The Sacrament of Trust*. (filmstrip) Minneapolis: Winston Press, 1978.

Roccapriore, Sr. Marie, M.P.F., *Anointing of the Sick and the Elderly*, Canfield: Alba Books, 1980.

Schmitz, S.S., Walter and Tierney, Terence E., eds., *Liturgikon: Pastoral Ministrations*. Huntington, Indiana: Our Sunday Visitor, Inc., 1977.

Westerhoff III, John H. and Willimon, William H., *Liturgy and Learning through the Life Cycle*. New York: The Seabury Press, 1980.

Winstone, Harold, ed., *Pastoral Liturgy*. London: Collins Liturgical Publications, 1975.

Rite for the Anointing and Pastoral Care of the Sick: Background Catechesis. Washington, D.C.: Federation of Diocesan Liturgical Commissions, 1973.

Periodicals

Liturgy 18:4 (April 1973), and 24:2 (March/April 1979), and new series: 2:2 (1982), Washington, D.C.: The Liturgical Conference.

Liturgy 70 5:4-5. Chicago: Liturgy Training Program.

Modern Liturgy (Anointing) 5:3 (April 1978). San Jose: Resource Publications.

Pastoral Music 3:4 (April/May 1979). Washington, D.C.: National Association of Pastoral Musicians. See also: 6:2 (December/January 1982): "Musical Liturgy for the Elderly," by Edward McKenna.

CHAPTER SIX: PASTORAL PERSPECTIVES ON THE RITES OF THE DYING

This final chapter is devoted to the rites for the dying. It treats of Part II of the ICEL revision of the ritual. Part II of *Pastoral Care of the Sick — Rites of Anointing and Viaticum* consists of chapters five through eight dealing with the celebration of viaticum, the commendation of the dying, prayers for the dead, and the celebration of the rites in exceptional circumstances. Part III of the ritual contains the additional readings, responses, and verses from sacred scripture. There is also an appendix which contains a rite for reconciliation of individual penitents. This final chapter of *Prophetic Anointing* concludes with some pastoral suggestions for the care of the dying and the bereaved and a brief statement on the meaning of death in a Christian perspective.

Part Two: Pastoral Care of the Dying
CHAPTER FIVE: CELEBRATION OF VIATICUM

This chapter contains a rite for viaticum during Mass as well as a rite for viaticum outside Mass. The rites have the following patterns:

DURING MASS	OUTSIDE MASS

Introductory Rites	*Introductory Rites*
	    Greeting
	    Sprinkling with Holy
	        Water
	    Instruction
	    Penitential Rite
	    (Apostolic Pardon)

Liturgy of the Word
    Homily
    Baptismal Profession
        of Faith
    Litany
	Liturgy of the Word
	    Reading
	    Homily
	    Baptismal Profession
	        of Faith
	    Litany

Liturgy of the Eucharist
    Sign of Peace
    Communion as Viaticum
	Liturgy of Viaticum
	    Lord's Prayer
	    Communion as Viaticum
	    Silent Prayer
	    Prayer after Communion

Concluding Rites
    Blessing
    (Apostolic Pardon)
    Dismissal
	Concluding Rites
	    Blessing
	    Sign of Peace

Although the ritual of anointing is not primarily for the dying, it tries to be pastorally sensitive to the needs of those in their final hours of life. And so Chapter Five deals with viaticum. Normatively, viaticum is to be administered within Mass. While the eucharist for the dying might ideally be given in a eucharistic celebration, it will usually be administered apart from such a liturgy. Thus, the ritual contains a rite for viaticum outside Mass. It is structured in such a way that it corresponds to the ordinary rite of communion of the sick. That is, there is the initial greeting, the sprinkling with holy water, the penitential rite, the reading from scripture, the Lord's Prayer, communion, a concluding prayer, and the blessing. In addition, the rite of viaticum has an instruction after the greeting, the granting of a plenary indulgence after the penitential rite, a baptismal profession of faith after the scriptural reading, a litany after the profession of faith, and the sign of peace after the blessing.

In place of the penitential rite the priest can hear the person's confession. Such a confession is preferably done before this rite, in which case the penitential rite must be retained. Since form B of the plenary indulgence contains the words, "I grant you a plenary indulgence and pardon for all your sins," form A which is oriented to the paschal mystery is to be preferred lest the impression of a second absolution be given. After the scripture reading a homily may be appropriate, although, when viaticum is given in a small group situation, the reflection on the scripture will be much less formal than the word, homily, suggests. In addition to the usual formula for communion, there is a special one for the person receiving viaticum: "May the Lord Jesus Christ protect you and lead you to eternal life." After the blessing the sign of peace is offered to the dying person by the people present. Robert Hovda has suggested that during the period of silence after communion, the group might join hands as a gesture of oneness in Christ. It is an excellent suggestion.

Viaticum has been restored to its position as the final sacrament. Historically, it had achieved such a position by the fourth century. It is now restored as the final passage rite for the Christian who is passing through death to new life. The liturgy asks the dying person to enter even more deeply into the paschal mystery at this time. It is to be a sign that death itself can be overcome through Christ's promise of final resurrection. For this reason, families should not delay to have the priest bring the sacrament to the dying person. It will be too late if the person is unconscious or impeded by all of the instruments one usually associates with intensive care. The person may receive only the wine if that is all that is possible, although communion under both kinds would be ideal. Those in attendance may receive even if they have already communicated that day. Such reception by those present should be encouraged.

Three elements in the new rite of viaticum emphasize that it is the sacrament of the dying: 1) the renewal of baptismal promises, 2) the A form of the plenary indulgence ("may almighty God free you from all punishments in this life and in the life to come"), and 3) the reception of the eucharist under both kinds. The relationship between baptism and death or entrance into community and leave-taking, needs special emphasis today. It might be advisable to bring the experience with the water, the sprinkling which may be done in the beginning of the rite, closer to the actual renewal of the baptismal commitment.

CHAPTER SIX:
COMMENDATION OF THE DYING

This part of the ritual is not a rite as such. It is a chapter of resource materials. It contains short scriptural texts, longer biblical readings mostly from the psalms and gospels, the litany of the saints, prayers for when the moment of death seems near, prayers when death has occurred, and prayers for the family and friends.[1] These last prayers may be concluded with a sprinkling of the body with holy water, a signing of the forehead with the sign of the cross, or with a simple blessing.

The texts contained in this chapter supply the material for communal prayer which should be simple and brief in this situation. But the rite of commendation is more than merely verbal. The sign of the cross should be made on the person's forehead as a reminder of baptism. If possible, the dying person should participate in the readings and prayers. Depending upon circumstances, music or singing might be employed. There is room for maximum flexibility in this

[1] For additional prayers for use at the commendation see Walter Schmitz, S.S. and Terence E. Tierney, ed. *Liturgikon: Pastoral Ministrations* (Huntingdon: Our Sunday Visitor, Inc., 1977). The texts in this book appear to be more conservatively oriented with considerable stress on the saints. Also, the language is sexist.

rite. Prayers may be added from other sources, especially familiar prayers, ones that people learned in their youth. This is one way for these people to get in touch with their origins in this rite of passage.

The purpose of these prayers and readings of commendation is to ensure the presence of the Church at the time of death and to assist the dying person to bring his/her Christian life to a conclusion. The Church should be represented at the deathbed by members of the family and close friends. An ordained minister need not lead this service. A lay person may do so and in many situations, this would be preferable. Through these rites the Church speaks of the meaning of the Christian life for one final time. Some of the contemporary theologies of death have emphasized the importance of these final moments as a time of summing up one's life and as a time of making a choice for eternal life.[2]

Along with the other rites of anointing, viaticum, and burial, the final commendation stresses the paschal character of the death of the Christian. There is the use of holy water in all of these rites with its obvious reference to baptism. In viaticum there is also the profession of baptismal commitment. In the Funeral Mass there is the use of the white pall and Easter Candle which are paschal symbols. The sign of the cross during the commendation ceremony is a non-verbal symbol which speaks of death in a paschal context. In the prayers and readings, paschal imagery is found in the recurring theme of Christ's victory over the power of death. What this rite is all about is summed up in the word, "commend." On the cross Christ commended his spirit to God. This commendation serves as the link between the death of Christ and the death of the Christian. Even when the dying person is not conscious, this rite fulfills the important function of speaking to those present about the paschal character of death.

[2]See as examples: Karl Rahner, *On the Theology of Death* (New York: Herder and Herder, 1961) and Ladislaus Boros, *The Mystery of Death* (New York: Herder and Herder, 1965).

CHAPTER SEVEN:
PRAYERS FOR THE DEAD

If the person has already died, anointing is not to take place. It would be a useless and empty ceremony. The rite of Christian burial is the appropriate liturgy in this case. But the need for pastoral concern does not cease. The family needs the presence of the Church at such an emotionally upsetting time. Such a situation calls for considerable sensitivity on the part of the minister. And so this chapter contains prayers which can be used to attend a person who is already dead. It may often be necessary for the priest to explain to those present that sacraments are only for the living and that the dead are helped most by their own prayers. ICEL's revision contains a structured rite for this occasion. It has this pattern:

> Greeting
> Prayer
> Reading
> Litany
> Lord's Prayer
> Prayer of Commendation

The rite may conclude with the sprinkling of the body with holy water, the signing of the forehead with the sign of the cross, or a simple blessing.

CHAPTER EIGHT:
RITES FOR EXCEPTIONAL CIRCUMSTANCES

This chapter contains liturgical formulae for three different situations: the continuous rite of penance, anointing, and viaticum; rite for emergencies; and Christian initiation for the dying. Clearly, less than ideal situations are envisioned here. However, such situations as these will arise and continue to happen for Catholics. The first situation is one where it is not possible to have a more developed celebration of the sacraments over a period of time because of sudden illness, an accident, or some other cause of the danger of death. It is the *Continuous Rite of Penance, Anointing, and Viaticum.* It has this structure:

> *Introductory Rites*
>   Greeting
>   Instruction
>
> *Liturgy of Penance*
>   Sacrament of Penance
>   (Penitential Rite)
>   (Apostolic Pardon)
>   Baptismal Profession of Faith
>   Litany
>
> *(Liturgy of Confirmation)*
>
> *Liturgy of Anointing*
>   Laying on of Hands
>   Prayer over the Oil
>   Anointing
>   (Prayer after Anointing)
>
> *Liturgy of Viaticum*
>   Lord's Prayer
>   Communion as Viaticum
>   Silent Prayer
>   Prayer after Communion
>
> *Concluding Rites*
>   Blessing
>   Sign of Peace
>   (Prayer after Death)

It should be noted that in such circumstances, the confession may be generic. As usual, if there is no confession, the penitential rite is retained. The priest may sprinkle the person with Holy Water after the baptismal profession of faith. Provision is made for the celebration of the sacrament of confirmation. Ordinarily, confirmation should not be combined with the anointing rite since a double anointing could be confusing. If required, however, confirmation could take place just before the blessing of the oil. In this case, the imposition of hands which is part of the anointing rite is to be omitted to avoid duplication. Confirmation and anointing are sacraments which should be celebrated at different times. Confirmation at the time of death is not envisioned as a normal practice. When viaticum is celebrated the prayer after anointing is omitted.

The second situation refers to those times when not even the continuous rite can be celebrated. Here the priest is asked to offer the ministry of the Church to a person who is on the point of death. He may be able to offer only the minimum of sacramental ministration. The ritual contains the outline of a rite, but the priest will have to judge how much of it he can use. The outline is brief:

> Sacrament of Penance
> (Apostolic Pardon)
> Lord's Prayer
> Communion as Viaticum
> (Prayer before Anointing)
> Anointing
> Concluding Prayer
> Blessing
> Sign of Peace

A generic confession would be usual here. Conditional anointing may be called for in which case the formula is introduced with the words: *If life is in you*. . . . Whether the person recovers slightly or whether the person dies, the priest or minister is urged to continue further pastoral care.

The third situation is concerned with the person who is near death but has not been initiated into the Church. Again this situation demands considerable sensitivity and adaptation. It may be that the person is at the point of death where only natural water can be poured on the head of that person with the usual sacramental formula. Or a fuller rite may be possible. In which case the ritual presents this structure:

Introductory Rites
 Greeting
 Dialogue

Liturgy of the Word
 Gospel Reading
 Litany

Liturgy of the Sacraments
 Renunciation of Sin and
  Profession of Faith
 Baptism
 Confirmation
 Communion as Viaticum
 Prayer after Communion

Concluding Rites
 Blessing
 Sign of Peace

The rubrics indicate considerable flexibility here. In some cases the person will have received none of the sacraments of initiation but will have been received as a catechumen. In other cases, the person will not be in the catechumenate. The dying child will require some special adaptations. The important thing is that the minister or priest ensure that the dying person, family and friends derive profit from the celebration of Christian initiation.

APPENDIX: RITE FOR RECONCILIATION OF INDIVIDUAL PENITENTS

ICEL's revision concludes with a form for the sacrament of reconciliation which is used during communion of the sick, the celebration of anointing, and the celebration of viaticum. The outline of the rite is simple:

Reception of the Penitent
 Invitation to Trust
 Revelation of State of Life

Liturgy of Reconciliation
Confession of Sins
Acceptance of Satisfaction
Penitent's Prayer of Sorrow
Absolution

After the priest invites the person to have trust in God, the penitent makes known to the priest whatever he needs to exercise his ministry. This would include mentioning one's state of life and the time since the last confession. A generic confession will often be appropriate. The nature of the penance will often be indicated by the circumstances.

Pastoral Care for the Dying

In those cases when anointing and viaticum come at the same time the liturgy will work more effectively if the proper planning for death has already taken place. Reconciliation of the sinner should have been taken care of in good time so that the final hours of one's life are not preoccupied with one's sinfulness. The culmination of one's life should be a gathering together of those positive and significant values that have structured one's personal history: relationships, work, special concerns, and the life of worship.

This is no time now for funeral plans and concerns about what is to be left behind. Plans for a simple and Christian funeral should be handled early in one's old age or prolonged sickness. Then there will be time to consider such things as the ministry of donating one's body to a medical school. The body need not be present at the funeral mass should such an option be made. Perhaps, after careful consideration, more and more Christians will choose cremation as a way of speaking about the resurrection from the dead as new life rather than as some kind of resuscitation of a carefully embalmed corpse. When cremation takes place immediately after death, the ashes could be integrated into the funeral liturgy with interment as part of the ceremony.

Part of the parish's ministry to the dying is to provide the families with sufficient information regarding the necessary decisions that must be made about funerals. People should be aware of various resource books and memorial societies which will enable them to provide a Christian perspective at this time. There is much that is not Christian in the culture's attitude regarding funerals. The expensive practice of "viewing" the body which has been cosmetically redone to appear to be alive needs to be challenged. It is not an easy thing to do. The cultural worldview which idolizes achievement finds it difficult to accept physical death. In a commercialized and materialistic society, it will take considerable planning to cultivate an attitude of simplicity. Parishes need to have established procedures and handy resources because usually funeral preparations need to be made quickly and in an emotionally charged atmosphere.[3]

Liturgy magazine contains a brief article detailing the use of hospices for the dying as a form of ministry to these people.[4] The author, Julia Upton, lists several principles employed by these hospices which can be of assistance to anyone working with the dying. They are worth reproducing here:

—to treat a dying person as a living being
—to insure the individuality of the dying
—to help a dying person maintain a sense of hope within this ever-changing, life-threatening situation
—to allow a dying person to express the feelings and emotions which well up from within
—to help the dying person participate in personal care as much as possible
—to be honest with the dying person
—to discuss the spiritual or religious aspect of death if the dying person desires this
—to allow the person to die in peace with dignity[5]

[3]For additional helps see: Arlene Hynes, "Practical Help for the Family," *Liturgy* 14:4 (April 1973):14ff. and Fred Kraus, O.F.M. CAP., *Liturgy in Parish Life* (New York: Alba House, 1979), pp. 135ff.

[4]Julia Upton, "A Place to Die," *Liturgy* 25:2 (March/April 1980):19.

[5]Ibid., p. 21.

Pastoral care for the dying on the part of the parish is an ongoing project. The final days before death are too late. The parish must remind its members that the meaning of death is found in life. Unless the entire Christian life is experienced as a dying and rising, it is difficult to see how it is possible to have the last moment of one's life carry the weight of such a meaning. Death education must be part of any religious education program so that people are not shielded from that reality which comes to all.[6] For this reason it is imperative to close this book with a note on the Christian significance of death.

The Meaning of Death

The point has been repeatedly made in this volume that anointing is not the last sacrament and that its administration during the final hours of the Christian's life must be experienced as exceptional. However, apart from the fact that serious illness often leads to death and so anointings need to take place in that context, there are those hopefully rare circumstances in which anointing is given because viaticum is not possible. Thus, the meaning of death for Christians necessarily becomes part of a comprehensive theology of the sacrament of anointing. Moreover, there is a special reason for concluding this book with a note on the paschal significance of death. And that flows from the particular perspective of this work, namely, that anointing's meaning is brought out most clearly in the experience of old age.

There is much about old age which has a sense of negativity about it.[7] This has always been true, although contem-

---

[6]For a helpful article dealing with the rituals that prepare us for death while we live our lives in the Church see Gabe Huck, "And maybe, just maybe, I'll be ready," *Liturgy* 18:4 (April 1973):6. Also see: "Rites for the Sick and Dying," *National Bulletin on Liturgy* 10 (January/February 1977):56ff.

[7]Much in this section on the meaning of death belongs to Christopher Mooney. His book, *Man Without Tears*, has already been referred to. For more of his thinking on death see chapter six of that book.

porary society has exacerbated some of these negative elements such as dependency and the loss of social and economic status. But none of these threaten one as much as death. This is especially true when death comes cripplingly.[8] The slowness of the final concluding moment of one's life encourages American society to conceal this reality. Even Christians hide from both the approach of death and the result of death: the bodily remains. They speak of dead people as being at rest. Funeral parlors become slumber rooms. Nature-Glo makes the corpse appear more presentable than when it incarnated the living person. Death is a void; most people try to repress it and when that cannot be done, they rage against it.

The very thing that is most frightening about death is precisely that which would most help the anointing rite take on a sense of honest confession of the paschal faith. Death makes one ask about the meaning of life. Because people do not know why they live, they find it difficult to die. Death has no parallel in calling humans to their uniqueness and individuality. Such stress on singularity is a challenge to understand themselves. Some have tried to find the meaning of human life in what comes after biological death: heavenly glory. More credible to the non-believer and more helpful in day to day living is the meaning of what precedes biological destruction. The task is not to learn how to die, but how to live. This is true not only for the explicit Christian community but the larger secular society. One of the ways in which both of these communities learn how to live is by ministering to the sick and elderly. A community which cannot deal with its old and infirm will not have the adequate means to deal with the presence of death in its midst. Monika Hellwig makes this point well when she says:

> Every parting and absence of friends and family members in the course of life is in some measure a rehearsal for the

[8]For some summary statements on the meaning of death at different age levels see "Rites for the Dying," *National Bulletin on Liturgy* 57:10 (January/February 1977):38ff.

great absence and parting of death. The manner in which all the absences and partings are experienced also influences the possibility of hope beyond death. . . . A Christian community that abandons to loneliness not only its widows and elderly, but also and more particularly its divorced and separated members, may be failing in the word of faith, hope and charity more extensively than at first appears.[9]

The purpose of liturgy is to articulate spirituality, to remove ambiguity in the community's relationship with God. For that reason the liturgies of anointing, the dying, and Christian burial should reveal what Christians so desperately want to conceal: the meaning of death. It is to help dissipate the anxiety about the possibility of non-being that the Church calls for celebration when one of its members is dying or has already died. If there is anything such as a special grace which comes in celebrating the sacrament of anointing, the rites for the dying, or the funeral service, it is what Paul Tillich calls the "courage to be." They speak of the acceptance of one's finitude. To worship on these occasions is to see death not as the end of life, but as part of life itself. The grace of the liturgy is to experience death as something which is always present. Death is part of what it means to be human. It is not something that puts an end to being human. Death is what makes human existence *human.* Death distinguishes the living person from sub-human life. Death calls all not so much to look into the future life as to look back on their past existence.

A person who is aware that she is dying during the whole of her life is forced to be aware of the way she is living. If death is not merely biological, then neither is life. The death experience in the present moment is not the same as regretting that one must die. It is to fear that one may not be living. To say that in death men and women find life is not to equate the meaning of life with a form of intellectual under-

[9]Monika K. Hellwig, *What are They Saying about Death and Christian Hope?* (New York: Paulist Press, 1978), pp. 84-85.

standing, although that may be part of it. Death gives them not the meaning *of* life, but meaning *in* life. Death says to all people: cherish now good human values. Do not denigrate friendship, sexual love, commitment to ideals, and imaginative adventures. It has already been pointed out by Kuebler-Ross that those who find life meaningful more easily embrace death. They need not pass through the four stages she describes: denial, anger, bargaining, and depression. They move immediately to acceptance. Few would quarrel with her findings on this point.[10] What would be a source of chagrin for many Church people is that religious faith, according to her findings, does not seem to be able to alleviate fear and conflict for a majority of believers. Is this due to the fact that the religious understanding of death was never run through the human relationships of family and friends? Was dying in terms of the Easter faith kept on the level of religious language and never allowed to find a home in ordinary human experience? The hope is that the rites for the dying and dead can provide the human context wherein the paschal mystery can become the meaning of the human passage into death.

The liturgical celebrations at the time of death can create an atmosphere where the worshippers can accept the dark side of the dying experience, both for themselves and the person who is leaving this life. Such darkness needs a cultic recognition. Some theologies of death depict it as moment of magnificence and energy.[11] While a defensible viewpoint, the death experience need not go that way. There is the danger of romanticizing what for many people is simply the running out of life's resources. The fact is that life will be taken away and one way to let go is not to rebel against one's

[10] For a summary of Kuebler-Ross' contribution to the pastoral care of the dying, see "Modern Science and Christian Rites," in *National Bulletin on Liturgy* 57:10 (January/February 1977):50ff.

[11] For some brief summaries of the contemporary approaches to the theology of death, see p. 44 of *National Bulletin on Liturgy* referred to in the previous footnote. But see especially Hellwig, *What are They Saying About Death and Christian Hope?*

own limits. Some theologizing about the afterlife gives the impression that the Christian faith knows more about death than it really does. The faith enables Christians to accept death but any information or suggestion about life after death or union with God is provisional. For this reason the liturgies of the dying as well as the Rite of Christian Burial use metaphorical biblical phrases to speak of the afterlife. References to individual eschatology are circumspect. And while traditional Church teachings stress the certainty of a life after death, the content of these teachings is communicated through figurative imagery.

The paschal faith does not take away the darkness of the Christian life; it helps the Christian to accept death with all of its opaqueness. What the liturgy of the dead can and should do is to proclaim that beyond physical death, something of the human person remains and that it has been worthwhile making these contributions which will last in the presence of God. Not to accept death means not to accept life with its greatest qualities of love, freedom, and fidelity. All that Christians can know about life after death is that what happened to Christ will happen to them. To claim any more is to make the Christian faith incredible. But despite the uncertainty, the liturgical rites can and should announce the paschal faith with clarity. These rites do this when they speak loudly of this last passage as one of the major tasks of human existence, when the liturgy helps the dying person to live his/her death in a human way and as a believer. Those who accompany people at this time need to experience the Christian aspect of this passing-over as well. For this reason, anointing, viaticum, and the funeral service see Christian death as the last stage of that which began at baptism.

> The initial immersion is continued in the final burial, which is itself only a passing over. On several occasions the Roman ritual of death refers to baptism and meditates on the connexion between sacramental life and eternal life. It is by means of a series of passages and initiations that man enters into life, and it is by virtue of a succession of sacramental passages that the Christian

gradually leaves the regions of darkness in order to proceed to the country of light.[12]

But the liturgy cannot speak of death in this way unless it first speaks of life. Thus, the presider and other ministers will need to make the experience of worship humanly credible. The religious symbols connected with the rites of the dying and the funeral must be intelligible to the fragmented congregations present at such services. The liturgy must be able to gather together enough belief to make the celebrations valid in a fully human sense. Monika Hellwig takes up this point when she speaks of the way in which the community can effectively minister in times of dying and death. She says:

> When one considers what to say to the dying, the important factor is really not the way the symbols are explained in words. The really important factor is in the analogies in life experiences by which the dying person can apprehend the images of our faith and hope. Any true pastoral effort must begin with the expectations and apprehensions which this individual's experiences have built up. The task will certainly be easier in a community that lives by a vivid faith and hope—a community in which life beyond death is already experienced as among the earliest followers of Jesus, who claimed to share in his resurrection before they themselves had died. A vital community of faith mediates an almost tangible presence of God and therefore an almost tangible pledge of consummating union with God.[13]

One way to accomplish this kind of community presence is by the shared conviction on the parish level that baptized Christians are not God, that they must accept their finitude and so accept death and to refuse to do so is the equivalent

[12]Philippe Rouillard, "The Liturgy of the Dead as a Rite of Passage," *Liturgy and Human Passage*, eds. David Power and Luis Maldonado (New York: The Seabury Press, 1979), p. 81.

[13]Hellwig, *What are They Saying About Death and Christian Hope?* p. 82.

of sinfulness. If death is accepted as part of one's life and not merely the end of it, then it must be accepted into one's life quality. To live with death is hoping that one is not alone. To accept death implies that the person in the end will not simply disappear. To integrate death into one's life means that a person becomes a better human being. It means that belief in life after death is best done by focussing upon belief in life before death. The anointing, dying, and funeral rites should explicate that Christian hope in the resurrection is tied to resurrection now, that in some experience of the fullness of life, of self-discovery, love, and creativity, people will be put in contact with the meaning of their lives. For the Christian Church the challenge of death is the challenge of what the believers are doing with their lives. It is the question that the liturgy of anointing, the rites for the dying, and the Christian burial service are asking of the living. That is a far more pressing question for the Christian community today than what will God do with people after death. What Christian liturgy celebrates here is simple: that the paschal faith and Christian hope make sense out of death when they say something about life.

BIBLIOGRAPHY:
PASTORAL PERSPECTIVES ON THE RITES OF THE DYING

Boros, Ladislaus. *The Mystery of Death.* New York: Herder and Herder, 1965.

Hellwig, Monika K. *What are They Saying About Death and Christian Hope?* New York: Paulist Press, 1978.

Kuebler-Ross, Elizabeth. *On Death and Dying.* New York: Macmillan, 1975.

McBride, Denis, C.SS.R. "Immortality, Old Age and Death." *Review for Religious* 37 (1978/5):717-729.

Power, David and Maldonado, Luis, eds. *Liturgy and Human Passage.* New York: The Seabury Press, 1979.

Rahner, Karl. *On the Theology of Death.* New York: Herder and Herder, 1961.